D0805784

THE BEST O
A.T. ROBERTSO

The Best of A.T. Robertson

A. T. Robertson

Compiled by David S. Dockery
Timothy and Denise George, Editors
Foreword by Herschel H. Hobbs

Nashville, Tennessee

Printed in the United States of America

4212-56
0-8054-1256–5

Dewey Decimal Classification: 286
Subject Heading: BIBLE / BAPTIST—DOCTRINES
Library of Congress Card Catalog Number: 96-24020

Unless otherwise stated all Scripture is from the King James Version.

Acquisitions and Development Editor: John Landers
Interior design by Leslie Joslin
Cover Design by Steve Diggs & Friends

Library of Congress Cataloging-in-Publication Data

Robertson, A. T., 1863-1934.
[Selections. 1996]
The Best of A. T. Robertson / Timothy & Denise George, editors.
p. cm. — (The Library of Baptist classics ; vol. 6)
Includes bibliographical references and index.
ISBN 0-8054-1256-5 (hb)
1. Theology. 2. Baptists—Doctrines. 3. Southern Baptist Convention—Doctrines. 4. Bible. N.T.—Criticism, interpretation, etc. 5. Bible. N.T.—Language, style. I. George, Timothy. II. George, Denise. III. Title. IV. Series.
BX6332.R63 1996
230'.6132—dc20 96-24020
CIP

01 02 03 04 05 00 99 98 97 96

To
Al and Kem Jackson,
special friends,
who envisioned and inaugurated the
Library of Baptist Classics
and to
Gerald Borchert, John Polhill,
James Blevins, David Garland,
Carey Newman, Mark Seifrid,
Harold Songer,
special colleagues in the
New Testament Department at
The Southern Baptist Theological Seminary,
who are faithful heirs of the
"Robertson tradition"

Contents

General Editors' Introduction

The Baptist movement as we know it today began as a small persecuted sect in pre-Revolutionary England. One critic labeled them as "miscreants begat in rebellion, born in sedition, and nursed in faction." Excluded by law from the English universities, Baptists developed their own structures for pastoral training. They also wrote hymns, preached sermons, published confessions, and defended their beliefs against skeptics, detractors, and rival religious groups of all kinds. From the popular works of John Bunyan and Benjamin Keach to the learned theology of John Gill and Andrew Fuller, Baptists wrote with a passion and with a purpose. In time, a large body of Baptist literature was developed, writings that both reflected and contributed to the emerging sense of Baptist identity.

The Southern Baptist Convention (SBC) was organized in 1845 for the purpose of "eliciting, combining, and directing the energies of the whole denomination in one sacred effort, for the propagation of the gospel." This was an ambitious undertaking for the 293 "delegates," as they were then called, who gathered in Augusta, Georgia, and embraced this far-reaching vision at the founding meeting of the Convention. Through the years the SBC has suffered numerous setbacks and distractions—the Civil War, Reconstruction, the Great Depression, social unrest, denominational strife, and much more. But through it all God has graciously blessed Southern Baptists in ways that future historians will surely record as remarkable. By the end of the twentieth century, Southern Baptists had grown into America's largest Protestant denomination, a fellowship of some fifteen million members in nearly forty thousand congregations supporting more than nine thousand missionaries.

Drawing on this rich heritage, the Library of Baptist Classics presents a series of books reflecting the faith and vision of Southern Baptists over the past 150 years. We are republishing in fresh editions and with new introductions a collection of seminal writings. These works have proven their worth as classics among Southern Baptists in the past and still speak powerfully to Baptists and other evangelical Christians today.

The Library of Baptist Classics includes writings of pastors, theologians, missionary statesmen, and denominational leaders from the past. Some of them are popular, others scholarly in form. They include sermons, doctrinal treatises, missionary biographies, and an anthology of Baptist confessions, covenants, and catechisms. Most of these writings have long been out of print. We present them now in the fervent hope that the Lord will see fit to use them again, as He has in the past, not only to remind us of the great legacy we have received, but also to inspire us to be faithful shapers of the future under the lordship of Jesus Christ.

Timothy George and Denise George,
General Editors

Foreword

DR. HERSCHEL H. HOBBS

I belong to the last generation of students whom Dr. A. T. Robertson taught. At 87 years of age, I realize that I am a vanishing breed.

Dr. Robertson was known to be hard on his students. He said one of his callings was to take the "starch" out of young Baptist preachers. But he did so with a benevolent purpose. It was customary for the first-year English New Testament class to present him with a silver goblet on his birthday. Leslie Williams, the teaching fellow, appointed me chairman of a three-member committee to purchase and present the goblet that year. The jeweler had to order it, and it had not arrived on Dr. Robertson's birthday, which fell on a Sunday. So that day we went to his home to wish him a "Happy Birthday" and explain about the gift.

He and Mrs. Robertson welcomed us graciously. As we were leaving after a pleasant visit, I said, "Dr. Robertson, I must say that it is nicer to visit you in your home than in your class." We all laughed. Mrs. Robertson said, "I've been telling him not to be so hard on you boys." To which he replied, "Huh! They will be preaching the New Testament the rest of their lives, and I want them to know it." "But," said she, "you don't need to embarrass them before the whole class." "Huh," he replied, "that's part of it. They know that they have to face the entire class as well as me!" With laughter on all sides, we returned to the seminary.

In those days we stood up to recite. His usual pattern was to ask a student two or three simple questions. If he answered correctly, Dr. Robertson would let him sit down. He was looking for someone unprepared to recite.

To him the almost unpardonable sin was chewing gum in his class. One day he called on a student who answered the simple questions. But as he was sitting down, Dr. Robertson saw him "whack" his gum one time. He asked, "Brother—are you chewing gum in my class?" "Yes, sir." "Don't you know that you are not supposed to do that? I'm giving you a zero for your recitation, sir!"

Leslie Williams told me that later in his office Dr. Robertson sat at his desk looking at that zero as a tear ran down his cheek. Then he rubbed out the zero and wrote in a "10," a perfect grade. Ironically he did not know that he had dealt with a future president of one of our seminaries.

It was a common saying among students that with impunity you could miss what Matthew, Mark, Luke, and John said. But woe betide you if you did not remember Dr. Robertson's footnotes in his *A Harmony of the Gospels*.

At times he liked to ask trick questions. One was "Brother—who is the greatest preacher where you came from since you left?" The poor student did not even hear "since you left." He would blurt out the name of the most prominent pastor in the area whence he came. This always evoked laughter from the class.

But one such backfired on him. He asked a student from Virginia if he was an FFV. The student replied, "Yes sir, a future farmer of Virginia."

One time some students in our class played a trick on him, though he was not aware of it. Dr. Robertson was cold-natured. Each time he entered the classroom he looked at a thermometer on the wall beside the door. One night a heavy snow fell. On the ledge outside the windows it was about six inches deep. Some students buried the thermometer in the snow. The classroom was on the second floor. When a lookout signaled that Dr. Robertson was starting up the stairs, they hung the thermometer on the wall. When he looked at it, the mercury was near the freezing point. As a result, while we basked in the room's warmth, Dr. Robertson endured the "cold."

In reciting for him, I was fortunate always to know the answers to his questions. At times when he called on one student after another seeking the answer to a question, it was like lightning striking all over the room. No one seemed to know the answer. Had he called my name, I could not have answered it either.

One morning when we were studying the apostle Paul, Dr. Robertson called on me to recite. He asked, "Brother Hobbs, where did Paul go to school?" I said, "His parents taught him at home until he was five years old. Then he went to the synagogue to be taught by the rabbi. At thirteen he went to Jerusalem to be taught by Gamaliel. But scholars agree that he never went to the University of Tarsus, since his father, a Pharisee, would not send his son to a Gentile school."

Dr. Robertson said, "You and the other scholars, huh?" I replied, "No, sir. I did not include myself." Then, "Well, Brother Hobbs, I don't agree with you. I think he did attend that school." If you hem a small dog in a corner, he will try to fight his way out. So I said, "Well, Dr. Robertson, all I know is that I told you what you wrote in your book *Epochs in the Life of Paul*." In return he said, "Yes. I did say that in my 'little Paul' book. But I've changed my mind since then. I just wanted to know if you had studied the lesson. Thank you, sir." And he gave me a "ten."

In those days it was customary near exam time for the fellow to conduct a "coach" class to prepare us for it. Exam questions in mimeograph form were given to each student. Through the years students had noted that Dr. Robertson often repeated the use of such. So these questions were handed down from generation to generation. It was thought that by getting the answers to these questions you could "spot" him on a given exam. The result was small attendance at "coach" classes.

On this occasion only about a half dozen came. Leslie Williams spent the hour in a thorough review of the life of Paul. In the following exam there were only two questions, with the value of each given: 1. Discuss in chronological order and in full detail the life of Paul from his conversion through his second visit to Corinth (80). 2. A simple question (20). The answers had to be exact.

When I received the questions my pencil hit the paper. For an hour I wrote furiously. Most of the students read the questions, sighed, and looked out the window. Finally they wrote something, hoping to get some sort of grade.

At the close of the hour many asked, "Hobbs, how in the world did you know the answer to that question?" "Coach class, brother, coach class!" From then on these classes enjoyed full attendance.

All the class passed the course. So I assume that "Dr. Bob" graded by grace, not by works. But he had made his point.

Dr. Robertson was also a fine preacher with a passion for souls. After going to Oklahoma City I delighted to ask former students if they could imagine him leaving the pulpit in a revival meeting, walking the aisles, and exhorting people to receive Christ as Savior. None could. But he did in the First Baptist Church, Oklahoma City. Shortly after my going there, an elderly deacon told me about it.

Finally, it was a Monday afternoon in a Senior Greek class. The time was September 1934. The previous Friday Dr. Robertson had asked me to give him the twelve rules he followed in his "Big Grammar." I did, and he gave me a "10." I still have the class enrollment card on which he wrote it.

But on that Monday afternoon he gave what was his last and, perhaps, greatest testimony about the New Testament. "I have been studying, teaching, preaching, and writing on the New Testament for more than fifty years. Yet I never open the Greek New Testament without seeing something I have never seen before." This prolific author also wrote two Greek words on the blackboard, the last words he ever wrote. I still have a picture of them.

It was a balmy September afternoon. Sitting at a front desk, I was not more than ten feet from him. But as he taught he perspired profusely. Drops of sweat fell from the end of his nose. His blue shirt soon appeared black, wet with perspiration. Finally, at 3:00, he said, "I don't feel well, so I am letting you go." He never dismissed a class early. I was the last student to leave the room. Dr. W. Hersey Davis, teaching in the next room, heard the class leaving. He came in and asked Dr. Robertson about it. When he said he did not feel well, Dr. Davis said, "I'll take you home." Had I known what would happen, I would have been like Elisha following Elijah.

By late afternoon, word spread that Dr. Robertson had died. I said, "If a tornado had destroyed the beech trees and buildings and left Dr. Robertson, it would be more like the seminary than with them intact and Dr. Robertson gone."

At this writing it has been almost sixty-one years since he died. But, like Abel, he has continued to speak through his former students and the more than fifty scholarly books he authored. The latter continue to be published and used. May it continue to be so until Jesus returns!

Introduction

DAVID S. DOCKERY

Archibald Thomas Robertson taught at The Southern Baptist Theological Seminary for more than forty-five years (1888–1934). Robertson, who was born on November 6, 1863, to John and Ella Martin Robertson in Chatham, Virginia, was the greatest biblical scholar in the history of the Southern Baptist Convention. He died on Monday, September 24, 1934, at his home on Rainbow Drive near the seminary campus. Characteristically, Dr. Robertson at his death was writing another book on the New Testament for Harper and Brothers.[1]

Robertson began a teaching career at Southern Seminary in 1888 which did not end until his death forty-six years later. His role as professor impacted the lives of hundreds, multiplying his scholarship and ministry through Baptist pulpits around the country and even around the world. Without question Robertson's teaching ministry was characterized by excellence and demanding rigor. Yet, it was his writing career, which extended even to the day of his death, that set Robertson apart as the greatest biblical scholar in Baptist history.

Both his teaching and writing ministry can only be understood and interpreted in light of Robertson's genuine evangelical piety and churchmanship. A churchman of the highest order, Robertson's scholarly pursuits were always in the service of the church, primarily for the preacher. He thought of himself first and foremost as a preacher. When asked which of the three kinds of service was the highest, preaching, teaching, or writing, Robertson replied: "Preaching! Yes, preaching is the greatest work in the world. The element in the other two that makes them worthwhile is the preaching that they contain."[2]

The Early Years

In 1875, the Robertson family moved from Virginia to Cool Spring, North Carolina, when young Archibald was twelve years old. For the next four years Robertson attended Boone Preparatory School, Statesville, North Carolina. From 1879 to 1885 he attended Wake Forest College, combining some high school subjects with the college core curriculum to earn the M.A. degree.

The Robertson family had little money. In fact, they, like other farmers, struggled desperately to make ends meet during the 1870s and 1880s. Yet, it was during this time that young Archie used to say, "I learned to work, to work hard, and to keep on working."[3]

When the Robertsons arrived in their new North Carolina town, there was no Baptist church. For three Sundays of the month they attended the Presbyterian church, and the other Sunday they attended Baptist services at the court house conducted by Rev. J. B. Boone. Pastor Boone was strongly attracted to the Robertson family. He sensed the interest that young Archie had in spiritual matters. Boone became a veritable Paul to this young Timothy. As the community grew and more Baptists came into the area, a church was formed. Baptisms were held in a pond at the edge of town, the first in the history of that strong Presbyterian center. Archie heard a neighbor say that she had seen the likes of a baptism before, but her husband had never seen the like, so she was going to let him go.

In March 1876, during a revival meeting led by Rev. F. M. Jordan, Archie "felt a change of heart." He was baptized along with his brother Eugene and two older sisters. Baptism by immersion was so new and strange that Archie was mocked by his Presbyterian playmates when he was baptized.

Mr. Boone prepared the equivalent of a college preparatory curriculum for young people not able to attend school. The plan focused on Archie Robertson, who was given free tuition. Archie began his studies in 1878 with courses in Latin, arithmetic, geography, and grammar. The school desk always had to be set aside when plowing and farm duties took priority. Boone's plan enabled Robertson to fulfill his educational longing and his passionate desire to prepare to serve the Lord. Archie's older brother, Martin, made great personal sacrifices that allowed Archie to pursue work with Boone, as well as eventual studies at Wake Forest College.

On his sixteenth birthday, November 6, 1879, Archie enrolled at Wake Forest, having borrowed ten dollars from a friend to purchase the train ticket. He arrived with two dollars in his pocket. Though he entered two months late (in November 1879 instead of September 1), he caught up with his classmates through his diligent effort. One of his former fellow-students made the illuminating observation that Archie, though arriving late that first year, soon led his class in Greek because of his "meticulous observation and a marvelous memory." These same great gifts served him well throughout his years of brilliant scholarship.

When Robertson entered Wake Forest, he had a serious impediment in his speech. He spent many hours alone, reading aloud and reciting choice selections of literature, which he memorized for that purpose. He enrolled in a special course to help eliminate this self-conscious problem. Eventually by learning to breathe differently, the matter was corrected. He later joined and participated in the Evzelian Literary Society to improve both his reasoning and speaking abilities. Robertson's mentors at Wake Forest included William Louis Poteat (languages), Charles Elisha Taylor (Latin), and William B. Royal (Greek). Robertson placed first or second in his class in French, Latin, and Greek, making grades of 95 to 100 in every course. He was co-editor of the renowned college paper, *The Wake Forest Student*, called by *The Cleveland New Era* "the best college magazine published in this country."[4]

Surprising as it may seem, it was in Greek, not French or Latin, that Robertson won the second place medal. What was then a keen disappointment became the motivating force for him in later years to excel in New Testament scholarship. His second-place finish was used as a stepping stone to higher achievement in forthcoming years. His six years at Wake Forest may well have been the most important of his entire career.

Robertson entered Wake Forest poorly prepared at the age of sixteen. He graduated in June 1885 as an accomplished student and budding scholar. Though offered a professorship at his alma mater, Robertson turned his efforts toward his calling to preach and headed for further training at The Southern Baptist Theological Seminary in Louisville, Kentucky.

The Southern Seminary Years

At age sixteen Robertson was licensed to preach. During that same year he preached his first sermon in a Black church in North Carolina. His journey to Southern Seminary was the next step on his lifelong pursuit of the "call to preach."

The seminary had been in its new home-city eight years when Archibald T. Robertson entered as a new student in 1885. As yet, the struggling institution had no home of its own. The Waverly Hotel served as dormitory, while the lecture rooms were up two flights of steps in the library hall on Fourth Avenue, an arrangement that continued until 1888.

Robertson worked hard his first two years, taking Senior Greek, Textual Criticism, and Patristic Greek, all courses normally taken in one's final year. He also found numerous opportunities to preach both in Louisville during the school session, and back in the mountains of North Carolina during the vacation periods. He also served the homeless in a downtown mission called the California Mission.

During the early days of the 1888 school year, D. L. Moody held a six-week campaign in Louisville. Robertson wrote in his diary of an encouraging opportunity he had in soul-winning. It was his privilege to lead a self-identified universalist from West Virginia to the Lord. Robertson was spiritually moved by that experience and the powerful preaching of Moody. Though Robertson was concerned about Moody's poor grammar and use of the English language, he nevertheless observed that "he [Moody] has a grip on the Bible, human nature, and God." He commented that Moody's exposition of the Holy Spirit was "the most enrapturing and heaven-inspired discourse" he had ever heard.[5]

As he neared the end of his student days, he recalled that on his fifteenth birthday his mother told him that she would still be prouder of him after fifteen more years. Yet, he wondered whether the Lord would fulfill his mother's prophecy. The answer came on April 7, 1888, when the faculty invited Robertson to become an assistant to Dr. John A. Broadus in Greek and homiletics. With this invitation Robertson's life course was set: he was to be "a man of The Book" and a teacher of preachers rather than a pastor. So it was that Archie Robertson, the student, found himself at age twenty-five at his desk, addressed as Professor Robertson, and affectionately as "Doctor Bob." His career as professor began October 1, 1888, and continued for the next forty-six years.

He joined the esteemed faculty of what was becoming the most significant seminary in the land. Those men with whom he had studied—Broadus, James P. Boyce, William Whitsett, Basil Manley Jr.—now became his colleagues. Upon joining the faculty, John R. Sampey observed that Robertson was clearly the foremost student of his period in the seminary. As he began his new work, the young professor remarked: "I am sure I do not know how to teach, but I am equally determined, by the grace of

God to learn how."[6] Nothing Robertson ever penned opens up for us his person as these words that describe his humility, his determination, and his dependence on the grace of God.

It was certainly the grace and providence of God that gave Robertson the opportunity to spend the first year of his professorate at the house of Southern Seminary's founding president, Dr. James P. Boyce. Unfortunately, Boyce would pass away by the end of the year. Still, the opportunity to spend his first year as a faculty member living with Boyce, and Boyce's successor in the department of theology, F. H. Kerfoot, instilled within Robertson a love for the seminary where he would spend the rest of his academic career. Not unlike Dr. Boyce, Robertson threw himself wholeheartedly into every enterprise in which he was involved.

In addition to his duties as a seminary professor, Robertson also became pastor of the Newcastle Baptist Church in Newcastle, Kentucky. His eagerness to fulfill the role of both teacher and preacher, however, soon placed Robertson's well-being in jeopardy. The aggressive schedule of preaching and teaching eventually caught up with the young professor, and threw him into states of deep melancholy.[7] Realizing his limitations, Robertson gave up his pastoral work at Newcastle. Nevertheless, Robertson saw his whole life as service to his God, stating, "After all, what is a man's life worth if it be not given to God, and his kindred and mankind?"[8]

There was no doubt that Robertson, however, was on the rise as an academician. The surrounding faculty admired his ability and motivation. Although already an original thinker and scholar, Robertson himself would have pointed to those same faculty members as the formative influences on his illustrative career. A.T. Robertson was gaining a solid reputation as a New Testament scholar in the already substantive Southern Seminary tradition. In particular, Robertson formed a special relationship with the famous Southern Baptist New Testament scholar, preacher, and co-founder of Southern Seminary, John A. Broadus, whom he affectionately called his "truest earthly friend." Later, Broadus' daughter Ella would become his beloved wife, and so Robertson truly became regarded as part of the Broadus family. Broadus himself thought of Robertson as his greatest discovery and modeled for the young professor two disciplines for which Robertson later became famous: New Testament interpretation and preaching. It was the model of Broadus' approach to the New Testament which later bore fruit in the interpretative method of Robertson in his mammoth *Greek Grammar*.

Broadus modeled for Robertson an interpretive method that took into account the recent developments in critical scholarship while still remaining true to the authority of Holy Scripture. Robertson's intimate acquaintance with Broadus' work, as seen in the critical textual notes he contributed to Broadus' *Harmony of the Gospels*, reveals his continuity with, and addition to, the Broadus legacy. One of the highest compliments Robertson ever received was from J. H. Farmer, of McMaster University, who observed, "Professor Robertson has worthily maintained the Broadus tradition."[9] Robertson's *Greek Grammar* and *Word Pictures* clearly reflect the imprint of Broadus upon the young professor.

It comes as little surprise then, that Robertson's first major publication was a tribute to the mentor whom he so greatly loved. *The Life and Letters of John A. Broadus* was first published in 1901. Robertson's esteem for the late Broadus and enthusiasm for the work were reflected in the length of the original manuscript. Robertson's original proposal was over one thousand pages in length! His high personal regard and appreciation for Broadus were clearly demonstrated in the content of *Life and Letters*. Evidence for this can be seen in Robertson's conclusion that his friend and mentor was "one of the finest fruits of modern Christianity."[10]

However, Robertson was not one merely to be a student of the masters; he became a master himself. He would come to be regarded as the greatest New Testament scholar ever to teach at Southern Seminary, and one of the greatest in the history of New Testament interpretation. Robertson's ardent dedication to study continually sharpened his keen mind, and he could always be found at his desk, between classes, pouring over his latest writing projects and research. Roberston's output of scholarly writings was exceptional. Edgar McKnight has observed that between 1914 and the year of his death in 1934, there were only two years in which Robertson did not have volumes published.[11] In addition, his scholarly contributions transcended his primary field of expertise in New Testament and included works of theology, preaching, history, and denominational analysis. Robertson also became a frequent contributor to numerous Baptist state papers in the South, Southern Seminary's *Review and Expositor*, as well as Northern Baptist periodicals such as *The Baptist* and *The Watchman-Examiner*. In all of these, Robertson dealt faithfully with the weighty, fundamental theological issues confronting Baptists at the dawn of the twentieth century.

Robertson also carefully blended level-headed, genuine scholarship with a passion for the seminary classroom. Students found his courses extremely demanding, but never boring. His keen wit and dry humor were among the most notable aspects of his teaching style, and the daily recitations he required in class always kept his students awake. William Mueller recounts a situation in which a student sought to come to blows with Robertson over something the professor had said in class, and asked "Doctor Bob" to take off his coat and defend himself. Robertson wisely replied "All right, all right, but let us first kneel down and pray!"[12] Even in the most difficult situations, Robertson was there, pointing his students to Christ.

The professor also played a critical role during one of the most turbulent times in the history of Southern Baptists' mother seminary: the Whitsitt controversy. Along with his fellow faculty, Robertson stood behind their president, William Whitsitt, in the heated theological and historical debate over Landmarkism. Robertson realized that Whitsitt's historical investigations and evaluations of Baptist successionism were not unfaithful to sound Baptist theology and a proud heritage. Robertson and his fellow faculty prided themselves on the "theological soundness" of Southern Seminary and urged caution in dealing with the issue at hand.[13] Their concern primarily was for a "faithful preaching of a pure gospel," coupled with sound scholarship.[14]

Robertson cared deeply for his students and the seminary, and the high calling of training ministers for the gospel ministry. Perhaps the greatest testament to this fact is that Robertson was teaching on the day on which he grew gravely ill, was taken home, and later died of a severe stroke. One student remarked that even before his death, students began to develop a historical consciousness concerning the import of their professor's work in the field of New Testament interpretation.[15] In spite of his established international reputation as a well-published scholar and theologian, the end of A.T. Robertson's life found him where he was preeminently dedicated and well remembered: in the halls and classrooms of Southern Seminary.

Theologian and Statesman

Robertson's work and influence were not limited, however, to the confines of seminary life and academic enterprise. Robertson gave himself to the larger work of Baptist denominational life, and especially the concerns of Baptists around the world. It was Robertson who originally suggested the concept for what would later become the Baptist World Congress. In 1905, a year after his suggestion in *The Baptist Argus*, the Baptist World Alliance convened in London, a meeting in which Robertson took part. In addition, he contributed to the life and thought of the Southern Baptist Convention, and especially its churches. Robertson had a passion for the centrality of preaching in the church and could regularly be found in pulpits throughout Kentucky, preaching on weekends and ministering the Word.

Robertson wanted to model for his students a careful, expositional approach to preaching the Bible. Like Broadus, he wanted his students to be "mighty in the Scriptures." On one occasion Robertson wryly observed, "The greatest proof that the Bible is inspired is that it has withstood so much bad preaching." Robertson's biographer Everett Gill recounts that when interpreting the Scripture passage, "a savor of life unto life or of death unto death," the professor asserted, "Preaching . . . is the most dangerous thing in the world."[16] Above all, Robertson's life and ministry had the edification and growth of the church of Jesus

Christ in mind. He once remarked to his students, "God pity the poor preacher who has to hunt for something to preach—and the people who have to listen." The wise scholar had a heartbeat for God's people. As William Mueller has observed; "The great New Testament Scholar seemed happiest when he stood before a congregation pointing men and women to the Lord Jesus Christ as their only Master and Savior."[17]

Roberston's influence was also felt throughout the North during the contentious Fundamentalist-Modernist debates in the Northern Baptist Convention. It was not uncommon for the reader of such papers as the *Watchman-Examiner* and *The Baptist* to find articles and essays with Robertson defending the supernatural nature of the Christian truth claim, and supporting the affirmation of the "fundamentals" of Christianity. Much like his colleague, President E. Y. Mullins, Robertson was a man in demand, one whose opinion Baptists would heed. Robertson proved to be a steady voice in unsteady times, a trustworthy scholar for all Baptists, in both North and South.

As a theologian, Robertson did not hesitate to state his conviction. His confidence in the historical reliability and complete truthfulness of Scripture can be seen clearly in Robertson's view of biblical inspiration. While Robertson certainly believed the Christian scholar should avail himself or herself of the most accurate historical data and interpretation, he simultaneously believed that all such human speculations must fall under the authority of the divine disclosure of the Scriptures. Robertson declares concerning the historical reliability of the Gospel of Luke in reference to the divinity and virgin birth of Jesus: "It remains that the whole truth about Jesus lies in the interpretation given by Luke in the opening chapters of his gospel. The view of Luke the physician holds the field today in the full glare of modern science and historical research."[18]

Thus, Robertson was convinced of the veracity of Scripture in light of the findings of modern historical methodology. As such, he was willing to use the best possible historical tools and research in demonstrating the full truthfulness of the Scriptures. Robertson felt that the tools of critical methodology, if cautiously used in reverence for the authority of Scripture, could aid the interpreter in understanding the biblical text. Consequently, Robertson's openness to the proper use of critical tools in interpreting Scriptures should not be viewed as an antithetical position to that of Robertson's forebears such as John A. Broadus and Basil Manly Jr., but rather as a contemporary exposition of that same tradition.

As such, Robertson became a standard in Southern Baptist circles by which New Testament scholarship and biblical fidelity would later be judged. Upon the occasion of his death, one of his students, Herschel H. Hobbs, remarked that if all the buildings of the seminary were blown down and Dr. Robertson alone were left standing "the seminary would have been more real than it was with him gone."[19] He was part of the impetus which brought Southern Baptist life and scholarship to the forefront of the theological world. In many ways, Robertson's reputation has yet to be paralleled. His legacy to his colleagues, students, and Southern Seminary was, in the words of his successor Hershey Davis, "inestimable."

Some of Robertson's writings, such as his famous *Word Pictures*, still are available in print and continue to be widely popular. His *Grammar* continues as a standard reference work in many circles. The essays and articles collected here are representative portions of Robertson's life and thought that have not, in recent memory, been widely circulated. As a body they demonstrate the breadth and quality of Robertson's scholarly and popular contributions. They cover his contributions in the areas of New Testament interpretation, biblical theology, lexical expertise, and denominational contributions.

Epochs in the Life of Jesus shows us a fundamental concern of Robertson: expounding and retelling the stories of the New Testament. In the light of the work of liberal scholars, like Albert Schweitzer, who were seeking to give their position on the historical Jesus, Robertson saw the need to write his own biography of the life of Christ. In place of Schweitzer's assertion that the titles of Jesus are mere "historical parables," Robertson clearly confesses him as the Messiah, the Son of God. In place of the confused identity with which "The Quest for the Historical Jesus" had sought to depict Jesus, Robertson reveals the unified witness of the Gospel material: that Jesus is in fact Lord and Savior.

In "The Bible as Authority," Robertson asserts that the Bible is actually the Word of God, and "since there is no ultimate authority in the spiritual realm outside of God," the Bible has the authority to command obedience, action, and belief. In this essay, Christ is revealed as the interpretive principle for all of Scripture. Robertson concludes that critical study of the Bible must be supplemented by the guidance of the Holy Spirit in its interpretation, stating "The Bible must be studied by the scientific historical method, but also with an enlightened soul in touch with the Spirit of God." What is more, Robertson affirms the historic Baptist principle that Scripture must be interpreted in light of Scripture, and that the Bible can be plainly understood, on its own terms, and in its own words. The Bible, he felt, has stood against so much criticism, unbelief, and misinterpretation, as to demonstrate through those facts alone that it must be the Word of God.

Robertson addressed the issue of the validity and importance of the supernatural conception of Jesus Christ in "Is the Virgin Birth Still Credible Today?" Robertson's answer to that question is a resounding "yes" as it appeared during the height of the Fundamentalist-Modernist controversy among Northern Baptists in the early 1920s. But Robertson's approach is not an uncritical literalism which hides away when the facts are presented. Rather, it embraces all of the truth God has shown us in the natural order as but further evidence of his powerful ability to accomplish his providential purposes. As such, Robertson declared with his Baptist predecessors that the Scripture "has God for its author, salvation for its end, and truth, without any mixture of error, for its matter."

The third part of this book shows how Robertson converted his mastery of Greek into practical applications for the believer in "The Greek Article and the Deity of Christ," and "Grammar and Preaching." In the former, Robertson refutes the questionable exegesis which has supplied false evidence to all those who seek to deny the deity of Jesus Christ by claiming a loophole in the grammatical construct of the first chapter of the Gospel of John. In "Grammar and Preaching" Robertson again weds the practicality of knowledge of Greek grammar with sound exegetical preaching that is faithful to the text of God's Word.

The final section of this work underscores Robertson's commitment to Baptist life and thought. It is a collection of his writings on issues that we call "Baptist Distinctives." Robertson was once reported to have said, "Give a man an open Bible, an open mind, a conscience in good working order, and he will have a hard time to keep from being a Baptist." This attitude was reflected in his labors both in denominational service to Southern Baptists, and as a resource to Baptists throughout the world. Robertson was a believer in Baptist polity and sought to bring Baptists, who might not have otherwise met, together through his support of the Baptist World Alliance.

Expositor. Theologian. Scholar. Statesman. A man gifted in several areas, A.T. Robertson faithfully taught the Bible in the spirit and conviction of his Baptist heritage, while simultaneously ushering Baptist scholarship into the twentieth century, and placing it on a solid but contemporary footing. The legacy of Robertson's work lives on in the lives of those whom he taught, and continues to teach, by his faithful witness and care for God's Word. Our hope and prayer is that this volume will introduce a new generation to that great legacy and motivate us all to a renewed commitment and faithfulness to "handle accurately the Word of God" (2 Tim. 2:15).[20]

PART I

New Testament Scholar Selections from *Epochs in the Life of Jesus*

CHAPTER ONE

The Messianic Consciousness of Jesus

"This is my beloved Son, in whom I am well pleased."
MATT. 3:17

There are many ways of approaching the life of Jesus. No other theme has produced so many books, and the steady stream flows on. The knowledge of Jesus is indeed the most excellent of the sciences. And yet no one has written an exhaustive or comprehensive discussion of Christ. It has always been so. No one of the Gospels gives a complete picture of the Master, nor do all four Gospels tell us all that we should like to know, nor, in fact, all that was once known of Jesus. Herein lies a strong argument for the deity of Christ, his inexhaustibleness. "The riches of Christ" are "unsearchable" and past finding out.

The Problem of Jesus

He is a constant challenge to men, to the greatest of men. It was so at the first and is true today. Men have grappled with the universe under the spell of a great theory of development. Orderly development has been found in the various spheres of human knowledge. But what about Jesus of Nazareth? Is he the product of the narrow ceremonialism and ecclesiastical bigotry of Palestinian Pharisaism? No connection can be traced between Christ and Plato, Socrates, Buddha, or any of the great thinkers outside of Judaism. Here is universal and absolute truth that sprang out of an atmosphere of intense racial pride and hate. Here is the man who laid most stress on the spiritual and moral aspects of religion in the midst of teachers who tithed mint, anise, and cumin.

But this is not all. Here is one who led a sinless life in the face of malignant enemies, whose character is the unapproachable ideal of all men who have ever read his story. Here is one who made the greatest claims for himself, who put himself on a par with the living God according to the testimony of the Gospels which bring us the story of his career. Here is one who asserts his right to the allegiance of all men, who offers to rescue all that come to him from sin and its effects. His perfect life and his lofty teachings give a serious aspect to what would otherwise be absurd claims.

The tremendous power of Jesus over the world commands respect, whatever the explanation. The men who are most loyal to Christ are just the men who have been foremost in the advancement of civilization and the uplift of the race. The nations where the influence of Jesus is greatest are those whose people stand highest among the kingdoms of earth. The Protestant nations which have freedom from priestly domination have long led the world.

Even those who reject the claims of Jesus to deity on philosophical grounds, like Professor G. B. Foster (following Pfeiderer), or on critical grounds by disposing of the evidence for his career, like Professor N. Schmidt (following Bousset and Wrede), are reverent in their treatment of the person of Jesus, even enthusiastic about his character.

"What think ye of Christ?" He was indeed set for the falling and the rising of many not only in Israel, but in all the world. He is the loadstone of human hearts, the test of every person's life. Like Charles Lamb, we all feel that if Jesus came into our presence we should instinctively kneel. Jesus presses himself upon our hearts and upon our minds. He does not expect us to give up our reason when we come to settle the question with him. We need then all the intellect that we have. The difficulty is to see the problem as a whole and as it really is.

In this study we seize the main things in their historical development and seek to grasp their relation to each other and their results. No merely natural explanation of Jesus is possible. It is irrational, in view of all the facts, to attempt it. A "greater than Jonah" is here, the Son of God. Men have not always been able to show Jesus to those who asked to see him. Philip and Andrew were puzzled over the simple and polite request of the Greeks. Sometimes our sermons hide Christ, alas, instead of revealing him. Our theology may become a veil that rests on the heart so that Jesus is not seen when the Gospel is read. Our wranglings may picture an absent Christ and reflect the ecclesiastical ambitions of the first disciples instead of the spiritual elevation of Jesus.

The search-light of modern historical investigation has brought out into clearer relief the historic Christ and his environment. We can go back behind Calvin and Augustine to Christ. We can even go behind Paul, Peter and John to Christ himself. We can see how each of the apostles apprehended Jesus, what each contributed to our knowledge of the master. We can see how they at first were dazzled by the great light that bewildered them, how gradually they came to understand him and his message and their mission. The revolution wrought in the first disciples is the eternal miracle of Christianity and is repeated every day of the world.

It is the vision of the Eternal Christ. We cannot put mere historical limitations around Jesus in our study of him. While we follow the struggle, the greatest of the ages, which he made with the human and superhuman forces about him, we are conscious of a higher element in him. He himself spoke of this transcendent fact, and it puzzled and dazed all around him. His life did not begin when he was born, nor did it end when he died. Today the world bows not before a hero of hate whose body still lies on Golgotha's hill, but before the Risen Christ who sits on the throne of majestic glory at the right hand of the Father. That is the New Testament picture of the Redeemer who has triumphed over death and the grave and who is leading a victorious warfare against the hosts of evil. This is the Savior from sin who has spoken peace to our hearts and in whose name we work today. So, while we study together the human conditions and the various historic epochs in the career of Christ, let us not think that such an attempt can explain all that is true of Jesus then and now. But let our hearts burn within us as Jesus comes and walks with us and talks with us as we seek to explain some of the mystery of the Nazarene.

The First Glimpse of Jesus

When the boy Jesus comes to Jerusalem at 12 years of age, he knows that he is the Son of God in a sense not true of other men.

"Wist ye not that I must be in my Father's house?" His parents were astonished at the ease and powers he showed in such a place of dignity, teaching and amazing the doctors of divinity in the rabbinical theological seminary. But none the less is he astonished at their ignorance of the fact that this is the place of all the world for him. Who can tell a boy's golden dreams of the future till some day the sun bursts out in full glory? The boy has gone forever with the revelation of the man, and the manly purpose has come to fill the heart and life. The word "must" throws a long light back into the boy's quiet years at Nazareth. Modern theologians speculate learnedly on the time when Jesus first became conscious of the fact that he was God's Son and had a messianic mission to perform. That is idle speculation. We only know that at 12 years of age Jesus is aware that God has laid his hand upon him. He is at home in the Father's house and rejoices to discuss high and holy themes.

The whole problem of the person of Jesus is brought before us by this incident. By the side of this early Messianic consciousness lies the other fact that he grew in wisdom and in stature. He was a real boy for all the divine element in him, and an obedient one, too, for he was subject to his parents gladly after this event. The one boy that really knew more than his father and mother was a model of obedience.

The loneliness of the boy Jesus at this time impresses one. He was not understood by the theological professors at Jerusalem, nor by his parents, not even by his mother who had long ago been told of the future of her child. Had she hid her secret so deep in her heart that it was lost? But the time was long and he probably did little, if anything, out of the ordinary, certainly none of the silly things told by the apocryphal gospels. Only once is the veil lifted during the silent 30 years, and thus light shines on the Messianic consciousness of Jesus. He had a human education those years at Nazareth, in his home, in the synagogue, in the fields with the birds and flowers, with his playmates, at his work in the carpenter's shop.

Luke is the writer of this incident, and it is he whose introduction is so much like that of the Greek historian Thucydides. Luke it is who said that he had made careful examination of the sources and had taken pains to be accurate. The stamp of truthfulness is on the narrative with its simplicity and reality. Mary herself may well have told Luke what is here narrated. It is the fashion today with some to discount what John has to say about Jesus, but this is Luke the historian.

A word is needed in passing concerning the naturalness and reality of a life that is so soon conscious of a high mission. The explanation lies in the appeal to the facts. There is no vestige of artificiality, of playing a part, in the career of Jesus. We drop out of sight as wilfully blind those who deny that Jesus ever thought that he was the Messiah, who even say that the Old Testament does not predict a Messiah. This surprising result is obtained either by rejecting the passages or by marvelous exegesis of everything that points to a Messiah. It is not strange that God's Son should be acquainted with his Father. What better place for that consciousness to come to larger and more vivid activity than in the temple of the people of God, dedicated to the worship of God?

This boy of 12 who loved the birds and the flowers and worked well at the carpenter's trade grew in favor with God and with men. And no wonder. He combined early piety with popularity. When Joseph died he doubtless became in a sense the mainstay of his mother. Did ever mother's heart have so much to make her glad? Or so much that she did not understand in her wonderful boy?

Was Jesus Born of a Virgin?

We purposely passed over his birth till now. This has become an acute question in our time. The scientific temper demands to know everything and sometimes thinks it has succeeded; but this feeling of omniscience is not monopolized by the scientific spirit. The x-rays, wireless telegraphy, radium, and radiobes, to go no further, make it difficult today for the real scientist to say what can and what cannot happen in nature, even if God does not exist. If God does exist, there is no real difficulty from God's point of view.

Now Matthew and Luke both give the story of the supernatural birth of Jesus, but from different points of view: Luke from the standpoint of Mary, Matthew from that of Joseph. Evidently there are therefore two independent accounts of this great event, both of which come from sources near Jerusalem, while James and Jude, brothers of Jesus, still lived, and possibly while Mary, the mother, survived. Luke spent two years in Caesarea, and was a careful historian. In the opening chapters of his Gospel which tell of this wondrous event there are signs that he used an Aramaic or Hebrew document or heard the story from one who spoke Aramaic. The very first thing told, after his careful historical introduction, is the birth narrative. There are miracles here recorded, not necessarily beautiful legends to idealize or deify Jesus. Legends would be possible if the incarnation of Jesus were inherently impossible. But who can say that with confidence?

The silence of Mark cannot be turned against Matthew and Luke. This Gospel was probably written in Rome under the influence of Peter and away from the Jerusalem circle. It is not surprising that nothing should be said at first in public concerning the true birth of Jesus. He passed as the son of Joseph and Mary. The new Syriac manuscript of Matthew from Sinai does say that Joseph begat Jesus in one passage, but in another place the old reading is left. The text was probably under Ebionitic influence which denied the deity of Jesus.

If the prologue of John, with its wondrous survey of the pre-incarnate state of Jesus, does omit a discussion of the birth of Jesus and so has nothing concerning the virgin birth, it is not to give us an easier interpretation of the origin and person of Christ. Certainly John, for I do not doubt that he wrote the fourth Gospel, does not circumscribe the career nor the person of Jesus within purely human limits. The earthly career of Jesus is but a very small though momentous portion of the eternal existence of the Son of God, who was with the Father in heaven before the incarnation and who has returned to the Father since the resurrection and ascension. It is not mere ideal pre-existence that John has him in mind, but personal presence with the Father. John goes further still. He says pointedly of the Logos: He was God. That is a conception capable of comprehension, that the Father should have a Son, a necessary corollary of Father in fact. But John even says that this Son or Logos became flesh and dwelt among us. The Son of God, who was God and co-existed with the Father, became flesh. How? I venture to ask. Was it a mere theophany? Was Jesus a real man? Were the Docetic gnostics right after all who held that Jesus only seemed to be a man? The proper interpretation of John's language is found in the virgin birth, and only thus. He assumes it as well known and implies it. If he were in truth the son of Joseph, he would not be "God's only begotten."

The difficulty is just as great if we turn to Paul. He does say that Jesus was born of woman, and thus disposes of Docetic Gnosticism. He was a real man according to Paul. But did Paul hold him to be God as John clearly believed? He does not use the term God of Jesus unless we so punctuate Romans 9:5, and read church of God in Acts 20:28. But in Col. 1:15–18 and elsewhere (as in 2 Cor. 8:9 and Phil. 2:6) Paul so describes Jesus that he can be to him nothing else but God. Paul may or may not have faced the question of the virgin birth of Jesus. But the real deity of Jesus is taught by Paul, and that is the crux of the whole matter. He has nothing inconsistent therewith, nor has John. All the positive testimony of the New Testament is in favor of this explanation, and there is not a word against it. Indeed, the theological conceptions of Paul and John demand it. Professor Briggs boldly claims that to give up the virgin birth is to give up the philosophical basis for the incarnation of Christ. One may still believe in the deity of Jesus and be illogical. That does not disturb a good many people. Logic cuts a small figure in a good deal of theology. But it is not possible to think of God becoming man except by the virgin birth and not thereby have two persons in the one into whom God has entered. The heresy of Nestorianism or two persons in Christ is then inevitable. And even if God could thus enter such a man, he would not thereby affect any other man. If Jesus is indeed the God-Man, Son of God and Son of Man, the virgin birth is the only conceivable way for that great event to happen. And, indeed, this problem is no more difficult than anything else connected with the deity of Jesus. That is the problem after all. The ancient deification of the Roman emperor and other heroes and demi-gods does not prove that this is what happened with Jesus.

So let us take our place with the shepherds on the hills of Bethlehem and hear the angels sing about peace on earth to those who receive the good pleasure of God. Let us fall under the spell of this transcendent mystery. The Child in the manger has brought new hope to every mother in the world, new glory to every child on earth, new dignity for every person who has felt the touch of the Son of God. He will indeed save his people from their sins. Zacharias and Mary, Simeon and Anna caught a glimpse of the Light that brightens Jew and Gentile. They sang the first Christian hymns. They had seen the salvation of Israel. The wise men still fall at his feet, and the Herods and Satan are still trying to compass the ruin of the Christ. But not priest, nor king, nor devil can stay the march of the Kingdom of God.

Who is Jesus then? No doctrine that we can frame meets all the facts. The Kenosis theories of the humiliation of Christ put into Paul's word in Phil. 2:9 more than he had. They multiply, not minimize, the problems. They fade away into dimness and vagueness. Of what did Christ empty himself when he left the place beside the Father on high? Did it apply to his divine nature or only to his divine glory? How much of God's knowledge and God's power did Christ have while he was man? How could the infinite Son of God tie himself up in human flesh with human limitations? How could the sinless one dwell in flesh and not have sin? If he had sin, he could not save us from sin. If the true theologian is humble and reverent here, it must be recalled that the true scientist is not boastful about life, ultimate life, the Source of all things. We do not understand either half of this problem, God or man. It is not strange that the combination causes new difficulties. Perhaps when we do reach clearness of vision about both God and man, we shall approach the subject of the God-Man with more confidence. At any rate, we are sure that this sublime union of God and man does offer the only real solution of the career and character of Jesus of Nazareth. It is in personality that God and man can properly meet. Philosophy can help a little way here by the new emphasis on the problems of personality. We can in Christ form an intelligible conception of God. Without Christ our ideas of God tend to fade away into abstractions.

The Father's Sanction of the Son

The news came to Jesus in Nazareth that strange things were going on down by Jordan river. He was a man now, the man Jesus, and the news had a fascination for him. It was not the call of the wilderness, but the call of his Father that he heard, though he must go to the desert. A new prophet had appeared in the wilderness, a man with odd garments, strange habits, and a marvelous message. But the charm of John was not in his garb nor in his diet. Greatness cannot be counterfeited by imitating eccentricities. It was the spirit and power of Elijah, not the hairy raiment of Elijah, that most characterized the Baptist. The message was the most wonderful thing about the man. He said that the Kingdom was at hand, no longer in the distant future. Was it true? The news spread till all Jerusalem and Judea went out to see what was more than a reed shaken in the wind. Finally the preachers and teachers went also with the crowd to hear this mountain prophet, some perhaps to scoff and sneer. It was amazing, the audacity of the man! He said that even the preachers must repent like common sinners, publicans and Gentiles, and be baptized. As if we were not the children of Abraham! But this prophet spared not high nor low, soldier, publican, nor priest. Those that repented he immersed in the Jordan, and the new rite made many suppose that he was the Messiah himself. For a little while then John was taken at more than his real value (as reformers often are), but he soon dispelled such false estimates by bluntly saying that he was not the Messiah. He was only the voice of the herald crying in the wilderness. He was not worthy to unloose the shoes of the Messiah, who would have the baptism of the Holy Spirit. But where was the Messiah?

Did Jesus tell his mother where he was going when he left Nazareth? His crisis had come and he knew it. John and Jesus met by the water side. John had had a sign given him by which to recognize the Messiah. Doubtless he had each day watched for that sign as he baptized the multitudes and eagerly scanned each upturned face. He probably had not seen Jesus, certainly not for a long time, and he did not know who the Messiah was. But before the sign came he had an instinctive feeling that here was he! It was incongruous that the Messiah should ask baptism at his hands. John had not, it seems, been himself baptized. His baptism called for confession of sin, and in the presence of the sinless One, John felt afresh his own unworthiness and asked baptism at the hands of Jesus. But Jesus held his ground. It was right enough for John to feel that way, but Jesus was a man and a Jew and must obey the call that his Father made on all to be baptized on confession of sin. The fact that he had no sin to confess did not relieve him from the obligation to do this righteous act of obedience. Let us never forget that Jesus thought it worth while to come from Nazareth to the Jordan, not to be saved, for he needed no saving, and baptism saves no one except symbolically. He gave the sanction of his own example to baptism in the

Jordan, and later he enjoined it upon all his disciples. He was indeed in a symbolic way setting forth his own death and resurrection also, but John in all likelihood did not see that point.

John soon saw that Jesus was right in being baptized, for the Father spoke audibly to the Son, and the Spirit of God in the form of a dove rested on Jesus as he came out of the water praying. It was an august moment. Father, Son, and Spirit join in celebrating this event. Clearly the baptism of Jesus had a wonderful personal significance. It has been variously interpreted. Some imagine that now for the first time Jesus became aware of the fact that he was the Messiah, the Son of God, but that interpretation is not justified by the facts. His protest to John just before the baptism was no disclaimer of the Messiahship. His whole bearing with John was that of one who had faced his destiny and had settled it. Some of the Cerinthian Gnostics imagined that the Christ as an Aeon or Emanation of God came down on Jesus at his baptism like a dove, and that it was this Aeon Christ that was divine, while Jesus was himself a mere man. His baptism was, however, the beginning of the public Messianic work. Jesus was now stepping out into the open. He had crossed the Rubicon and there was no turning back. He had put his hand to this plow and he must follow it to the end and sink the plow in deep. It was the coming of the Holy Spirit that constituted the anointing of Jesus, and not the baptism. Let us not confuse the two things. We may compare the prophetic endowment in the Old Testament.

The Moral Issue in the Temptation

The Gospel writers can only have gotten this narrative from Jesus himself. He probably told the disciples long afterwards about this fierce struggle with the prince of evil that met him at the threshold of his ministry as it often comes just then to the young preacher. Mark barely mentions the fact, while Matthew and Luke tell the details of the titanic struggle. The time of the occurrence could only be at the beginning of the ministry. Satan would wish at once to challenge the Messiah. Like a lion of the jungle he challenges the newcomer into his domain. Rightly or wrongly the devil claimed this world as his own. He had done much to make it a jungle of sin and woe. He felt that there could only be enmity between himself and Jesus. The synoptic Gospels all agree in putting the temptation just after the baptism. It was the psychological moment. Every new convert has a fresh struggle with the devil after his baptism. "Now, you have gone and made a fool of yourself," the devil will say.

We may not pause to discuss whether it was an objective visitation of the devil or merely the pressure of devilish suggestion on the mind of Jesus. Most probably both elements existed. It is no more difficult to think of the devil making a visible manifestation of himself to Jesus than to believe in the existence of the devil at all. That is the real problem. If there is a real spirit of evil who has access to and power over the soul of man, we need trouble ourselves little about the rest. It would be comforting to believe, as some writers do, that the devil is dead. Certainly sin is not dead. If there is no devil, it is not complimentary to man to make him originally responsible for all the evil in the world. But, whether the devil appeared objectively to Christ or not, it was in the realm of spirit that temptation took place. Mark even says that Jesus was led of the Spirit into the wilderness to be tempted of the devil. This is at first a hard saying, but probably it only means that God wished his Son to meet the tempter at once and have it out once for all. Not that the devil would not try again, but the line for future conflict would be clearly defined.

The devil has an evident allusion to the approval of the Father at Christ's baptism when he said "if thou art a son of God," as God had said. Not that the devil denies that this is so; in fact, the form of the condition implies that it is true, and he says "a son of God," not "the Son of God," as God had said. But he suggests to Jesus that it would be just as well for him to test what God had said. That would do no harm. He would then have personal experience to sustain him. He was very hungry and, if he was God's Son, surely he could do creative work as God did. It was a subtle appeal. Jesus would work miracles for others. Why not begin by working one of himself? In a word, shall Jesus be a selfish Messiah? But the temptation would have been no temptation put in that form. That is the peril with a temptation, that its real character is at first concealed and difficult to see. There was here concealed distrust of God.

The Jews expected the Messiah to come with a great spectacular display. They will often ask Jesus to do a sign, not merely work miracles, but some great portent in the heavens, for instance. The devil suggests that Jesus accommodate himself to the popular expectation and let them see him come sailing down from the pinnacle of the temple, right out of heaven. They would hail him with acclaim. But Jesus was to be no mere performer of tricks, no balloon or parachute aeronaut. The devil grows pious and quotes Scriptures, not misquotes it as some good people do, but he misapplies it. In that also the devil has no monopoly. But Jesus saw that he would be presumptuous and not trustful if he dared such a feat. Besides, he might as well settle now as later whether he was to be the kind of a Messiah that the people wished or the one that the Father had planned. Every preacher in a humbler way has to meet a similar problem. It is so easy to fall in with the drift of things, so easy as to fall over a great height when nervous and afraid.

But the devil was not done. He appealed to the ambition of Jesus. He would help him to be king of the world. The devil was an old hand at it. He would not exactly abdicate; he and Jesus could run it together. That would be better than open war. He offered Jesus all the kingdoms of the world and the glory of them. It was a fascinating picture as it passed before the mind of Jesus. He only asked in return that Jesus bow down before him up here on the mountain. Nobody else was there, and it would merely be a recognition of the facts of the case. The devil did have the kingdoms of the world in his power, the great Roman Empire, for instance. Was it not better to make peace and be friends than to fight it out? He could turn this great Roman Empire against Jesus, who had no disciples as yet, and, if he should win some, he could use this empire against the Kingdom of Jesus. This was the heart of the temptation. Jesus wanted the world. In fact, he had come to win the world, but he was to win the world from the devil, not take the world on the devil's terms and with the devil as dictator. Christ was not confused by the issue. He knew what his decision meant. But he loved the world too well to betray it in that fashion. He would not have a mixture of the kingdom of heaven and the kingdom of the world. He would die for the world. Strange to say, the devil did fight Jesus with the Roman Empire and did graft much of the world on the church of the Middle Ages. But Jesus brushed aside all compromise and surrender and ordered Satan to go hence. He did go, cowed for the moment, but he will bide his time and wait for another chance. Death then faces Jesus at the very beginning. He must be willing to die for men before he can save them. So Jesus chose the high and stony path that led to Calvary, a lonely way and a weary one. His decision meant eternal conflict with Satan till he has conquered and the kingdoms of this world have become the kingdom of our Lord and of his Christ.

The Johannine Presentation of Jesus

It harmonizes with the synoptic picture as seen in the temptation, for instance. In John, Jesus is represented as conscious from the very start that he is the Messiah charged with a mighty work for God, conscious also of his death for men. The point of note is that this conception of Christ is given also in the synoptic Gospels. John has merely accented what is implicit in the temptation and expressed by the Father at the baptism. Jesus is the Son of God. John represents Christ as addressed as Messiah and even claiming to be Messiah at the first. That is not strange, but natural. Just as John tells of the early baptizing done by the disciples of Jesus, which apparently ceased because of the popularity of Jesus with the people and consequent hostility of the Pharisees, so he narrates the early Messianic claims which were soon stopped in terms and for the same reason. The collision with the rulers at Jerusalem at the very first Passover made it plain that matters would come to a focus at once if Jesus persisted in openly claiming to be the Messiah or in allowing himself to be so called. The Messianic restraint of Jesus, therefore, became a necessity. But this restraint does not at all mean that Jesus began his public career merely as another rabbi or even a prophet like

John looking for the Messiah, finally drawn by popular expectation to think he was the Messiah or to pose as the Messiah. Those alternatives are alike inconceivable and inconsistent with all that we know of Jesus. He was no mere dreamer, no fanatic, no play-actor, no demagogue, no charlatan. There are difficulties in thinking of Jesus as knowing at the beginning of his ministry that he was the Messiah and would be put to death, but that fate is before every true soldier. Jesus goes on bravely to meet his hour and live out his day. Actual experience shows that the highest type of manhood is developed in a time of stress and storm.

The Terms Used of Jesus Have a Peculiar Interest

His own favorite word, Son of Man, had a Messianic import, though not generally so understood at the time. It served as a claim for his office, and yet in a veiled form. It was certainly more than the jejune Aramaic "barnasha," a man. In some passages that idea is positively ridiculous. Besides, the term accents the incarnation of Christ. He is the representative man. A few times Jesus called himself the Son of God (Synoptic as well as Johannine) in a sense not true of other men. This claim the Jews regarded as blasphemy, for he claimed to be equal with God and received worship as God. After the opening ministry he did not allow himself to be called Messiah in so many words till he pointedly asked Peter to say what he thought of him. Even then he warned Peter and the disciples not to call him Messiah in public. And yet on oath before the Sanhedrin, Jesus did say that he was the Messiah, the Son of God, and the son of Man. He paid the penalty of that confession by death. It would not be blasphemy for the real Messiah to make this claim. And Jesus had been identified by John the Baptist as the lamb of God that taketh away the sin of the world. The last time that the Baptist saw the Messiah he stood looking, rapt with the glory of the vision. "He standeth in the midst of you," he had said, "and ye know him not." And that is often true today of the unseen and unrecognized Christ.

CHAPTER TWO

The First Appeal of Jesus

Come, and ye shall see.
JOHN 1:39

We are told in Hebrews 5:8 that, though Jesus was a son, yet he learned obedience by what he suffered. He had to be made perfect by the discipline of experience (Heb. 2:10). Thus alone he could become the Captain (or Author) of salvation, and thus he could gain power to help the tempted (Heb. 2:18). Experience does not come as a gift or an inheritance, nor can it be bought. Already Jesus has settled accounts with the great tempter as to the character of his work. The long war for the rescue of the world has begun, for Jesus came to bring not peace, but a sword.

Connection with John the Baptist's Work

Christ was not wholly alone in his work for the kingdom of God. A few spirits like Simeon and Anna, Zacharias and Elizabeth, of a former generation, lingered on, waiting for the consolation of Israel, though as a whole the "seed-plot of Christianity" in Sanday's words was in uncongenial soul. But John the Baptist, as the forerunner of the Messiah, had brought to the surface some choice spirits who would hail the Messiah with joy.

John the Baptist never wavered for a moment about the Messiah. He could take his own measure perfectly, a very difficult thing to do. We make mental misfits very easily. He did not allow flattery or intrigue to turn him from the hearty loyalty to Jesus as the true Messiah, the Hope of Israel. The Gospel of John does not narrate the baptism of Jesus by the Baptist, though it implies it in alluding to the sign of the Holy Spirit descending on him (1:33). After the baptism of Jesus, John only saw him twice, so far as we know, and that on two successive days. But on each occasion his soul was rapt with the vision. There is the Lamb of God! Nothing else was worth seeing while Jesus was to be seen. "He looked upon Jesus as he walked" (John 1:36). He rejoiced to bear his testimony of identification, "I have seen, and I have borne witness that this is the Son of God" (John 1:34). He saw truly also the sacrificial aspect of the Messiah's work. He is "the Lamb of God that taketh away the sin of the world" (John 1:29). The Baptist did not, as some maintain, wholly mistake the work of the Messiah, for he expressly said that Jesus would perform a spiritual ministry (baptize with the Spirit), though his coming did bring inevitable judgment upon the world.

The First Disciples

These were disciples of the Baptist, Andrew and probably John the Evangelist, who took the Baptist at his word and went with Jesus. It was a moment of great significance for Jesus. Here at least was a beginning, two souls prepared by the Baptist's work. John the Evangelist wrote of it when an old man, but he never forgot across the years the event nor the hour of the day, ten o'clock in the morning (Roman time). They spent the day with Jesus, the first of many like days. The leaven of the Kingdom was already at work. To Andrew belongs the distinction of moving first to win another. The correct text (John 1:41) indeed says that this is the first thing that Andrew did after his communion with Jesus. He put first things first. He had no time for anything else. To Simon, his brother, he says simply: "We have found the Messiah." It was a piece of tremendous news. Could it be true? Simon is soon face to face with Jesus. At once the eye of Jesus was taken with the man. He "looked upon him" with all the penetration of human nature so characteristic of Christ. He saw in Simon what nobody else had ever seen—saw indeed the instability, the impulsiveness, the weakness of his nature, but saw beyond all that the deeper and stronger possibilities of this man and appealed, as he always does, to the best in him. He prophesied a new name for Simon, that of Cephas or Peter. He did not now deserve to be called a Rock, but he will. What Jesus did with Simon he does with every person. The most remarkable thing about Jesus is what he puts into a person, not what he sees in him. Thus Christ has lifted up the world, by finding the best thing in a person, developing that, and putting new life into him, the kingdom of God.

On the next day Jesus finds Philip and pointedly says "Follow me." It was a strange command. Philip did not know Jesus. Why should he follow this stranger? He may have been a disciple of the Baptist, but at any rate Philip came from Bethsaida, the town of Andrew and Peter, who were now with Jesus. This fact gave weight to the demand of Jesus. So it is today. We follow Christ partly because our friends do. Besides, there was a tone of insistence in the words of Jesus. He seemed to have the right to ask this supreme service of Philip. People will listen to the plea of Jesus, it is now clear. It will be possible to win them to the Kingdom of Christ in opposition to the kingdom of the devil.

As Andrew (and probably also John the Evangelist) was stirred by the power of the leaven, so Philip is stirred to find Nathanael. Each one wins one. Why not? That is the normal work of the kingdom of God. "We have found him," Philip says. It was the greatest of earth's discoveries. Not gold, nor diamond, nor planet, nor new sun, nor radium can be mentioned beside this discovery of whom Moses and the prophets did write. But Nathanael was not impulsive like Simon. He was a skeptic. "Can any good thing come out of Nazareth?" (John 1:43). Like many other skeptics, he settled the whole matter on a side issue. Philip had called him "Jesus of Nazareth, the Son of Joseph." Nathanael lived not far from Nazareth. To be a citizen of that town was enough for him. Nazareth had a bad name, and was the wrong place anyhow according to the Old Testament; therefore the Messiah could not lie there. Logic is after all a poor coach to ride in. One has said that the best thing in the world came out of Nazareth. But Philip was patient. He only asked a trial. "Come and see." The claims of Jesus are not to be settled finally in the realm of abstract discussion. The argument from experience is a scientific argument. Philip rested his whole case right there. He knew what Jesus had done for him. Nathanael could not refuse to come. So he came to investigate Jesus, but found that Jesus had already diagnosed him and pronounced him "an Israelite indeed in whom there is no guile." Thus it is a personal issue between Nathanael and Jesus. "Whence knowest thou me?" It is the first time that Jesus exhibits to men supernatural knowledge. Nathanael's skepticism vanishes before this personal experience. He takes Jesus as the Son of God and the King of Israel. He leaps to the full length and recognizes the divine element in Jesus "the Son of Joseph." Jesus prophesies greater things than these which Nathanael will see, for Jesus is the bond of union between earth and heaven. The angels ascend and descend upon the Son of Man, as Christ calls himself now for the first time. It is significant to note how the chief terms used of Jesus afterwards come to the front right at the beginning. He is the Messiah, the son of Joseph, of Nazareth, the Son of Man, rabbi or teacher, the King of Israel, the Lamb of God, the Son of God.

The First Miracle

The devil had tried to get Jesus to work his first miracle for himself. He never wrought miracles for himself simply, though he was and is himself the great miracle. John the Baptist wrought no miracle, so that we cannot say that a prophet was expected to work miracles as a matter of course. The miracles of Jesus do present difficulty to the modern scientific mind. They created difficulty then also, so much so indeed that the enemies of Jesus attributed them to the devil. But the modern approach to the subject of miracles is through the person of Christ. If he was in reality the Son of God, it is not surprising that he should exercise the power of God. The remaining difficulty lies in the relation of God to the world. If God has not exhausted his power in the laws of nature known to us, we may not limit the expression of his will. The more real and spiritual God is, the less reason we have for denying his power in nature. The suggestion for this miracle came from the mother of Jesus, and shows that she knew that he had entered upon his Messianic work and that she believed in him. And yet, while the suggestion was perfectly natural and indicates an intimate relation of fellowship between mother and son, a demand was created by it for an outline of the new situation. The very fact that he had entered upon his Messianic work made it impossible for Mary longer to exercise a mother's power over him. Jesus had no harshness in the use of the word "Woman," but it was necessary for her to understand the new relation. Perhaps his "hour" had not come for a public demonstration or issue as will come later in Jerusalem. Hc did adopt the suggestion of his mother and change the water into wine, real wine. Jesus thus had power over nature. His first miracle is as hard as any. He is Lord of nature, and the water recognized that fact and responded to his will:

"The conscious water saw its God and blushed."

Jesus knew how to mingle in social life in such a way as to bless and gladden. He was no recluse who held aloof from men. He lived in the world, but was not tainted by the world. The lover of temperance, as Jesus was, is not driven to false exegesis of this beautiful incident to justify his plea even for local option of prohibition. The light wines of that time were taken with three parts of water and were about like our tea or coffee in effect. Jesus was no advocate of the modern saloon with its traffic in human souls. The glory of Jesus was manifest to the little group of a half dozen disciples who now exercised fresh faith in the new master. A brief visit to Capernaum with his mother and the band of disciples followed the wedding feast at Cana.

The Issue with the Jerusalem Authorities

It was proper that Jesus should go to the feast of the Passover. There was no better time for the Messiah to meet the religious leaders of the people than at this great feast. Here first we come to a note of time in the public ministry of Christ, and it is John who gives it, not the Synoptics. For all that they tell, the work of Christ might have culminated in a year, though a crowded one. But John, if we take his Gospel to be fairly chronological, makes at least two and a half years with three Passovers, with the possibility of three and a half years. So it was in the spring of A.D. 27, let us say, that Jesus is in Jerusalem for the first time since his baptism some six months before. He is in the temple, where he loved to be when a boy of 12, the house of his Father. Here also he realizes that it is his Father's house that is desecrated with the barter and sale of doves and sheep, the clink of money, and the clamor of the money changers in the corridors of the Court of the Gentiles. He is not engaged in theological discussion as before, but this outrage, this graft which enriches the priestly rules, so stirred Jesus that he turns reformer at once and asserts his prophetic and Messianic authority. It is objected that the Synoptics give this incident at the close of Christ's ministry and not at the beginning as John has it. But surely it was of such a nature as to make it likely to occur again when the tradesmen returned to their desecration. The influence of Jesus was only personal and momentary. The men rallied and wondered what they went out for anyhow. The Jews demanded a sign in proof of his claims in doing what only the Messiah had a right to do. So here at the start the issue is drawn between Jesus and the ecclesiastical authorities. He could have wrought a great sign and made verbal claim to be the Messiah. Would they have accepted him? No, rather they would have killed him now instead of three years hence. He does give them a sign, but one which they do not understand, nor the disciples. He gave the sign of his death and resurrection, the great sign on which he staked his whole career. It was in symbolic and parabolic form, but for that very reason stuck in the minds of the people, though with a misunderstanding, as is shown when at the trial of Christ this misinterpretation is all that the enemies of Jesus can find against him. And on the cross it will be flung in his teeth that he had said that he would destroy the temple and raise it again in three days. He had not said that. He had said a great deal more. He had said that, if they destroyed the temple of his body, he would raise it up in three days. This is not merely John's interpretation of the parable of Jesus. It is the only interpretation in harmony with the career of Christ.

It is objected that it is an anti-climax for Jesus thus at the start to announce his death, that he could have no spirit to go on if that was the foreseen end. But this objection takes too narrow a view of the career of Jesus and makes his soul too small. He came to earth at all to die for sinners. He would not commit suicide. He would let events work out their course. He would not hasten his "house," but would go bravely on to meet it. To take out from the mind of Christ this early knowledge of his death would rob him of the chief element of transcendent heroism, would make him a blind groper after the good, rather than the great constructive spirit who saw that the only hope of the race was for him to lay down his own life for it. But in doing so and before doing so he will do a man's part also. He will attack the evil conditions all about him in religion and in life. He will set up the ideal before men, both in word and deed. His death will rest upon a life worth living, and that will be to men the appeal of the ages. This is a conception worthy of Christ, and it is the one given in the Gospels. He will begin with the house of God. That calls for cleansing. Even if men with vested privileges granted or winked at by the rulers profane the house of God, he will protest. He will protest even if they come back. He will lift his voice and his hand against the violators of law and decency. That hand is lifted yet and scourges every breaker of law and order.

An Interview with a Jewish Scholar

Nicodemus felt drawn to Jesus as one scholar is to another. Here was a kindred spirit, a man versed in the deepest things. But there was more. The signs that he wrought in Jerusalem proved to him that God was with the new teacher. And yet Jesus was persona non grata to the Sanhedrin, of which Nicodemus was a member. Christ was already a man taboo with the doctors of divinity. It was partly due to the fact that Jesus was not a technical schoolman in their sense, not a graduate of the rabbinical seminary, had not learned from them; but partly also to an element of novelty in his teachings. His standpoint was so unconventional and so different. They could not at first place him. He was unsafe for their theology. His collision in the temple accented it all. The rabbis apprehended trouble. But all the more Nicodemus was drawn to him.

We may picture this timid and inquiring scholar going by night to a tent on the hill outside of the city, with many a covert glance by the way. His introductory remarks pave the way for more intimate conversation. Here is a very different man from either Simon or Nathanael. He is the inquiring scholar hedged about by custom and intellectual abstraction, drawn by truth if only he can see his way through the maze. Nicodemus is the slave of the ceremonial system, and does not know it. So Jesus at once puts before him the heart of the whole matter, the necessity of the new birth for entrance into the Kingdom of God. The helplessness of Nicodemus before that fundamental idea in the kingdom of grace shows how much he was entangled in the meshes of legalism. Jesus attempts to help him by suggesting an advance from his own point of view. There must be not only ceremonial new birth, which was easy to Nicodemus, but spiritual new birth, which is axiomatic with us. "Ye must be born anew."

Nicodemus had come for light and he had received more than he knew what to do with, though it was destined to bring him into the Kingdom. But Jesus insisted that this was a mere elementary earthly truth in the Kingdom and not a heavenly truth that reached back to the eternal purpose of God as shown in the necessity of the atoning death of Christ. This "must" took Nicodemus in too deep, and we still wonder over the depth of love as set forth in John 3:16, whether it is the Evangelist's own interpretation or the closing words of Jesus to Nicodemus.

The work of Christ in Judea was more successful than that in Jerusalem, though even there more people believed nominally in

Jesus than he could trust. In Judea the tide of popularity rose so high that the jealousy of the Pharisees was aroused. But the Baptist did not let jealousy enter his heart when Jesus passed him in popular favor. The arrest of John merely showed what was in store for Christ when the issue was sharply joined.

An Interview with a Samaritan Woman

It is hard to put ourselves in the place of Jesus as he talked with the Samaritan woman by Jacob's well. Everything was against his endeavoring to win this one, lone woman. He was worn out with a long day's mountain travel. He was hungry. She was a woman, and a rabbi was not expected by the Jews to talk in public with a woman. She was a Samaritan, whom the Jews hated all the more cordially because she was half Jew. She was a woman who had had too many husbands and whose character and reputation made a very delicate and difficult case to handle. Surely here was a more hopeless proposition than that of Nicodemus. Every reason of race prejudice and personal inclination argued for letting her alone. But Jesus never rose to greater heights than when he roused himself to win this sinful woman. He began with a drink of water, the one common topic between them. There is no finer study in the method of soul winning than in the supreme skill shown by Jesus here in overcoming every obstacle and finally reaching the conscience of the woman herself. She was eager for theological controversy when she suspected that Jesus was a prophet. That was her use for a preacher, a dispute. But Jesus held her to the point and revealed to her the highest word that he had to give about God and worship, and told her plainly that he was the Messiah, a thing he had not told Nicodemus. The result justified the patient perseverance of Jesus, for her conversion led to that of many others. Jesus saw in the saving of this Samaritan woman the promise of victory. The harvest of the world was indeed ripe for the sickle of the reaper when such a woman as this could be converted. The harvest is still ripe, waiting for the reapers. But the soul of Jesus fed on this blessed fruitage. He cared not for food and water now. The will of God was enough. He was now becoming the Savior of the world, for even Samaritans can be saved.

The Call to Nazareth

It is not surprising that Jesus should wish to visit Nazareth. Indeed, he made a second visit later, according to the accounts in Mark and Matthew. It was only fair to give Nazareth, the home of his childhood and youth, a good opportunity. True, Jesus remained away after his baptism till his ministry was well under way. He came then with an acquired reputation as a rabbi, and with even more, for many had heard of his miracles. But with some there was lingering doubt how a young carpenter, reared in their town, whom they knew, could do all the things ascribed to him. There must be a mistake somewhere, they felt. But at the start Jesus was treated with every courtesy. When he read the famous passage in the scroll of Isaiah and gave it back to the attendant, Jesus sat down by the reading desk. That was the sign that he was going to make an address, and instantly all eyes were fastened on him. They were on the *qui vive*, for now they would be able to tell for themselves what there was in him to justify his sudden reputation since he had left them.

They had not long to wait, for Jesus claimed the fulfillment on this day of the Messianic promise just read. The very boldness of the claim won a sympathetic hearing at first. Just to think of it! The Messiah has arisen in our town! Their pride was aroused, and they fell under the spell of his wondrous speech. But still, was not this Joseph's son? Incredulity was expressed in their faces and perhaps in whispers. It is a mortal offense with some people for their neighbors and friends to succeed beyond them. The idea of superior gifts and work is out of the question. It is this underlying resentment that Jesus meets when he interprets it by the parable or proverb, "Physician, heal thyself." They were longing for him to do some of the miracles of which they had heard. After all, talk was easy. Work a miracle or two. Jesus could interpret accurately the psychology of a crowd. But instead of accommodating their idle curiosity, he gave them a stern rebuke, with the example of the sovereignty of God as shown in the case of the widow of Zarephath, and Naaman the Syrian. Nazareth had no natural privileges in the Kingdom above any other town. They took this as a thrust at their town pride, and instantly anger filled them all, so that they attempted the life of the hero of the hour before. It was a sad outcome, but Jesus was not surprised, for he said, "No prophet is acceptable in his own country." It was now clear that Nazareth could not be the center of the Galilean work. Jesus had been too popular in Judea and so had to cease his work there. But he is not too popular in Nazareth.

The New Home

Where should Jesus now make his headquarters? It must be somewhere in Galilee. Judea had become impossible, and Samaria was obviously out of the question. In Galilee no town was more cosmopolitan than Capernaum. The Pharisees had less influence in Galilee than in Judea, and here at least was an opportunity of sowing the seed of the Kingdom free from the dominating ecclesiastics of Jerusalem. The Gentile element in Galilee was still considerable, especially around the Sea of Galilee, which was the center of a large trade. The outer world pressed upon Capernaum, though the Jews had a synagogue there, the gift of a generous Roman centurion. Nazareth itself was near one of the great caravan routes between Egypt and Syria and Mesopotamia. Aramaic and Greek were the languages chiefly heard, both of which Jesus and the disciples probably spoke according to occasion, as was true of Paul also.

The half dozen disciples who had been with Jesus in Judea and Samaria seem not to have gone with him to Nazareth, but rather to their several homes. Four of them, two pairs of brothers, were back at their fishing. When Jesus came to Capernaum to live, he soon found Andrew and Simon, James and John. They had not indeed had any luck on this occasion, and were mending and washing their nets. To Simon Jesus suggested that he put out in his boat and try again. A fisherman can always try once more. But Simon had no further hope. "But at thy word I will let down the net." If it pleased Jesus, he would try once more, though he had toiled all night and caught nothing. The result humbled

Simon and enabled Christ to draw a valuable spiritual lesson for Simon and the rest. Will he have as little faith as a fisher of men? This is the second time these four men follow Christ, though not yet as apostles. They continue with him, leaving their fishing for good.

In the synagogue at Capernaum Jesus is before a strange audience, though not a hostile one. What astonished the assembly was the personal independence of Jesus as a teacher. He was not the slave of the past, as the usual rabbi was who was afraid of a new opinion that did not have the support of some learned rabbi of old. But Jesus taught not as the scribes, but as one having authority. He had the authority of truth and not the dictum of some self-appointed custodian of orthodoxy. It had been a long time since a new idea had been expressed in this synagogue and it created a commotion. What the world needs is the truth, whether new or old. A lie is no more true because hoary with age. A pulpit should not have the dry rot nor the itch for the merely new. In this case the truth was a sensation. "What is this? A new teaching?" We have here also the first incident of many when Jesus healed a poor demoniac. The demon recognized Jesus as the Holy One of God, but his testimony was not welcome for obvious reasons. It would not help Jesus to have such attention. But the people were amazed at his power to cast the demon out. There are serious difficulties connected with the subject of demons, their reality and their relation to disease. We know too little of the spirit-world and psychic phenomena to be able to deny the reality of demons. If the devil exists, demons may without doubt. Missionaries in China today claim to have met similar phenomena in modern times. One is slow to credit Jesus with merely humoring the illusions of the time. The Babylonian and Persian teachings of demons do not prove necessarily that the idea of Jesus was illusion or delusion.

The life at Capernaum was manifestly a busy one. On this very Sabbath Jesus raised Peter's mother-in-law from a fever. Please observe that no protest is made on this Sabbath against the cures wrought on this day. The Pharisees have not yet begun to work against him in Galilee. One of the most beautiful scenes in the life of Jesus is at the close of this day. As the sun was setting, he stood in the door of the house and healed all who passed by. His name and fame filled all the town.

The Lines Drawn in Galilee Also

The strain upon Jesus was now very great. We find him rising a great while before day to secure a quiet place for prayer, and then the multitudes seek him. Jesus no longer lingers in Capernaum, but makes a tour of most of Galilee, apparently with these four disciples. We have no incidents recorded of his first formal tour of the country, though the healing of the leper may be one. We must expand the general statements made in the Gospels and imagine the vast amount of work done. In the case of the leper so much excitement arose that Jesus had to withdraw again to the desert places to pray. He had strictly charged the man not to tell, but, as often happens, all the more the report spread.

We are told, however, several incidents of this period falling in Capernaum after the return home. One of them is the case of the paralytic let down through the roof because of the press at the door. The significant thing here is that the Pharisees are present, and eager to find fault and make charges against Jesus. This is the first time that the Pharisees appear in opposition in Galilee. Christ will no more have a free hand even here. It is to be observed also that they come not only "out of every village of Galilee," but also "out of Judea and Jerusalem," these "Pharisees and doctors of the law sitting by" (Luke 5:17). The recent tour had stirred up the waters in Galilee, and the local theologians had evidently appealed to Jerusalem for help. What was Jesus to do in the midst of so much traditional orthodoxy? They had already condemned him in their hearts as guilty of heresy. Their eyes gleamed with envy and they smiled with satisfaction, the long-bearded hypocrites! He will not attempt any hocus-pocus now that we are here, for we are ready for the impostor! Jesus gave them a handle at once. He offered the paralytic forgiveness of sins. This rankled in their hearts, for according to their theology no one can forgive sins but God. Hence Jesus had claimed to be God. But even so they only felt and looked their indignation.

They were not so brave as they supposed. But Jesus knew their hearts and accepted the unexpressed challenge. He bade the paralytic take up his bed and walk right then and there as a proof of his power on earth as the Son of Man to forgive sins. It was audacious. The worst offence of all was that the palsied man did get up without even asking their permission! "We never saw it on this fashion," the people said. And the Pharisees? They now feared him, but were the more bent on his ruin. If let alone he will overturn all Pharisaical theology. That calamity the world could not survive.

Jesus won a notable disciple when Levi the publican responded to his invitation. The Pharisees would not have asked him to be their disciple. "Publicans and sinners" were branded together as the lowest of men. This was worse than to pick up ignorant fishermen to follow him. Perhaps Levi was impressed by the very fact that Jesus broke over social caste and sought him. There was a real man in this publican and he instantly went with Jesus. He was very grateful to the new teacher and loyal to his old friends. So he gave Jesus a feast and asked a great multitude of publicans and other sinners, and Christ accepted. He did not ask the Pharisees, but they went! They would have declined a formal invitation. They were too pious to associate with such "trash." It was a custom then for all who wished to come to the feast and stand by the wall and watch, if they liked. These pious Pharisees and their scribes (students) did this. They stood off and made remarks about Jesus while he enjoyed the feast, a delightful occupation. "He eats and drinks with publicans and sinners." Jesus heard their talk and said: "Go ye and learn." This to the doctors of theology! Yes, go ye and learn that spirit is more than form with God, though not with you. Taking the Pharisees at their own estimate of themselves, Jesus had come to heal the sick, not the well.

Growing out of this dispute comes the discussion about fasting. Even some of the disciples of John the Baptist are led by the Pharisees to complain that the disciples of Jesus do not observe the stated fast. They are, therefore, not orthodox. This complaint gives Christ an opportunity to draw in outline by three illustrations (bridegroom, new garment, wineskin), the vital distinction between Christianity and Judaism: Christianity is spirit and Judaism is form. It is impossible to graft Judaism upon Christianity. The failure to see this nearly wrecked Christianity in Paul's day, and did ultimately make a hybrid type of religion dominant through the Middle Ages, to the lasting injury of the cause of Christ.

For the first time we see Jesus in the chamber of death. He took only Peter, James, and John, and the little girl's father and mother. He took her by the hand and she arose. Death could not stay where Life was when Life spoke. If this miracle seems hard to believe, we may remind ourselves that all are hard to us and all are easy to God. Jesus was anxious to keep this great deed quiet, because the envy of the Pharisees had already been aroused and he foresaw renewed hostility on their part. So in the case of the two blind men, he charged that no man know it, but to no effect. The result was what Christ expected. Already the Pharisees dare to say, "By the prince of demons casteth he out demons." They did not deny the cure, but they attributed it to the devil. The demons merely obliged their master.

Jesus is no longer obscure nor unknown. His appeal has been heard all over the land. He is the cynosure of all eyes. But has he won in the rapidly growing struggle with the Pharisees?

CHAPTER THREE

The New Departure

John takes up the narrative again, and we are in Jerusalem at a feast (John 5:1). We do not, however, know what feast it is, nor what time of the year Jesus is here. All things considered, we may take it as a Passover, though with much reservation and uncertainty. If so, the ministry of Jesus has been going on a year and a half. At any rate, it is the second time that we find Christ in Jerusalem, both occasions being described by John, who gives as a rule the Jerusalem or Judean ministry, while the Synoptics largely present the Galilean work. When Jesus was here before he had a certain popularity with the people, both in the city and in the country. But the rulers were hostile to him. Jesus now comes no more as a teacher and miracle worker who has stirred all Galilee. He has a great reputation already.

Conflict over the Sabbath

The Pharisees not simply held to the literal and ceremonial regulations in the Old Testament, but they had added many more. Indeed, they had made the day a burden instead of a blessing. A large part of Pharisaic religion consisted in seeing to it that other people carried out to the letter all the pettifogging rules which they had laid down. One could hardly turn around on the Sabbath day without running against one of the Pharisaic laws. If a woman looked into a mirror on the Sabbath, she might see a gray hair and be tempted to pull it out. To wear false teeth on the Sabbath was to carry a burden. But in the case of Jesus the Sabbath question was more occasion than cause. They had long ago decided to oppose him and his teachings. In Galilee they found fault with him for eating with publicans and sinners, for not making his disciples fast, for assuming to forgive sins and hence for blasphemy, for being in league with the devil. Each new link that they can forge in the chain is welcome.

Jesus was not asked to heal the man by the pool of Bethesda. He was a stranger to the impotent man who had long waited by the pool for a cure. It was the Sabbath day and Jesus took the initiative. Though the poor man did not know who it was that told him to get up and walk away with his bed, the very thing that he could not do, yet he somehow was impelled to try. The Jews, who saw him, cared little about his being healed. That was a comparatively small matter. The important thing to them was that he was carrying his bed on the Sabbath. The man felt that he was guilty and laid the blame on the man who had healed him—strange gratitude surely. To cap it all, when he did learn who had healed him, he went and told the Jews.

Jesus had not courted trouble over the matter, but he would not run from it. We are not told what the form of persecution was which they first used against Jesus, but he defended himself by the example of the Father. The defense was worse than the offense. Now they sought to kill him because he made himself equal with God, calling God his own Father. Jesus did not deny the accusation. Rather, he admitted it and proceeded in the first formal apology of his person and work that we possess (John 5:19-47) to prove that he is equal with the Father in all essential things, though he does nothing contrary to the Father. On the other hand, he joyfully does the Father's will, and the Father has set his seal upon him, and will do so to the end. It was, as we say, throwing down the gauntlet to his enemies, though they did not take it up. They did not know exactly how to proceed, for the man who was healed was a tremendous argument for Christ. They were no match for him in debate, with all their dialectical subtleties. But the wedge had gone in deeper.

The Battle Renewed in Galilee

To the Jerusalem Pharisees Jesus was not a common Sabbath breaker. On his return to Galilee the Pharisees appear again. While going through the wheat fields on the Sabbath, his disciples pluck some of the heads and rub the grain out in their hands. The technical offence to the Pharisees was the rubbing out of the grain. That was work. Instantly the Pharisees make the attack upon the disciples. It is wearisome and pitiful to think of having to deal seriously with such hair-splitters. But Jesus proceeded to defend what his disciples had done by five arguments. He appealed to the historical example of David who ate the shewbread on the Sabbath when in flight. He reminds them that the priests worked in the temple on the Sabbath, and Jesus claims to be greater than the temple. He recalls the message of God in Hosea: "I desire mercy, and not sacrifice." The ceremony counted for nothing with God unless the spiritual worship went along with it, a lesson that scribes had obscured and one that the prophets had great difficulty in enforcing. Besides, man was not made for the Sabbath, but the Sabbath for man, an obvious truth, but one often hid from view. It is true of the Bible itself. Men are not saved that there may be some to obey the Bible, but revelation is given to help men to come to God. And, to end the whole matter, Jesus is Lord even of the Sabbath. Jesus observed the spirit of the Old Testament teaching, but was not a slave to the mere form. He denied that what the disciples had done contradicted the real import of the Old Testament. But even if it did, he claimed the right to institute a new order of things, for he is greater than the Sabbath. This point he did not expand, but in it is contained the gem of the New Testament attitude towards the day of rest. He had brushed off his enemies, but left a rankling sting by his supreme claim concerning the day.

The Sabbath controversy goes on now in various parts of Palestine to the end, and yet the enemies of Christ are not able to make out anything against him serious enough to stand. One difficulty with the rabbis was that they did not themselves strictly observe what they so diligently preached to others. They had Pharisaic orthodoxy, but not Pharisaic orthopraxy. Hence they could never go to the limit in the matter. On the very next Sabbath, however, in a synagogue in Galilee the storm breaks out again. This time the Pharisees are ready beforehand. They seemed to know that Jesus would attend this synagogue, and were watching to see if he would dare heal the poor man with a withered hand who was there. Would he do it when they were on hand to expose him? They felt their importance keenly, these regulators of the faith. But Jesus knew their thoughts—solemn thought to us—and made a point of the matter. He made the man step out where all could see him. Then he joined issue with his enemies. Much depends on the way a thing is put. Jesus asked if it was right to do good or to do harm on the Sabbath. That was unanswerable. Then he asked if a man was of more value than a sheep. This was the crux of the whole question. They feared to answer this. Jesus' eyes flashed with anger over them as he bade the man to stretch forth his hand, right before and almost at the Pharisees. To the Pharisees this utter rout was unendurable, and yet what could they do? They could not keep the man from stretching out his arm. There was but one thing left. They would kill Jesus. A man will never forgive you for giving him an unanswerable argument. It is a mortal offence. They even counsel with their old enemies, the Herodians, on the subject, so bitterly do they now hate the Nazarene.

The New Organization

The need of it is now manifest. We need not speculate on what was Christ's plan before this time, nor say that now he made a radical change in his views. There is nothing to justify such a statement. What is clearly true is that now he can no longer wait for things to take their course. There was organized opposition to Jesus with headquarters in Jerusalem, a regular conspiracy bent on leaving no stone unturned to compass his downfall. Satan is carrying out his threat with speed. He has arrayed against Jesus the religious leaders of the time, the exponents of the traditional orthodoxy of the day. The devil becomes anxious to preserve the harmless faith of the Pharisees. He poses as the champion of the faith. Jesus is put in the light of an innovator, a heretic. If Jesus is to win, he must conquer rabbinical Judaism as well as the powers of the world of sin. However much Jesus foresaw all this, there was inevitable isolation in the result. He came as the Messiah of his people, and the accredited teachers of the time shut the door in his face.

Now is this all. He had some true believers, but as yet no organized band of followers, no force bound to him by hooks of steel. It was a worldwide and an age-long conflict. Steps must be taken looking towards the future. Already half of the public ministry was over.

The purpose of this band is stated in Mark 3:14. They are to be with Jesus, to preach, and to have authority over demons. This body of preachers was not a local church, nor the church general. It is a special body of men chosen for a special purpose. They are to be charged with the work of starting Christianity upon its world career. They are to be with Jesus till he returns to the Father, so that they may learn Christ and be true exponents of him and his ideas. These men must be teachers of the Kingdom. The policy of Jesus evidently, then, is to teach the teachers. Thus he will guarantee the proper interpretation of his message and mission and the work of the kingdom of God. It is true that the work of Jesus with these men will need the further teaching of the Holy Spirit, but the foundation on which they will build will be laid by Jesus himself. When this group of men shall be trained by Jesus, he can leave the work to their hands under the guidance of the Holy Spirit. The great teacher then had a class of twelve to go with him constantly for nearly two years. The choice was made under very solemn circumstances. Jesus had spent a whole night in prayer. It was a crisis, for, humanly speaking, all depended on the choice of these men. He talked with the Father all night about it. In the gray dawn of the morning he came down the mountain side with the dew of heaven on his brow. A great multitude of believers and of unbelievers was assembled already in the early morning. He seems to have called the men, "whom he himself would," up to him out of the crowd. Then he appointed them as apostles. It was an old term, but henceforth it was to have with them a new meaning. Afterwards he came down with them to a level place on the mountain. Here at least is a nucleus. Will they justify the choice of Jesus? He had risked his all on them and had chosen them, as he afterwards said, because he knew them. Some of them, a majority indeed, had been with him already a good while. The rest Jesus had probably noticed carefully.

But who are these men? Six of them probably, Andrew and Simon, James and John, Philip and Nathanael, became disciples at the beginning at Bethany, beyond Jordan. Another, Levi, left his publican's seat some while afterwards. The other five, James, the son of Alpheus, and Thaddeus, Thomas, Simon the Cananean, and Judas Iscariot, meet us here for the first time. They are all of Galilee save Judas Iscariot, who comes from Judea. This fact marks him off from the rest at once, but he seems to have business capacity (thought a preacher) and soon becomes the treasurer of the band. There are three groups of brothers, Simon and Andrew, James and John, James the son of Alpheus and Judas the brother of James. The four lists that we have of the Twelve were evidently made according to later developments in the group. Simon Peter always appears first and Judas Iscariot last, save in Acts when he has dropped out entirely. They fall into three groups of four, Philip, heading the second, and James the son of Alpheus the third. Nathanael appears as Bartholomew, and Thaddeus is also called Judas the brother of James. Simon the Cananean, or Zelotes, had belonged to the party of zealots who later brought on the war with the Romans. Four of them were fishermen. None of them had theological training until now. With Jesus they were to be in the greatest school that earth has ever seen. Aristotle taught Alexander the Great, but Jesus was the teacher of these men. They had less to unlearn than if they had been to Jerusalem to school, but they still shared in the common theological views of the time. It will be a task even beyond the power of Christ to lift these men up to the spiritual interpretation of the kingdom of God before his death and resurrection.

Did Jesus make a mistake in choosing these men? Where could he have gotten men better adapted to his purposes? Not in Jerusalem nor in Judea, and Judas came out of Judea. They were all men of ability, as the sequel shows. No rarer spirit has ever lived than John. Simon Peter was versatile and alert. Andrew was a man of counsel. Thomas was cautious. Nathanael (Bartholomew) was a man free from guile, if a bit skeptical. Levi was a man of methodical business habits. Simon, the zealot, had zeal in abundance. James, the brother of John, was one of the chosen inner circle of three, and a man to be trusted. Philip seems to be practical and prudent. Of James the Less and his brother Judas (Thaddeus) we are not able to form a very clear picture, though we cannot assume that they were negative characters. Judas once shows a lack of spiritual insight (John 14:22). There was thus great variety in personal traits, and each had his strong points. Even Judas Iscariot was not without special aptitudes, else he would not have been treasurer (so as to absconding treasurers today who would not have been trusted if they had not shown capacity). He had his opportunity, poorly as he used it.

The Declaration of Principles

The Sermon on the Mount has been the occasion of much discussion and even controversy. No other words of Jesus stand out quite so sharply as these. They are commonly taken as typical of the mind of Christ. The ideal of righteousness here set forth is still the goal of the civilized world in spite of the notion of a few that the teachings of Jesus are wholly out of sympathy with modern life.

The occasion of this discourse seems to have been the choosing of the twelve apostles. Luke so represents the matter, and he is usually chronological. According to Matthew the Sermon stands at the beginning of the Galilean ministry, more as a type of the teaching done by Jesus. But both Matthew and Luke give it as a real discourse at a definite place. They do not differ essentially in the circumstances, for Luke's "plain" need only be a "level place" as the revised version has it, probably a level place on the mountain such as one finds on the Horns of Hattin near Tiberias. From this level place Jesus probably went up on the mountain side a little way and sat down to address the people.

But we are not to think of Jesus as speaking only to the twelve or simply to believers, for both Matthew and Luke mention the presence of the multitudes, Luke indeed recording the fact that they came all the way from Jerusalem to Tyre and Sidon. Many Gentiles were probably on hand, or certainly many Greek-speaking Jews. It is possible, though not certain, that Jesus on this occasion spoke in Greek. But while the discourse was general in its nature and suitable for all, it had a special application to the twelve and may be compared with the closing address to them on the night before his death, as given in John 14:17. It is a long journey between these two occasions. The reality and unity of the Sermon may therefore be assumed. Matthew had much more than Luke, but chiefly things that concerned his attitude towards the Jewish teaching. The reports in Matthew and Luke begin and end alike and agree in general argument. It is possible, though not necessarily true, that some of Christ's later sayings may have been put into this great address. But it is far more probable that the same or similar sayings occurring at other points were simply repeated by Jesus on other occasions. Repetition is not simply allowable; it is necessary for effective service, especially in the case of a popular teacher who had to meet different audiences in various parts of the land. This sermon is admitted by all to have essential rhetorical unity as reported by Matthew and Luke. The Sermon on the Mount is a fine example of the teaching of Jesus. The element of the parable is not as pronounced as in some of the later discourses, but it is here in the case of the two ways, the two builders, and in numerous figurative allusions. Here are sharp distinctions drawn, antithesis, invective, paradox, illustration, precept, warning, appeal. But one must not make the mistake of supposing that Jesus had on this occasion said all that he has to say in condensed form. By no means. Many great ideas taught by Jesus are not even alluded to here. Others are merely assumed or implied, as the new birth, for instance. The disciples were not yet ready for all Christ had to say, nor will they be ready for all by the time Jesus comes to die. The Holy Spirit will take up the teaching and carry it on. But Christ has laid down a platform of very important principles pertaining to the kingdom of heaven. He by no means wishes men to understand that this is all the teaching that they need, though one can readily admit that this is enough, and too much for many. Those who decry theology the most and appeal to the Sermon on the Mount as the sole standard for men are likely to be the very ones who fall farthest short of the ideal of human life here outlined. This ideal of righteousness is impossible save to one who has a new heart to begin with and the help of the Holy Spirit all through to the end. But this clear-cut epitome of ethical principles made a pronounced impression then and does today soar above all human ethical standards. The people wondered at these words, and the world is wondering still. This is probably not a complete report of the Sermon, but a brief abstract, the most striking things that were remembered and told over and over.

There is some difference of opinion as to the theme of the Sermon (as often today about sermons), because Luke does not give what we have in Matt. 5:17–20). There Christ's idea of righteousness seems to be set forth as the theme. And even in Luke this is the implied subject of discussion. It is introduced by the Beatitudes and illustrated and discussed from various points of view. Christ's idea of righteousness is today the world's ideal of righteousness, though one cannot say that the world as yet approximates its ideal. But this much is gained, to have put the goal before the world. At one blow Jesus struck down the standards set up by the scribes and Pharisees. He even said that if his hearers did not do better than that, they had no hope at all. The scribes and Pharisees were the religious leaders of the time. The pity and the pathos of the situation! The boldness of Christ's conceptions is here manifest. He did not compromise nor hesitate. He was laying foundations for all time. He went to the heart of things and saw them as they are. Hence his teaching is universal, pervasive, eternal.

The Beatitudes form the introduction to this great discourse. It is not a new style of speech, occurring often in the Psalms. There are two parts to each Beatitude and special significance in each. Luke gives only four which are balanced by four woes. The most outstanding thing about the Beatitudes is that Christ's conception of happiness differs so radically from that of the teachers of the time, both Jewish and Greek. The formal ceremonialism of the Pharisees was set at naught by the lofty spirituality here insisted upon. The mere Sadducee would find little to attract him in this transcendental spiritual philosophy. If any Greeks were there, they would be equally puzzled. The Epicurean would prefer the world of sense to this happiness of the spirit. The Stoic would understand the spiritual plea better, but it was all too altruistic for him. All of them had rather do the persecuting than endure it. Vengeance was sweeter to them than mercy, pride than humility, self-conceit than craving to be better. Purity of heart was too inconvenient for a work-a-day world. Only in portions of the Old Testament, especially the Psalms, do we find an approach to this sublime spiritual idealism. The Beatitudes imply a new heart or regeneration. The kingdom of heaven belongs to those who rejoice in these qualities. In truth no one else will rejoice in them. It should never be forgotten that the possession of the spiritual renewal lies at the basis of Christ's idea of righteousness. It is impossible to all others. It is mere mechanical imitation to seek to reach this ideal without beginning with the foundation laid by Jesus. The kingdom of God comes before the righteousness. "Seek first the kingdom of God and his righteousness."

The ideal of righteousness is unfolded from various points of view. It must exceed the standard of the scribes, the accepted teachers of the time among the Jews. These scribes taught the Old Testament plus their own interpretation of it, a second Bible covering up the first. One specimen of that teaching is here condemned by Jesus, "and hate thine enemy" (Matt. 5:43). But it is not enough to seek mere formal obedience to the Old Testament. Revelation is progressive. Jesus does not set aside the Old Testament teaching on these points as wrong. It is merely inadequate for the new time. He carries the teaching further in the same direction, from letter to spirit, as illustrated by murder, adultery, oaths, retaliation, enemies. His own words here are not to be pressed literally at all points. He used paradox and even hyperbole to make an impression. But his point is plain. In fact, the ideal of Christ's teaching is the Father. "Ye therefore shall be perfect as your heavenly Father is perfect" (Matt. 5:48). Mere labored conformity to this or that detail will not answer.

Nor is the practical righteousness of the Pharisees one whit better than this unsound teaching of the traditionalists. It was vitiated by a grievous fault, that of self-consciousness. Alms, prayer, fasting were all done to be seen of men. Missing that, all was lost to the Pharisee. Virtue to him was not its own reward. A man must be known to give alms. If necessary, sound a trumpet before you, so as to attract a crowd and be seen! The model prayer of Jesus brings all life into relation to the Father and puts this Kingdom first. It is not original in many of its phrases. How could a model prayer be wholly original?

The warning against worldliness hits a sensitive place. Trust in God may be all very well, but the worldly-wise had rather keep one eye on the main chance. But the good eye is when both eyes focus on the same point. It is not forethought that Jesus here condemns, but anxiety. It is not work, but worry that wears out the machinery of life. It is always a sign that something is the matter when the machines makes too much noise. The birds sing as they take what God sends. Most men assume that they are themselves right. Hence they have the privilege of passing judgment on others. It is second nature, if not first. It is easier to see the mote in the brother's eye than the big beam in one's own. Jesus does not mean that we shall not form opinions about people. That cannot be helped. He does mean that we shall not be hasty, captious, nor unjust in our criticisms. The habit of criticism is very vicious. One can so easily be snappish and disagreeable.

The Golden Rule is not original with Jesus, though he first put it so crisply in the positive form. The practice of it is the original thing with Jesus. The man who says that this is his religion has some justification in theory, for Jesus said that it is the law and the prophets. Clearly, however, Jesus meant that this was the sum of the law and the prophets as they bore upon our relations with our fellows. If it be extended toward God, everything would be included with no reservations. However, a word of caution is needed to one who is so easily satisfied. This inclusive principle of life is the very hardest one to live up to. It means far more than mere good-natured well-wishing for everybody and everything. It is the practice of love towards God and man in the widest sense. It is more than mere abstinence from harm to our neighbors. It is to be an exponent of every positive grace and virtue.

The narrow gate and the broad way are favorite images in ethical teaching. The idea is in Psalm 1. It appears in the Two Ways, in Barnabas, etcetera. It is an obvious parable of life. It is the straitened, not necessarily the straight, way. The supreme test is that of life. Character, not profession, is the element that endures the crucible of this examination. Many will glibly say then who are not willing to do now. Excuses and explanations are always handy, and mere talk is very easy. One is not to imagine that Jesus has changed his theology by this demand that the tree be judged by its fruits. If the kingdom of heaven with the new birth lies at the basis of Christ's idea of righteousness, the man whose house stands because built upon the rock pictures graphically the consummation of that righteousness. The good tree does bear some good fruit. There is a note of confidence as well as of warning here. Jesus differs from all other ethical teachers in just this. He gives the power to put into practice these ethical ideals. It is just because the Kingdom is in a man that he can finally reach Christ's ideal. He can and he will. The final and supreme test of the seed is the fruit. The man whose perfected life conforms to the real ideal is indubitably one whose heart was renewed by the spirit of God. Here, then, is a vital system of ethics. It is righteousness applied to life, and that bears fruit. The teaching is no longer in the clouds, but is brought down to men. No wonder that the people were astonished at such words. It was the glint of the sunshine through the clouds and fog of rabbinism. Jesus actually had ideas of his own and spoke with the authority of transparent truth, not the mechanical repetition of former rabbis. His words still challenge our admiration and appeal to our highest selves. To be what Jesus here commends is to be the noblest type of man that was ever presented to the world, for the conscience of Jesus has become the delicate standard for all the world. His condemnation leaves no further appeal.

The Despair of John the Baptist

At the very time that Jesus was planning for an aggressive campaign with some organization, John the Baptist was languishing in the prison at Machaerus. His friends were allowed to see him, but it was a dreary life, so utterly different from the wild freedom of the wilderness and the favor of the great multitudes. After all the excitement to come to this dark solitude was too much even for a robust nature like John's. Doubts would come even about Jesus whom he had baptized and identified as the Messiah. Logic in a cell and out by the Jordan is not the same thing. If Jesus was the Messiah, why was he so slow in setting up the Kingdom? Why did he let John stay in prison? Perhaps after all there was some mistake. Maybe Jesus was only another forerunner like himself, came to John occasionally. Probably the account of the raising of the son of the widow of Nain reached him and quickened his depressed spirit into fresh interest. So he sent two of his disciples with the pathetic appeal to Jesus for more light. Jesus was busy at the time with his cures and kept on till he was done. Then he bade these two disciples to go tell John what they had seen and heard. He added a beatitude to the effect that he was blessed who found no occasion of stumbling in him—a gentle rebuke to John. Jesus was not without sympathy for John at such a time, but the most effective reply was work, not words. He was doing the work of the Messiah. Jesus treated this request from John seriously. There is nothing to indicate that it was mere make-believe on John's part. If we wonder that John could fall into doubt, let us recall the case of Elijah, the prototype of John, and even the mother of Jesus later. After all, Jesus was not the conventional Messiah, and hid in the dark as John now was he could easily go astray.

But Jesus took occasion to pass a wonderful tribute upon John, one that would have cheered him greatly could he have heard of it. He recalls the multitudes who flocked to the wilderness to see, not a reed shaken in the wind, not an effeminate man of the city, but a son of the soil, a prophet and more, a man as great as any born of woman, an epoch-making man who divided the past from the future. He was the close of the old age and the beginning of the new, so that in one sense all those in the new have an advantage over him. He is Elijah that was to come. True, he was not accepted by all men, as Jesus was not. The Pharisees and Sadducees rejected his baptism, while the masses and even the publicans justified and glorified God because of John. To the leaders John was too much of an ascetic. He was peculiar, different from other folks. His dress, his diet, his home all marked him from men. But to the same men Jesus was equally objectionable. He did live with men, ate their food, lived in their homes. They called him therefore a wine-bibber and a glutton, a palpable falsehood. But they had to find fault with him somewhere. They said he was too much like other people for a rabbi! So it goes. What is a preacher to do? How can he please the people? It is doubtful if he can succeed, and he ought not to succeed if he makes merely that his aim. The best that one can do is to do right and let the results speak for themselves. Wisdom is justified in the end by her children (or works). In the long run the man wins who goes straight ahead and does his duty. It was not long now before Herod yielded to the wiles of his wife Herodias and was caught in her trap to kill John. She had never forgiven him for rebuking her. She held it against him. The disciples of John "went and told Jesus." He would understand.

The Son's Relation to the Father

In this great crisis of his career Jesus is fully conscious that the Father is with him. In Matt. 1:25–30 we have a section that is identical in tone and point of view and even in style with the Gospel of John. Chorazin, Bethsaida, Capernaum will reject him and be punished, but Jesus sees victory in the future. All things have been delivered into his hands by the Father. No one really knows him but the Father, as no one really knows the Father but the Son. The way to the Father depends on the will of the Son, a marvelous claim of elective power. On the basis of that power he extends the most gracious invitation to the weary and heavy-laden. He invites all to come to school to him and promises that his yoke will be easy and his burden light. The twelve apostles are already in his school. He asks for more pupils who are willing to learn of one who, though the son of God with all knowledge and power, is yet meek and lowly in heart. Who can refuse to learn from such a teacher whose words linger in the mind like sweet bells at eventide? No teacher ever made such an offer as Jesus does here. He will indeed put us under the yoke, but the yoke is, after all, easy and the burden grows light.

CHAPTER FOUR

The Galilean Campaign, or the Rejection of a Spiritual Kingdom

Would ye also go away?

JOHN 6:67

Jesus will now endeavor by vigorous work to win a foothold for the Kingdom in Galilee. He has already preached much in various parts of the country, but the results have not been large. The crowds are great and excitement is intense.

He Makes a Second Tour of Galilee

He takes the Twelve with him, which is his new band of disciples. It will be an experience of much value to them. Certain women, a noble band of workers, followed also during this preaching tour. How early the women began to work for Jesus, and how faithfully they have served him! The church is never better than its women, and not always as good. These good women ministered of their substance for the support of Christ and his company. Perhaps Judas later was influenced by this fact when he resented Mary of Bethany's spending so much money for the ointment, though he spoke of the poor at the time Mary Magdalen was one of this band, and is now mentioned for the first time. She is not the woman that was a sinner who at the Pharisee's feast washed the feet of Jesus. That legend is an unpardonable slander on Mary Magdalen. Nor was Mary Magdalen the same woman as Mary of Bethany, the sister of Lazarus. We know nothing of this journey save the general statements made, but we can easily imagine the character of the work done.

Jesus Repels the Attacks of His Enemies

He has a new cross to bear, that of misunderstanding at home. His mother and his brethren have become puzzled over all this stir and confusion. The crowds are so great that they fail to eat. The family conclude that he is beside himself and come to take him home. He has gone crazy! Poor Mary! It must have been a sad hour for her. Even John the Baptist had doubted, and now his mother has given up hope about him. It has all turned out so differently from the way that she expected the Messiah would do. He was still just a mere preacher, with great crowds, it is true, but he was not now claiming in so many words to be the Messiah. Mary doubtless heard this explanation of Jesus' conduct from some of her friends who wanted to put the best face possible on the situation. Our "friends" sometimes are excessively kind in explaining our conduct. The people were all seeking to explain the career of Jesus, while he studiously avoided saying anything that would give his enemies a handle. So the mystery about him grew and deepened.

But the Pharisees were not so charitable in the construction that they put upon the matter. They had already hinted at their view. One day when the multitudes in their amazement went so far as to ask, Is this the Son of David? The Pharisees retorted that he was in league with Beelzebub, the prince of demons! That is the true explanation of his miracles, they said. It was a shock to the multitude and was a public attack right in the presence of Jesus which could not be passed by. They were at some distance from him, but he knew their thoughts and called them to him. They had made a bold shot and a desperate one. Jesus claimed to be the servant of God; in reality he was the agent of Beelzebub. The issue was fairly joined. Jesus replied with a string of sententious aphorisms (parables) that cut to the quick. He points out the absurdity of their charge, for Satan would be casting out Satan, a thing he would never do. He uses the *argumentum ad hominem* on them. They claimed also to cast out demons. By whom did they do it? It was a fair turn. Jesus could use this weapon without committing himself to the reality of their claim. Here is a *reductio ad absurdum*. Christ then pressed the alternative that he cast out demons by the Spirit of God rather than by the devil. The conclusion is that the kingdom of God has come upon them. It was a complete turning of the tables, but Jesus is not done yet. They have themselves committed the unpardonable sin of attributing the manifest work of the Spirit of God to the power of the devil. That was inexcusable and would never be forgiven. They were guilty of an eternal sin. It was more excusable if one blasphemed Jesus, who was man as well as God. He was the Son of Man. Even now Christ is not through with his arraignment. With something of the fire of John the Baptist and of his own later denunciation of his enemies (Matt. 23), he turns upon them and calls them "offspring of vipers." They are evil and can only speak evil.

One would have thought that the Pharisees would have withered away under this righteous denunciation. But some of them blandly stepped up and asked that Jesus work a sign! They probably meant it in ridicule, but they got still more denunciation. Christ calls them "an evil and adulterous generation." They repeat the usual Jewish idea of the Messiah, that he will come with spectacular display. Jesus gives them the sign of his death and resurrection, with a reference to the story of Jonah. The sign of Jonah was, of course, lost upon them, though Jesus expressly said that the Son of Man should be three days and three nights in the heart of the earth, that is, three days as men count days, not meaning to accent unduly night from day. He reminds them how the men of Nineveh repented at the preaching of Jonah, a thing which they were not doing.

The mother and brethren of Jesus press up to the house to have a word with him and take him home. Jesus "looked round on them which sat round about him" and said: "Behold, my mother and my brethren." He was no longer to be commanded even by his mother. He had entered a larger fellowship of the Spirit to which he admitted every one who did the will of God. His disciples were his real kindred, for at this moment those bound to him by the ties of the flesh had failed to understand him. Mary, though so close to Jesus, just now had lost her way. But she will find it again and some day even his brothers will believe.

Jesus Adopts a New Style of Teaching

It is not the first time that Jesus used parables, but the first time that he had made a point of doing so. Those used theretofore had been brief and isolated. On this occasion they are many and at much length. But from now on they form a marked characteristic of his teaching and make a definite turn in his method of instruction. Jesus will bear the closest scrutiny as a teacher who followed the deepest laws of nature in his efforts to reach the hearts of men, followed them naturally and almost artlessly, while we blunder on and painfully discover some of the great principles of teaching. It is one of the hopeful signs of modern times that we are seeing the importance of studying the pupil as well as the subject to be taught. Jesus in this very context urged his hearers to take heed what they heard and how they heard.

The parable is not an invention of Jesus. The Jewish rabbis were fond of using this form of instruction. There is nothing to prevent any modern teacher from using the parable, and some do. But the parables of Jesus so far surpass those of all other men that the rest sink away into oblivion. His parables ring clear and true and perfect. They are not overdone nor underdone. They illustrate rather than darken the point. This is by no means the least noteworthy fact. The term *parable* is used in a variety of ways, but the essential idea is that of an objective parallel to moral and spiritual truth. On this occasion, as usual, the parables of Jesus grew out of the circumstances. The hostile attitude of friends and enemies on this busy day gave the tone to this entire group. They had accused him of being in league with the devil. Hence they did not deserve to receive more of the teaching of Jesus. The use of parables now served to hide the mysteries of the Kingdom from his enemies, while the spiritually minded would remember the wonderful story and by and by understand the teaching contained in it. The harshness of this judgment upon the enemies of Christ is much relieved when the actual circumstances of this day are perceived. The day will come when the Pharisees will see the point of those parables directed against them.

It is no wonder that Jesus wished to get out of the stuffy hostile atmosphere of the house and into the bracing air of beautiful Galilee. But even here he found a crowd and sat down in the boat and taught the multitudes on the shore. The people were astonished as he taught them in parables, and even the disciples could not understand him. We are such slaves to routine and intellectual ritual that the new gives us a jolt. We do not know how many parables Jesus spoke on this day. Matthew gives seven and Mark one more, but he spoke "many such parables," it is added. Things new and old Jesus brought out of his store. Some were spoken after he left the shore and went back to the house. Two of them (the sower and the tares) were explained by Jesus at the request of the disciples. They serve as models for the interpretation of the parables that are not explained.

The eight that are preserved for us from this day's teaching fall into four pairs: the sower and the seed, the tares and the net, the leaven and mustard seed, the hid treasure and the pearl of great price. They illustrate together many sides of the Kingdom of heaven, which is indeed like a diamond with numerous facets; and again the kingdom of God is a vital growth and cannot be analyzed, as life refuses to be put under the microscope. The kingdom of God has various results due to the diversity of soil, and the secret of its growth in the heart is like that of nature.

The line of cleavage between those who have the Kingdom and those who have not is not made perfectly clear as yet. They grow in the same field (the world) till the harvest time. The growth of the Kingdom, while slow and from small beginnings, is sure and pervasive. It will ultimately cover the earth. Meanwhile, in spite of much evil and discouragement, many will find joy in the Kingdom and consider it the greatest treasure of earth. There will be other great groups of parables, but none will surpass in suggestiveness this first one.

Jesus in Heathen Territory

It had been a day of stress and storm, the sample of many in the life of Jesus. The wedge had entered deeper and the cleft was wider between Jesus and the rulers. The iron had indeed entered the soul of Christ. With a heavy heart and a weary body he sank down into the stern of the boat "even as he was" and pushed out with the disciples at eventide to cross over the lake. Perhaps the wind and the waves would bring rest. No wonder that Jesus was soon asleep. When the sudden squall from the north fell down upon the little lake and tossed the water into fury, Jesus slept on till the excited disciples awoke him with a cry of despair. He spoke to the wind and the sea and they obeyed him; they did, though the Pharisees had just reviled him. The disciples marvel as to what manner of man he is. They had taken him to be the Messiah, but it was not perfectly clear to their minds what the Messiah would be. They grew in perception of the content of the term *Messiah* to the end of their career. There was, therefore, a twofold development. Jesus revealed himself more and more to the disciples, and they grew in apprehension of him. On the shore the Master had an experience of horror. It was in the region of Decapolis at the village of Khersa (Gerasa) not far from Gadara. The wild demoniac rushing along among the rocks was not a sight to give rest of spirit. And even the sea had turned to storm. But at least Jesus gave peace of heart to this unfortunate man. The mystery of the demoniacal possessions never appears darker than in this incident. The destruction of the swine added to the ravings of the man make a dreadful background in the twilight on this heathen shore. The mystery of evil is not relieved by the denial of the devil and demons. The presence of disease here may or may not be in conjunction with the power of the evil one. The assumption that Jesus was merely accommodating himself to custom in speaking of demons cannot solve all the difficulties concerning the demon possession. As previously said, we know too little about psychic matters to say the final word here. But let us at least rejoice that Jesus is Master over both sin and disease. He will sometimes bless those who do not appreciate it. The people of the community begged Jesus to leave their shores for good, but the picture of the man, once so wild, sitting clothed, in his right mind is a comfort to those who battle with sin in country or in city. Here, where no Pharisees are to molest, Jesus tells the man to go to his house and tell what great things God has done for him.

Jesus Makes a Last Visit to Nazareth

Nazareth did not deserve this second opportunity. Some scholars indeed deny that it was so, but on the whole it seems probable that this is not the early visit recorded by Luke. It is not surprising that Jesus should once more come to Nazareth, the home of his childhood, in spite of the treatment received the last time. It was his own country. True enough, as he finds, a prophet has no honor, no lasting honor, in his own country, among his own kin, and in his own house. But he would give them their chance. They are astonished. They are incredulous. How can it be? Where did it all come from? We know his family and we know him. They stumbled at him and even refused to believe what they saw with their own eyes. In such a skeptical atmosphere Jesus did few mighty deeds. So great in fact was their unbelief that he marvelled at it. And this at Nazareth. It must have been a sad look that Jesus gave Nazareth as he saw it for the last time and passed over the hill and out of sight. Who will welcome Jesus now? The heathen region of Decapolis had turned him away. His own home had pushed him aside. Jerusalem was bent on his destruction. Will Galilee endure him, when she knows the truth?

A Third Tour of Galilee

This tour will settle the matter so far as Galilee is concerned. It will be the last. The occasion was the compassion of Jesus for the multitudes. He had indeed a little band of laborers, but they were utterly unable to cope with the situation in Galilee. The harvest was great and the laborers few. The remedy suggested by Christ for this new recruiting dilemma is prayer to the Lord of the Harvest. Somehow we fail to emphasize the one item laid upon preachers by Jesus, that they pray for other preachers to be raised up. There can be no jealously here, for it is a world need.

But these twelve must go and reap what they can. So Jesus sends them forth for the first time without him. They have had much instruction and observation. Now they can put it into practice. It is one thing to study about preaching. It is quite another thing to preach. Will they succeed as they go and preach the kingdom of God? Will sinners be converted under their preaching? Will the demons go out at their command? Who does not recall his first experience in leading a soul to Christ? The Master will follow them to see how their work turns out, for much depends on these men. In the struggle with the Jerusalem authorities they had the power and prestige of state and the strength of prejudice. What if the disciples fail utterly after all their training?

Jesus renews his instructions to them, or rather gives them in condensed form the main ideas that they will need for this tour, incidental details as well as fundamental principles. Some of the things here enjoined were afterwards expressly changed by Jesus, as the direction not to go in the way of the Gentiles or the Samaritans. The "Hardshell" spirit has always made a literal interpretation of the words of Jesus on this point, but with blind obscuring of the historical situation and the later commands of the Master. But let no one think that common sense details as to food, clothing, manners have little value. They go largely to determine the ultimate success of every minister.

The point that Jesus laid most stress on was the spirit with which they should go. They go forth as sheep in the midst of wolves, a vivid picture of helplessness. But they are not to fear the wolves. If they are persecuted in one city, they will go on to the next. The one to fear is God, not man. After all, Jesus came to send a sword, not peace. This seems like a flat contradiction of what Christ had said elsewhere. But we must put together all that he said, however paradoxical it may appear. Then the result will be clear. The man who cringes with fear to save his life from the wolves will lose his life. This is the paradox of courage and sacrifice, but it is the law of life. Along with dove-like innocence, they are to have the wisdom of serpents. It is the combination that Jesus commands, not the isolated possession of either quality. So the new preachers of the gospel went forth into all Galilee. They did cast out many demons and preached the gospel of the Kingdom.

The dread of Herod Antipas was one result. The disciples manifested due courage and achieved some degree of success. Galilee was apparently stirred to the foundation by this concerted campaign. News of the commotion reached Herod Antipas who was already the victim of his fears. He had never felt right about the death of John the Baptist, and was anxious to see if it was not John come to life again. Others thought Jesus was Elijah or another of the prophets. But Jesus studiously kept out of the way of Herod, a name that boded no good to him.

Will the Galileans Accept a Spiritual Messiah?

As yet they do not fully understand what Jesus claims to be. They know him as a wonderful teacher, a worker of miracles, a man who has won the enmity of the ecclesiastical forces in Jerusalem, who is reviled by the Pharisees in Galilee, but who is immensely popular with the people. He had not said to them that he was the Messiah. Who is he?

Great as was the favor in which Jesus was held by the people, the feeding of the 5000 men, besides women and children, carried the enthusiasm beyond all bounds. Christ and the disciples had just returned from the great tour of Galilee and were seeking the hillsides near Bethsaida Julias for rest. But a great host of people awaited him there. They lined the mountain eager for his words and his works. Jesus stood out in full view of all who had come. His heart was tender towards the multitude. He taught them, and he did more. He offered to feed the entire host with a few loaves and fishes from a lad who was there. It was a glorious scene as with their colored garments they reclined in rows like garden beds on the green grass. They saw the constant dispensing of fish and loaves from the hands of Jesus, and, what was more, they ate them. There was but one conclusion. He was the Messiah. We will take him to Jerusalem and make him king. No matter what the Pharisees think. We know that Jesus is the Messiah. We will set up the messianic reign in Jerusalem and drive out the hated Romans and win the world for the Jews. That was the Messianic hope of the Pharisees. It was the voice of the people, but not the voice of God. The voice of the people is *vox dei* if not *vox diaboli*. This time it was the same temptation that Satan had offered Jesus in the beginning. Christ saw that he must act quickly. So he dismissed the people to their homes and sent the disciples back in the boat. He himself went up into the mountain to talk with the Father who alone would understand him and his loneliness. There he found the sympathy that he needed. He won his victory again over this fresh temptation, but he lost the Galileans as we shall soon see. To the disciples Jesus at first seemed like a specter as they see him gliding over the water towards them. Peter was bold enough to wish to walk on the water with him till he saw the wind coming and his heart sank, and so did he. In the boat the disciples worship Jesus as the Son of God.

Christ was now at the height of favor with the Galileans. He was the man of the hour with the people; yes, the man of the hour. Was he the man of all time with them? Jesus was determined to let the multitude know his true character. They labored under a misapprehension. He will not employ terms to give his enemies a club to use on him, but the Galileans must know that he does not claim to be a temporal Messiah. He has not come to fulfill their political dreams. He has come to give them eternal life, a far greater blessing, if they only knew it. So Jesus makes a point of coming over to the synagogue the next morning in order to tell the people the truth. He would like to have their love and loyalty, but on proper terms. The master bluntly told them that all they wished was to get the loaves and fishes. Step by step he seeks to lead them on to wish for the meat that abides to eternal life, to eat the true bread of God, which is Jesus himself, to take him as the bread of life, in a word to "eat" him. A perfect storm at last broke loose in the synagogue when it dawned on the people that he claimed to have come down from heaven and to be himself the bread of eternal life. Their rage was assisted by keen skepticism which scouted his claims and the possibility of eating him. These rationalists finally wrangled with each other and strode out in disgust. One thing was now certain. Jesus had deliberately broken his hold on a large part of the Galilean populace. He was no longer a popular idol with them.

But the matter did not stop here. Christ had in the audience of professed disciples those who found this a hard saying, especially hard now that so many had gotten up and gone out. Their theological difficulties increased till they too began to leave. People go in herds. They, too, stalked out. Finally all had left Jesus save the Twelve. This then was the outcome in Capernaum when the people began to understand what Jesus really claimed to be. If that is the kind of a Messiah that he is, we do not want him! The campaign in Galilee has definitely failed. Christ had no sure foothold in Judea nor Samaria. It is only one year now till the end. He has labored probably two and a half years, and almost nothing is the spiritual result. He knew crowds, but it saddened Christ when under the fatal test this assemblage melted away.

Jesus turned to the Twelve. What will they do? It was a solemn moment in his ministry. Once more all hinged on them. Had they, too, succumbed to the outgoing tide? They were still here in the house, but did they wish to go? Were they loyal yet in heart to Christ? "Would ye also go away?" Simon is the speaker. His reply indicates that they had considered going. How could they help it? But they had decided to stay with him. For one thing, to whom should they go? There was no hope back with the Pharisees. Besides, they have a settled trust and experiental knowledge that he is the Holy One of God. It is not a new experience with them. They have had it from the first, but with varying lights and shadows over this lesser hope. Now, as he has told most about himself, they are drawn most to him. They would come closer and learn more. This then is the joy of Jesus. He has these men at any rate. But even one of them is a devil.

The Jerusalem Pharisees Renew Their Attack

It was an opportune time after the breach between Jesus and the populace in Capernaum. So the regulating committee from Jerusalem boldly challenge the orthodoxy of Jesus on the question of eating with unwashed hands. His disciples had been found guilty of this heinous crime. To their minds it brought up the whole question of ceremonial religion. The disciples of Jesus had transgressed the tradition of the elders. They did not say, but assumed, that this was also the command of God. Now right here is where they missed it. Jesus did not object to washing the hands before meals. That was a good and a proper thing to do. What he did object to was making a doctrine out of this very proper custom, a doctrine on a par with fundamental spiritual matters.

With keen irony the Master exposed the hypocrisy of these champions of ceremonial orthodoxy who violated with impunity the command of God and bound upon others the tradition of men, who knew how to get the credit for punctilious observance of these traditions without the trouble and privation of strictly keeping them, whose orthodoxy consisted in seeing that other people obeyed them, and not in observing them themselves. You make void the word of God by your tradition "and many such things ye do." This sword cut through the armor of self-righteous complacency with which they had approached Christ. They would even wink at robbery of father and mother under the traditional use of "Corban," especially if part of the money came their way.

Jesus was not content with this terrible exposure and arraignment, for he felt that the whole case between him and the Pharisees was summed up in this motto, a spiritual religion versus ceremonialism. He called the multitudes to him and warned them specifically on the point. It was not external observance that made a man good or bad, but the state of the heart. Jesus here laid the axe at the root of the tree of the current Judaism. It was a conflict, in a word, between spiritual truth and mere traditionalism. So strongly had Jesus spoken that the disciples grew uneasy. In the house they ventured to ask Christ if he had not noticed that the Pharisees were made to stumble at what he had said. They still cherished a wholesome dread of the power of the Pharisees. They were afraid that the Master had gone too far. But Christ had no notion of retracing his steps along that line. He saw that it was impossible for him to cooperate with these sticklers for the p's and q's of mere religious observance to the neglect of the spiritual life. "Let them alone: they are blind guides." This is the pathetic description of the Pharisees in the reply of Jesus. They pose as religious lights to point others to the truth, when they themselves are blind and are merely stumbling around in the dark. Luckless travellers are those who follow such spiritual guides. Peter even insisted that Christ explain this parabolic description of the Pharisees, and received a rebuke from Jesus for his dullness in not understanding what he had said about the difference between the spiritual and the ceremonial. In plain terms he tells Peter that out of the heart come forth all evil thoughts and deeds. This lesson, so difficult of apprehension then, is a commonplace now with all evangelical Christians. But even yet the majority of those who name the name of Christ have bound themselves to the externals, to the obscuring or even the destruction of the spiritual realities.

Mark adds that in saying this Jesus made all meats clean. It was, indeed, a revolutionary position to take from the point of view of the average Jew, not to say Pharisee. It is, perhaps, not strange that the disciples themselves stumbled at it. It is worth noting that Peter is the one who will receive the vision on the housetop of Simon the tanner when he will be invited to eat all kinds of meats. The stoutness of his protest then will show how far he is here from fully comprehending all that Jesus had in mind when he spoke. But the seed has been sown that will bear fruit. However, the first result of this conflict was to sharpen the issues between Christ and the Pharisees. They have one more definite ground of complaint against him. The struggle for spiritual religion will not be won in a day, has not indeed been fully won yet in all parts of Christendom. But Jesus is clear that the path of duty lies straight ahead. He has, however, reached a real crisis in his ministry. Evidences multiply that his effective work in Galilee is over. More and more his hopes center in the Twelve. To them he must devote himself more exclusively if they are to be qualified to carry on the work without him and to meet the crucial events now rapidly coming on. Are they now ready for the gloom of his death? It is less than a year to that awful event.

CHAPTER FIVE

The Special Training of the Twelve

But who say ye that I am?
MATT. 16:15

The Reasons for Such Training Are Obvious

It is now less than a year till the end will come. For nearly six months Jesus will devote himself chiefly to the chosen band of men whom he has gathered around him. If these men come to understand him, it will not matter so greatly about the rest. As yet they do not fully appreciate either the Messiah or his message. It is supremely difficult for one to rise above his environment. One's standpoint has much to do with what he sees. One of the greatest proofs that Jesus is more than man is just this, that in an environment of cold ceremonialism and external punctiliousness he came with abundant life and spiritual power. So far Jesus has sought to teach mainly the great ideas concerning the

Kingdom. He had indeed, in a vital way, outlined the theology of the Kingdom. The disciples did not now understand all that they had heard, nor would they till later. But meanwhile it was necessary that they should learn more of the Messiah himself. Henceforth Jesus will speak more concerning the King and less concerning the Kingdom. This is not a wrong historical order, but the right one. The early Messianic disclosures were personal and they largely ceased for obvious reasons. On the broad foundation of the Kingdom teaching Jesus had built, till now they ought to be able, however far the people fell short, to rise to the true idea of the Messiah. The disciples had to expand before he could tell more. But now he must tell more. The time had come when he could not wait longer. The shadow of the cross was coming rapidly towards him. The total eclipse would find the Twelve wholly unprepared for the catastrophe. It is not certain that even now the disciples are capable of appreciating all that Jesus has to say about himself and his mission. They have shown signs of development of late which are encouraging. At any rate they must be told the truth.

Jesus sees that it will be difficult to devote himself so exclusively to the disciples in Capernaum or in Galilee. The distractions are too many and the interruptions too frequent in the midst of the excited multitudes. Besides the tension is acute now in Capernaum since the crisis in the synagogue. The issue will be sharper and the lines more tightly drawn between him and the Pharisees. There is danger of a fanatical outburst on the part of his followers, as was shown after the feeding of the five thousand. Besides, Herod himself had grown jealous and uneasy and was likely to cause trouble. So Jesus spends the hot summer away from Galilee, chiefly in the mountain districts. He has a summer school in theology. What a joy to have been one of that little company. They appear in several places and are not entirely alone even in the heathen regions. But, on the whole, it is a summer of freedom from disturbance and of intimate fellowship. Jesus unburdens his heart to the men of his choice as far as they will allow him.

The Trip to Phoenicia

The work of Jesus was limited mainly to the Jews for clear reasons. They were the chosen people, the people of promise. They must have the first chance. To work much in Samaria or in Phoenicia would prejudice the Jews generally against the gospel. Hence Jesus spent most of his ministry in Jewish territory. Now he is on heathen ground and will be for most of the summer, but his work is chiefly with the disciples.

Jesus is the Savior of the world as the Samaritans saw and as he himself accented, but he was to begin with the Jew. To the Jew first and then to the Gentile. All this must be borne in mind, and yet Jesus did mingle with the Gentiles and was destined by his gospel of grace and liberty to break down the middle wall of partition between Jew and Gentile, as he had already indicated in his teaching concerning eating with unwashed hands. He even seems to have entered a Gentile house (Mark 7:24), though he would have no man know it. However, his seclusion seems due to a desire for quiet from the crowds rather than to any sense of ceremonial defilement such as Peter felt in the house of Cornelius.

The reluctance of Jesus to heal the daughter of the Syrophoenician woman is not hard to understand in the light of what has just been said. It was not hardness of heart on the part of Christ. It is to be noticed that Jesus did not abruptly send her away as the disciples suggested. He heard her plea, though he made it plain that his mission was first to the lost sheep of the house of Israel. He tested the woman and brought out the greatness of her faith. He did grant her request, a thing that the disciples would not have done. The disciple is often narrower than his master. The cleverness of this woman is as striking as her faith. "Even the little dogs eat of the crumbs which fall from their master's table." She deserved a hearing for that bright turn to the Master's protest. Jesus did not long tarry here, but went on from Tyre up north to Sidon, though we have no further details of this journey. One would infer that the work done was less than in Galilee, though it is to be recalled that when Jesus preached the

Sermon on the Mount there were people present from the seacoast of Tyre and Sidon. Hence Jesus was not an entire stranger to the Phoenicians and many more had heard of the wonderful Galilean Rabbi.

In Decapolis

They kept to the mountains after leaving Sidon. Mark briefly sketches the journey as from Sidon through the borders of Decapolis to the seacoast of Galilee. This would mean probably a journey east from Sidon, then south and to the east of the Sea of Galilee into the high cliffs to the southeast. This is still heathen territory. The Decapolis was a league of Greek cities which were practically entirely Hellenized after Alexander's conquest. The teaching of Jesus in this region as well as in Phoenicia shows that he used Greek when necessary. The people here "were astonished beyond measure" at the healing of the deaf and dumb man, and they wondered as they saw the dumb speaking, the maimed whole, and the lame walking, and the blind seeing: and they glorified the God of Israel. As elsewhere, therefore, so here also the work of Jesus made a marvelous impression. In the modern sense of the term Jesus was here a foreign missionary. These Greeks glorified "the God of Israel." It was to the north of this section a little that Jesus had come when he healed the wild demoniac with a legion of demons. As a result of that excitement, though no Pharisees are here, Jesus charges them all not to tell about the healing of the deaf and dumb man. "But the more he charged them, so much the more a great deal they published it" (Mark 7:36).

There was here also a feeding of 4000 similar to that of the 5000 at Bethsaida Julias. Some critics cannot see how such a thing could have happened twice, although Mark and Matthew mention in detail both incidents and each records that Jesus referred to both incidents as separate. Other distinctions, like the name of the baskets on the two occasions, are preserved also. One can be too particular as well as too credulous. Nature works in great variety, but with marvelous similarity also. It is remarkable how in each great region where Jesus labored similar events take place, as in Judea, Galilee, Perea, and to a lesser extent in Samaria, Phoenicia, Decapolis, and the region of Caesarea Philippi. People are very much alike after all. Christ delivers the same teaching in these regions with modifications here and there, and he works the same kind of cures. The people are astonished everywhere. The slowness of the disciples to obey the Master in the case of the 4000 after their experience with the 5000 is not to be wondered at too greatly. The dullness and forgetfulness of the disciples concerning these two incidents were pointedly condemned by Jesus. Besides their slowness here is not an isolated instance, but is a characteristic of their whole experience before the coming of the Holy Spirit. The surroundings in the case of the 4000 are quite different and the points of likeness are such as belong to the nature of the case.

A Brief Visit to Galilee

One day Jesus went with the disciples over to the other side into Galilee. We do not know exactly where the parts of Dalmanutha or Magadan were, except that it was on the western side, possibly down towards Tiberias. He has been absent from Galilee for some time now. How will he be received? Instantly, the ubiquitous Pharisees came forth and began to question him, as if they had missed him and were so glad to see him back. The Sadducees are with the Pharisees, a strange combination. The Herodians had already taken sides with the Pharisees against Jesus and now the Sadducees do so. Christ had united all three parties on one point at any rate, hostility to himself. This is the first time that the Sadducees are mentioned in the Gospels and the only one till the Passion Week. On the last day of Christ's ministry in the temple these three parties will appear together against Jesus. Here they have nothing new to say. They ask for a sign from heaven as proof of his claims as the Pharisees had done before.

Jesus "sighed deeply in his spirit." So this is his reception in Galilee! It is as hopeless as ever, in fact more so. Jesus answered them with reproach and denial. They could tell the weather, the face of the heavens, but not the signs of the times. They could not tell a sign from heaven if they saw one. He repeats this answer to the same demand made in Capernaum. He will give them the sign of Jonah. This enigmatic allusion perhaps only puzzled them. It was useless to explain. So Jesus abruptly left them and Galilee. He took a boat with the disciples and turned up towards Bethsaida Julias on the northeastern shore.

On the way he pointedly warned the disciples against the leaven of the Pharisees, the Sadducees, and Herod. He had just been in the land of Herod and had been attacked by the Pharisees and the Sadducees. The disciples are hopelessly at sea with this simple simile and rather jejunely rely, "we have no bread!" (Mark 8:16). They did not have any kind of bread and so Jesus need not caution them against the particular brand of the Pharisees, Sadducees, and Herod! No wonder Jesus was led to rebuke them sharply. He asked if they had a mind, if they had eyes, if they had ears. Their dullness seemed incomprehensible. Perhaps every teacher has moments of sympathy with this mood of Jesus here. Christ patiently explained about the 5000 and the 4000 and then said that by leaven he meant teaching. Did they now understand? They saw dimly like the poor blind man who at first saw men as trees walking.

The Examination of the Twelve

It was time for examination. They had now had a special summer course with Jesus in addition to all the rest. So he took the disciples up to the slopes of Hermon in the region of Caesarea Philippi. He still kept away from Galilee. Philip was a milder ruler and a better man than Herod Antipas. He had tried Galilee (Bethsaida, Chorazin, Capernaum, and all the rest) and it had been found wanting. But after all it mattered little what Galilee thought of him, provided these men were clear and loyal. They had been true that day in Capernaum, but a deeper probing was necessary. They are here by themselves and Jesus had been praying alone.

So on the way he took it up with them. He first asked what men thought of him or said he was. He knew that well enough already, but it served as a background for their own attitude. It was a crucial moment when Jesus abruptly asked: "but who say ye that I am?" (Matt. 16:15). They had taken him as the Messiah at the start, it is true, but they knew little about him then. They had their own preconceived ideas as to what the Messiah would be like. He had not come up to that. The discovery of that fact had sent the Galilean populace away in disgust. The Twelve had been loyal. He had told them much more about himself. What do they think now after they know so much of the truth about him? Do they still think him to be the Messiah, the Son of God? Or have they felt the force of uncertain popular opinion which is now much divided? Few among the people now hold him to be the Messiah, though many consider him John the Baptist come to life or Elijah or Jeremiah or one of the prophets.

It was Peter who found his tongue first and spoke as he had done that day in the synagogue in Capernaum. He rose to the dignity of the occasion. Jesus had said that Simon would be a Rock. "Thou art the Christ, the Son of the living God" (Matt. 16:16). They are noble words and rightly expressed his conviction and that of the rest. They did not indeed fully understand all that these words signified, but they could joyfully use them as their creed about Jesus. The heart of Jesus was made glad by these words and he made no effort to conceal the fact. Now Simon was worthy of his name. On this truth, trust in Jesus as the Son of God, rested the kingdom of God, his glorious church. What Peter has done, all will do who come into the Kingdom. They will take Jesus as the Son of God and Savior. In this clear confession Jesus sees the sure promise of victory. Satan had often tried to overturn him, but it is now clear that these men will be true and will carry on the work of the Kingdom. The gates of Hades will not be able to prevail against the church or kingdom of Christ. Peter and all the rest, all teachers of Christ, have the keys of the Kingdom, all who proclaim life to men on these terms. God will stand by the acceptance or rejection of Christ as his Son.

Not yet does Jesus wish them to tell others what is a great secret. It would set the land ablaze if the great truth came to be preached as yet. There is much more that they themselves need to know. They have made good progress on this point. Will they be true when they learn this "more"? When they learn of his death, what will they do? So a shadow comes over the hour of joy, but Christ does not doubt the final outcome. The present situation has vindicated what Christ said. Look at the Kingdom of God today in the world.

The New Great Lesson

It seemed like a mockery of all their hopes that now just as they had made afresh the great confession, Jesus should announce his death. There was no mistaking his words. He had indeed heretofore used symbolic language that pointed to his death, but it was all so veiled that little impression was made. It is in fact a distinct epoch in the career of Jesus, and Matthew says that "from that time began Jesus to shew" (Matt. 16:21) that he must be killed at Jerusalem. Observe "must" and "at Jerusalem" and "at the hands of the chief priests and scribes." So he expects the Sadducees and Pharisees to kill him after all. All this was not only disconcerting to the disciples; it was absolutely depressing. It is true that Jesus said also that he would rise on the third day, but this ray of hope was always obscured by the dreadful darkness of his death. That overshadowed all else. The eclipse was coming and they were in the penumbra. Jesus spoke of his death "openly" and without parable.

Peter felt so strongly this chilling of their Messianic hopes that he even took Jesus aside and dared rebuke him for talking so. Of course Peter knew more of what Jesus ought to do than Jesus himself! This audacity was grounded in solicitude to be sure, but none the less it was inexcusable. Besides, he was grossly in the wrong. He did not understand the philosophy of the Messianic Kingdom. He did not know that self-sacrifice was the law of life, that one who tries to save his life shall lose it, that every man must take up his own cross if he means to follow Jesus. Already his cross is before the eye of Christ, as it was a familiar figure to all the Jews in Roman times.

All this goes to explain the sharpness of the rebuke that Jesus administered to Peter for his presumption. "Get thee behind me,

Satan" (Matt. 16:23). It was a hard name, to call a disciple Satan, and especially Peter who had so recently been the spokesman in calling Jesus the Son of God. He is acting the part of Satan now as he was like a rock then. "Thou art a stumbling block to me." That was the point. Peter was tempting Jesus to do the very thing that the devil had urged. The most prominent of the disciples was actually persuading him not to die for the sins of men! It was a strange coalition, Peter and Satan! The devil had used Peter once and he will try again. He has discovered a way to handle the very foremost of the disciples. If he could only win him wholly! Peter was minding the things of men, not the things of God. Unconsciously he had taken the devil's point of view about the career of Jesus. It was a shock to Christ to have it come from Peter. It was a rude awakening to Peter, this agony of Jesus, but a necessary one. It was now clear that the disciples were far from being ready for the great catastrophe. Can they be made ready in time? How can they reconcile his Messiahship with his death? That was a theological knot difficult of solution.

Heavenly Light on the Subject

From the human point of view Jesus was absolutely without sympathy in the deepest things of his life. The circle had once widened, but now it was very narrow, and almost a point. The apostles were indeed faithful to him, but they could not comprehend the spiritual nature of his mission nor the necessity and significance of his death. They were in poor plight to be left alone in a world that understood him still less. How could they pass through the dark hour of his death? One can little imagine the loneliness of Jesus at this time. The Father was his only sympathizer. About a week after Peter's rebuke Jesus went up into a mountain one night to pray. He took with him Peter, James, and John, the inner circle within the Twelve. Jesus cherished no hard feeling toward Peter. After all, did the rest know any more? There is no indication that Jesus was expecting what came, though, of course, that is possible. Certainly the three disciples were not. In fact, while Jesus was praying they went to sleep, or were on the point of sleeping at any rate. If the spirit was willing, the flesh was very weak as it was in the garden of Gethsemane. The transfiguration of Jesus took place as he prayed. Was it the glory brought from heaven by Moses and Elijah? Or was it the restoration of Jesus to his pre-incarnate state as he talked with these heavenly visitors? The miracle consists not in the glory, but in the presence of Moses and Elijah. If genuine, as I believe, we have full proof of life beyond the grave, and of heavenly recognition.

There was something unusual in the death of both Moses and Elijah. God buried Moses and took Elijah up in a chariot of fire. But Moses stood for the law and Elijah for prophecy. Both law and prophecy have representatives to speak with Jesus who is the gospel of grace. They spoke of the decease of Jesus, of his exodus from earth. They at least understood, and Christ's heart was comforted at this dread hour. No doubt the Father graciously sent Moses and Elijah to console the spirit of Christ in this time of darkness. In the strength of this meat he could go on steadily to the cross. We do not know the words that were said, but they were words of comfort beyond a doubt.

It would seem that another object in view was to help these three disciples to look at the death of Christ from the standpoint of heaven rather than from that of the world or Satan. A glimpse of the larger vision was offered them here, but they were so heavy with sleep that Peter blundered again. He did indeed like the glory all about him, so much so that he wished to stay there always. Luke says (9:33) that he did not know what he was saying when he suggested three tabernacles, but though dazed he was talking. They were afraid when they saw the cloud overshadow and envelop them and heard the voice out of the cloud. The voice not only identified Jesus as the Son of God, but exhorted that the disciples hear him, hear him especially in the matter of his death.

But it was soon over, and with Jesus they went down the mountain. Christ broke the silence by telling them not to speak of what they had seen and heard till the Son of man should rise from the dead. Then they might tell for the consolation of others. Meanwhile it was to be for their own strength. But once again they missed the point and went to questioning among themselves as to what the rising from the dead should mean. They did notice now his allusion to the resurrection. But if he referred to the resurrection at the end of the world, that was a long way off. So they relapsed into confusion again. They did ask Christ about the coming of Elijah, but not about the real problem in their heart.

At the bottom of the mountain they found the rest of the disciples harried by the scribes because they had failed to heal a demoniac boy. When Jesus succeeded they learned that their own failure was due to lack of prayer.

Back in Galilee and Fresh Teaching About His Death

Jesus wishes no one to know that he is in Galilee now (Mark 9:30). His real work in Galilee is over. He attempts again to explain about his death and resurrection: "Let these words sink into your ears!" (Luke 9:44). They did get in, but "they understood not." It seemed concealed from them somehow and they were afraid to ask further, though they were exceeding sorry. It was really hopeless and the hour was drawing nigh. The Galileans did find out that Jesus had returned, at least the tax-collector did, for the demand was made that he pay the half-shekel for the temple tax. Jesus paid the tax for himself and Peter, though in a rather unusual way.

Rivalry Among the Twelve

Surely the cup of Jesus was full enough without this. And yet, after all the careful teaching about his death and resurrection they go on parcelling out the chief places in an earthly kingdom among themselves. They get into a quarrel on the great ecclesiastical question as to which of them is greatest in the kingdom of heaven! Ecclesiastical jealousy is rife, therefore, right among the bosom friends of Christ and in his very presence. When he asked them what they were disputing about, they would not say. They had already asked him who was the greatest in the Kingdom.

They did not wish him to know of their envy. So Jesus called a little child. Was it Peter's child? This little child should teach them. They had missed it all again and did not know the law of service that the least was the greatest, the one who humbled himself most to serve.

This is a pathetic incident, but the saddest part of it is that the lesson was not learned then or now. Soon John, the beloved John, showed a spirit of narrow intolerance that caused a rebuke from Jesus. John had seen a man casting out demons in the name of Christ. He actually cast them out, too! What was his offence? He did "not follow us!" That was all. John expected to be promoted for extra zeal in orthodoxy! Here we have a needed lesson in tolerance about methods of work for Christ. How little John here understood the spirit of Jesus. But Christ was patient with the narrowness of John as he is today with ours. What poor earthen vessels we are after all, with our bickerings, jealousies, and prejudices. The wonder is that Jesus can use any of us in his service. We preach the spirit of service for other people and practice too often self-aggrandizement and self-seeking. It was pitiable then and it is lamentable now.

Christ cares for his little ones, those who are weak and tender in the faith. It is easy to be heedless and reckless of consequences to those who love Jesus. Sometimes the millstone is hung around the neck of those who wrong the people of God. It is not God's will that one of those little ones perish.

The spirit of forgiveness of injury is in opposition to that of self-aggrandizement. Jesus does not mean that a brother shall injure as a matter of policy and then turn around and demand that we forgive him. That is rather a cold-blooded proceeding. But he does mean that genuine repentance shall be followed by forgiveness. And real forgiveness is "from your hearts." The eternal need of this spirit is accented in almost every church in the land.

There are some who are very officious in their service of Christ, not to say flippant. Jesus discourages such loud followers and reminds them of the privations ahead of them. At this particular time Jesus had no where to lay his head. He was an outcast in the land of his people. On the other hand, if one wishes to follow Christ, he will not turn back after having put his hand to the plough. He will not turn back even to stay with a father till he die. This is what the expression "bury my father" means. That was a pious duty, but the father might live many years and service for God was imperative.

Light Advice from the Brothers of Jesus

Was Jesus going to the feast of tabernacles? It was near that time now, the last of September. It had apparently been a year and a half since Christ had been in Jerusalem. To go now offered little of hope. The brothers of Jesus had noticed his long absence from Jerusalem at the public festivals. They probably knew also about his long and recent absence from Galilee. So they come and taunt him with being a secret Messiah as if he were rather ashamed of it. They tell him to go up to Jerusalem and to do his work "openly." There are always plenty of people who know how to manage our business better than we do ourselves, especially if they dislike us a bit. It is amazing how much wisdom is misapplied. It looks sometimes as if all of us have the wrong task, to judge by the advice so freely and generously given. But Jesus asserts his independence. He will go to Jerusalem when he pleases and conduct the affairs of the Kingdom as seems good to him. He went up privately and not publicly, as they had suggested, and at his own time.

Facing Jerusalem

So he was going to Jerusalem again. It is a significant event in his career. He has returned from his seclusion, but not to make new campaigns in Galilee. He has higher ends than that. He will go to Jerusalem and bring matters to a focus there. When that is done, the end will not be far off. Will he win Jerusalem? He goes through Samaria again and excites the hatred of the Samaritans because his face was set towards Jerusalem. When he went north it was all right.

Once more James and John show a spirit of bitterness and lack of self-control as they wish to call down fire on a Samaritan village. They did not know what spirit they were of, and certainly they missed utterly the spirit of Christ. Is it with a heavy heart that Jesus goes on to the storm center of militant and hardened Judaism? They will not have him in Galilee and he had already been rejected in Jerusalem. Heretofore Christ had been on the defensive as to his enemies in the Holy City and had kept aloof from them not only in Jerusalem, but lately in Galilee also. But now the Master boldly appears in Jerusalem, not on the defensive entirely. His appearance then is in the nature of an attack upon the enemy's country. Will it succeed? Suppose Jesus should win Jerusalem to his cause. Is it worth trying?

CHAPTER SIX

The Attack upon Jerusalem

O Jerusalem, which killeth the prophets and stoneth them that are sent unto her.

LUKE 13:34

Jesus will not make a series of attacks upon Jerusalem itself. He had come here in the beginning; he will finish his career here. He will not, indeed, be able to stay in Jerusalem continuously, else the end would come at once. But there is nowhere in Palestine where Jesus can gain a permanent foothold so long as the city of Jerusalem is wholly in the hands of his enemies. They are entrenched behind ages of tradition and walls of prejudice and pride. Somehow the idea had gotten out that Jesus might come to the feast of the tabernacles this time, possibly from his brothers, possibly from the Galilean multitudes. But in the opening days of the feast he is not present. All at once Jesus is the chief topic of conversation. Will he come? Where is he? What do you think of him anyhow? The Galilean multitudes are divided over him. They had once been almost unanimously on his side, but now it is not so. In the murmuring like that in the synagogue at Capernaum, some take up for him and say: "He is a good man"—this at any rate, whether he is the Messiah or not. But others stoutly protest: "Nay, but he leads the multitude astray." This controversy was largely in an undertone because all knew that the Jews of Jerusalem hated Jesus. No one from Galilee wished to be mixed up in the affair. But one day in the midst of the discussion Jesus settled all speculation on this point by appearing in the temple and teaching.

The Jerusalem Conspirators Outwitted at Home

There he is! What will his enemies do? This was their opportunity.

They fail to arrest Jesus at the feast. The first effect of his teaching is the astonishment of the hostile Jews that he can talk so well since he did not attend their rabbinical seminary in Jerusalem. He had attended God's school, if they but knew it. But that alternative they would not admit. Jesus cut matters short by boldly charging them with wishing to kill him. They are hushed to silence, but the Galilean multitude protest that no one sought to kill him. They little knew; but the people of Jerusalem understood all about it and a group of them comment on the fact when they see Jesus (John 7:25) and even poke fun at the rulers for not arresting Christ. Their theology as to the origin of the Messiah is interesting and Christ took notice of it. His enemies resented the ridicule of the people of the city and actually sought to seize him then and there. But Jesus bore a charmed life as yet. His hour had not come. Some of the Galilean multitude become outspoken champions of Christ. At this time the Pharisees and Sadducees (chief priests) ordered some officers to arrest him. Jesus, meanwhile, in mystic language announces his independence of them, which his enemies fail to understand, thinking he will teach the Greeks (as he did indeed!). The people become more excited over his words, taking sides for and against, some even ready to seize him. But the soldiers sent for that purpose stood and heard his wondrous words and came back sheepishly to the Sanhedrin without Jesus. The Sanhedrin stormed at the officers and sneered at them and at the ignorant rabble who followed Christ. The officers had fallen under the spell of the speech of Jesus, a tribute to his character as well. It is to the credit of Nicodemus that, when Jesus was there under fire by the Sanhedrin, he dared to make a point of law in his favor. He has more courage now than when he went to see Jesus by night, but he received scorn for his courage.

The rulers are exasperated by Christ after the feast. The multitudes had left for their distant homes, but Jesus remained a while in the city and continued to teach in the temple. His teaching consisted of short, crisp sayings that drew attention. One of these stirred the Pharisees mightily. "I am the light of the world" (John 8:12), he said. It is an astonishing saying, if one is not prepared to go to the full length of the deity of Christ, indeed otherwise an impossible saying. The Pharisees took it up instantly. The dispute turned on the claim of Jesus that God was his Father. That was its justification and that the Pharisees would not admit. Jesus stung them again by saying that, if they did not believe in him, they would die in their sins. "Who art thou?" they demanded. If he would only say a plain word that they could lay hold of! But he points to the cross as the proof that he is what he claims to be (John 8:28), a proof that to them was only a stumbling block. Still some of the Pharisees were impressed and said that they believed on him. But Jesus had been suspicious of the Jerusalem converts the first visit (John 2:24), and proceeded to test these new believers. He offered them the freedom of truth, which they resented; he offered to make them true children of Abraham, but they were insulted; he showed that they were not children of God in the full sense and they proved it by trying to kill Jesus, a man who told them the truth. This sublime claim of existence before Abraham was to them unendurable.

The Pharisees are twitted by a blind man who had been healed by Jesus. He had been a well-known beggar and had a regular place to sit. The opening of his eyes by Jesus created a stir among the man's neighbors. They were not satisfied with his simple narrative. They took the man to the Pharisees who knew everything, but it was pitiful, the embarrassment of these pious wiseacres. It was done on the Sabbath and therefore God did not do it. But then it was done, and who else but God could do it? Some argued that Jesus was a sinner, else he would not have done it on the Sabbath; others that the man was never blind at all. They proceeded to settle the facts in the case by logic! The doctors differed and the man's parents were appealed to. They identified the man and proved his blindness. So the Pharisees were in a corner. Their logic and theology were bound to be correct, but how to explain this miserable fact without admitting the natural impression as to Jesus was a puzzle! They had appealed to the devil as the explanation of the expulsion of demons, but that fallacy had been exposed. The devil at any rate would be more likely to put eyes out rather than open them. They took this new turn. We admit the fact, but deny the conclusion. You just admit that Jesus is a sinner and we, well, we will admit that you can see! The man saw the humor of the situation. He was no theologian, but he could see a point as plain as this. He opened my eyes and you cannot tell whence he is! That is strange, when you know everything! Besides, we all know God does not hear sinners. But my eyes are open! They turned on him in a rage. "Thou wast altogether born in sins, and dost thou teach us?" He had cut to the quick. They cast him out of the synagogue, but Jesus then led him into the kingdom of God and gave him spiritual sight also.

The enemies of Christ have their picture, drawn by Jesus. They did not sit for it voluntarily, but provoked the characterization by asking Jesus, "Are we also blind?" (John 9:40). He told them the allegory of the Good Shepherd who knows his sheep, and whose sheep know him. There are thieves and robbers who want to get the sheep, but who will run at the sight of a wolf like a hireling. But the good Shepherd will die for his sheep, and the one flock has Gentile as well as Jewish sheep. It was a vivid picture and some of them cried out: "He hath a demon, and is mad." Yes, but others said, "Can a demon open the eyes of the blind?"

A Campaign in Judea

There had been an early Judean ministry which was only too successful. Now, when Jesus has to leave Jerusalem, he turns again to the country round about. As yet no permanent impression had been made here. Judas Iscariot had come from the town of Kerioth, and in Bethany Jesus had one home that he could almost call his own. He needed it, too, as a place where he could find rest and sympathy. Lazarus, Martha and Mary all loved Jesus though they had different ways of showing it, and Jesus greatly loved them.

This Judean ministry is recorded only by Luke who fills out largely the events of the last six months, his distinctive contribution to the life of Christ. Many of the events are similar to those in Galilee and many of the teachings are almost identical. All this is perfectly natural. There were Pharisees in Judea and hence the blasphemous accusation is repeated. Some of the Pharisees showed courtesies also to Jesus here as some did in Galilee. But the breakfast with the Pharisee did not turn out well. He put on airs because Christ did not bathe before the meal so that he and his lawyer guests were all sorely rebuked for insistence on the externals to the neglect of the moral and spiritual. The breakfast seems to have been broken up in disorder. One of the sharp lawyers who tried to entrap Jesus fell into the pit himself, but we forgive him since he was the occasion of Christ's telling the parable of the Good Samaritan which has so richly blessed the world. It is not strange that Jesus should send out a band of preachers in Judea with similar instructions to those given the Twelve. Christ followed after them also and their success was to him a prophecy of the downfall of Satan.

Some of the sayings of Jesus during this period (Luke 12) are much like portions of the Sermon on the Mount. One must never forget that he repeated his sayings often and as a teacher ought to have done so. In the abstract it is possible that Luke has here recorded what Jesus said in Galilee, but it cannot be assumed that Christ would not repeat his teachings in different parts of the country, or even in the same region.

The eagerness of Jesus to meet his fate comes out (Luke 12:49). He longs to see the fire blaze, to receive his baptism of blood. One cannot wonder at this when he recalls what the Master has already undergone and how hopeless the task seems. So few understand what he has to say and fewer still seek to put it into practice. This outburst is not impatience, but it helps us to catch a glimpse of the volcano of emotion locked in the Savior's heart.

In Jerusalem Again

Without the blare of trumpets Christ comes again. It is winter (the feast of dedication), about our Christmas time, and he is walking in the corridors of the temple. The hostile Jews gather round him at once with a petulant question of impatience. They want to know who he is and what he has to say about himself. Evidently his last visit made a profound impression on them, and they are still talking about it. "If thou art the Christ, tell us plainly" (John 10:25). The question was a legitimate one, but they wished to make a bad use of his answer. They knew very well who he claimed to be, but they wished to charge him with blasphemy. But Jesus would not say the word Messiah for another reason, because it would inflame the populace beyond control. So he stood his ground and repeated his claim of oneness with the Father. They jumped at this and hurled the charge of blasphemy at him for making himself equal with God. He did do that, but it was not blasphemy, for he was equal with God. He would not argue that point, however, but he used an *argumentum ad hominem* by showing how in their law the rulers with God's authority are termed gods. It was a deft turn, but did not appease them. If they could not argue with him, they could kill him. But he was swiftly gone.

Beyond Jordan Again

The stay of Jesus in Jerusalem had been brief and the collision was sharp and soon over. He did not stop in Judea, but went first to Bethany beyond Jordan where John the Baptist had identified him and where he had won his first disciples. What memories would come to Jesus as he thinks over the past. In a sense he is now a fugitive from Jerusalem. Had he made a mistake in joining issue so quickly and so persistently with the Jerusalem religious leaders? Could he have been more conciliatory and more effective? The devil had offered him compromise and power. He will go on as he began. There is one item that glorifies the preaching of John the Baptist. These people knew Jesus because of what John had said about him. That is a pertinent and a piercing test of modern preaching.

Luke alone gives us the story of this Perean ministry, save a few verses from John, but not much is preserved. We have to think over what we know about the work in Galilee and Judea and imagine similar scenes here. There was a man who had a theological point that troubled him. He wanted to know how many would be saved. Jesus told him that he had better try to get to heaven himself. One point that comes out is the anxiety of the Pharisees lest Jesus shall fall into the hands of Herod Antipas in whose territory he now is. Christ understands "that fox" very well and asserts his independence both of Herod and of the Pharisees. It is difficult to make out the frame of mind of these Pharisees, whether they were really friendly to Jesus, whether they were mere cat's-paws of Herod who wished Jesus to move on, or whether they were trying to inveigle Jesus back to Jerusalem. Christ saw all that was involved and said that he would go to Jerusalem to die at the right time. Meanwhile his heart went out in sorrow over Jerusalem.

A Pharisee in Perea also invites Christ to breakfast and three parables were spoken by Jesus, one to the guests, one to the host, and one to a guest who made a pious and platitudinous remark (Luke 14:15). There were great crowds here also and Jesus put them to the test much as he did in Galilee and probably with the same result. The hard conditions of discipleship, like hating one's father, etcetera, are to be interpreted in this light. If the issue is made between father and Christ, one must not hesitate.

It was in Perea also that the scribes and Pharisees sneered at Jesus for receiving sinners and eating with them as he had done in Galilee. In the formal defense made by him for his conduct in seeking to win the publicans rather than the Pharisees, he takes them at their own estimate of themselves, not meaning that it was correct. But his answer was complete. They assumed that they were righteous. Well and good, therefore; they did not need Christ, while the publicans did. Hence Christ came after the lost sheep, the lost coin, the lost son. They were like the elder brother and were sulking because publicans and harlots were entering the kingdom of Heaven. When he spoke further the story of the unjust steward, the Pharisees scoffed at him, for they were lovers of money. But they ceased scoffing when he told the parable of the rich man and Lazarus, though they hated him all the more. We may thank the Pharisees for one thing. They furnished the occasion for the most marvelous parables in all the world.

The Sanhedrin in Desperation

The raising of Lazarus was for the purpose of glorifying God and Jesus the Son of God (John 11:4). It was premeditated and so a deliberate expression of divine power right in the teeth of the enemies of Jesus. The miracle has been fiercely attacked in modern times, but if Christ is divine, the argument for its reality stands. The larger purpose of Jesus here explains his apparent indifference to the request of the sisters and then his seeming recklessness from the point of view of the disciples and especially of Thomas who had the courage of despair. When he comes it is Martha who hints that Jesus has power with God even now. It is to Martha that he uses the supreme language of deity: "I am the resurrection and the life." It is Martha also who makes a confession of faith in Jesus as noble as that of Peter (John 11:27). With Mary he exhibits great emotion in spite of himself, and even at the tomb he has difficulty in controlling his feelings. Martha recoils at the last moment, but Jesus is now calm and masterful. It was a majestic moment when at his command Lazarus stepped forth out of the tomb. The bearing of Jesus was never more dignified nor more serene than at this instant. He knew that Lazarus would come forth.

The Jews had come in great numbers from Jerusalem to console the sisters, for Lazarus was a man of wealth and position. Many of those that saw Lazarus come out of the tomb believed on Jesus. Others went and told the Pharisees what had occurred, as if in search of help. They were on the point of believing too. It was clear that something had to be done, and that at once, or all would be lost and for good.

It was indeed outrageous. Jesus had done this wonderful deed right at Jerusalem without their help or permission. A meeting of the Sanhedrin was called to deliberate over the situation. They each asked the other: "What do we?" The answer was easy, for they were doing nothing. They predicted the loss of their place and of the nation by the Romans, putting place before patriotism. Caiaphas remarked that they knew nothing at all, in which he was correct. He suggested that they make a sacrifice of Jesus for the sake of the country. There was a deeper sense in his words than he knew, but his sense of the proposal was a failure. They did make a sacrifice of Jesus, but the nation was destroyed by the Romans and they did lose their places. It is an easy and an old way out of a difficulty to propose to get rid of the other man. By the death of Jesus there have been gathered into one the children of God scattered all over the world, but that was God's plan, not Caiaphas's purpose. But now at last a formal decision has been reached by the Sanhedrin to put Christ to death as soon as possible. It was intolerable that Jesus should raise the dead right at their doors. Of course, he was a deceiver! No amount of power or proof could change that fact!

In the Mountains of Ephraim

Back into the wilderness Jesus goes near the region where he had been tempted of the devil after his baptism. It was a dark hour from the human point of view. This then was the outcome of the Jerusalem campaign. Galilee at least had not tried to kill him save at Nazareth. True, Jerusalem had several times before attempted his life, but in a sporadic way. Now he had to meet the formal decision of the Sanhedrin. If anything, now the Sadducees are more active than the Pharisees in their hatred. One cannot doubt that there in the mountains of Ephraim the devil brought to the mind of Jesus all the points that told against him. He could remind Jesus how it might have been if his advice had been followed. It was just as he had predicted.

It was not too late now to mend matters on the same terms. The devil had influence with the Sanhedrin and could easily call them off from their murderous purpose! But Jesus had fought this battle long ago. He would go to meet his hour. He had the disciples with him now in the wilderness, but how little they understood the tragedy that was going on before their very eyes.

Going to Face the Issue

The hour is near at hand and Jesus leaves the hills of Ephraim. At first it looks as if he were going away from Jerusalem for he turns north through Samaria and into the edge of Galilee. But it is only to join one of the caravans from Galilee for the Passover feast. His brothers had once suggested that he go down in public. Now he will do so. He will go to Jerusalem as a king, the King Messiah. In the throng would be some followers of Jesus and many who were more or less friendly. The Pharisees who are along seem to feel that something is in the air. They ask Jesus when the Kingdom of God comes. He does not answer that question, but the one that lay back of it, the character of the Kingdom. Men will not see it with their eyes nor point it out as here or there. It is in the hearts of men, "within you" (Luke 17:20). The Pharisees make no reply, for the answer of Jesus made the gulf between them still wider. This was not the sort of a Kingdom that they wished. To the disciples Jesus proceeded to talk of his second coming. That subject looms up before his mind now as his death draws so near. The Son of Man will be fully revealed. Meanwhile he gave an immortal picture of the Pharisee who went up in the temple and gave the Lord a great deal of pious information about himself and called it prayer. The publican was "the sinner" and knew it, but the Pharisee had to wait till the next world to find out how big a sinner he was. The procession goes on through Perea. Now the story is told by all the Synoptics.

The Pharisees seek to catch Jesus on the question of divorce. They were divided on it themselves, one side favoring easy, the other, hard divorce. In either case Jesus would hurt himself. But they were amazed as he cut through their pettifogging scruples to the eternal principle of marriage and showed that Moses' bill of divorcement was due to the hardness of the hearts of the people and was a great advance for that time. The attitude of Jesus towards children comes out well here. Even the disciples regarded them as in the way. Christ has made the true place for the child in the world. No wonder they love him.

Jesus had to correct the ideas of the disciples about money. They actually supposed money proved that one was a favorite of heaven! The tendency today is to think that poverty is a proof of piety! One young man found out how much he loved money, more than he did Christ. Jesus makes another effort to teach his disciples about his death and uses the word "crucify" this time. His looks made the disciples amazed and afraid, but they understood them not. They were merely dazed for a moment and right away James and John with their mother come up and beg the two chief places for themselves in the Kingdom! What Kingdom? What places? It was pitiful, and at such a time! Jesus offered them the martyr's cup, the baptism of death, which they lightly accepted. How little they knew the philosophy of the Kingdom. Even the Son of Man had come to give his life a ransom for many (Luke 18:45). The ten, of course, were indignant, not that they were themselves innocent of the same spirit.

The Challenge to Jerusalem

Jesus is at Jericho and all is astir. Blind Bartimeus and Zaccheus are but incidents by the way. He was nigh to Jerusalem and the people supposed that the kingdom of God was immediately to appear (Luke 19:11). They felt it in the air. Their sort of a kingdom was now to appear. The real Kingdom had already come and was continually coming.

Jesus told the parable of the pounds to discourage their false expectations, and yet he had decided to gratify the people to a certain extent. He went on up toward Jerusalem to Bethany.

Here with the Bethany family he can spend the Sabbath in rest and quiet. Great events are ahead of him and he needs the respite. In Jerusalem itself all was on the *qui vive* as to whether Jesus would come to the feast or not now that the Sanhedrin had decided to kill him. They had made public request for his arrest, perhaps by placard in the temple courts. Out at Bethany many came not only to see Jesus, but Lazarus also. The feeling was tense at both places, in Jerusalem antagonism, in Bethany sympathy. In Bethany with his dear friends he had a sweet haven and the sun shone on Olivet, but the clouds hung low over Jerusalem.

Jesus knew that the people could not understand his claim to be Messiah without plainer language than he had used. He will now employ the language of action, well knowing that his death was the reward for his boldness. His enemies had long wished him to say in plain terms that he is the Messiah. That wish will now be gratified. The picture of Jesus that Sunday morning on the colt of an ass, as Zechariah had said the King Messiah would ride, was not one to strike terror to the heart. He was King of Peace, and yet as the multitude from the city joined the multitude from the village, and all turned down the slope of Olivet toward Jerusalem the Pharisees who saw it thought that all was over. This popular demonstration meant to them that Jesus had won. They would not dare lay hands on him while he had so many friends. So they turned and blamed each other for this outcome. "Behold, how ye prevail nothing: lo, the world is gone after him" (John 12:19). Others of the Pharisees sought to shame Jesus into rebuking his disciples for the uproar (Luke 19:39).

But they are hailing Jesus as the son of David. The kingdom of God has come at last. Hosannah. Peace in heaven and glory in the highest. If these had stopped now, the very stones would have cried out. The clamor grew worse, for in the temple courts the very boys took up the strains from the crowd, to the chagrin of the chief priests and scribes who even sought to get Jesus to stop that. With a look around upon all this scene Christ went back to Bethany with the disciples. What did they think of the

Master now? For the moment he was Master indeed, the hero of the hour and in Jerusalem at that.

A Foretaste of the Struggle

Jesus had crossed the Rubicon and now the issue was to be fought out. The exasperation of his enemies increased as he came to the temple next day to teach. He cleansed the temple again as he had done at the beginning and this maddened the rulers still more. The popularity of Jesus was unendurable. They came early to get standing room about the great Teacher and hung on his words listening. He was the center of all eyes. The rulers had found out where he was very well, but what to do with him was the problem, for they feared this multitude.

Some Greeks at the feast heard of him and courteously asked of Philip to be presented to him. But Philip felt embarrassed by the request and consulted Andrew the man of counsel. But even Andrew was not able to untie this knot. They bring the problem, but not the Greeks, to Jesus for his decision. The middle wall of partition between Jew and Greek Jesus had come to break down, but there was only one way to do it. Greeks will come to him indeed, as will all classes of men, when he is lifted up. The law of life is death, as Christ explains by the grain of wheat. Jesus in profound words sets forth the principle of his atoning death, the voluntary giving of his life for men. So vivid does all this become to him, as he contemplates his hour, that in agony as in Gethsemane he cries out to the Father to save him from this hour (John 12:27), but with instant submission. "Father, glorify Thy name." This, then, is Christ's idea of his death: it is a glorification of the Father's name. Once more, the third time, the Father speaks in audible voice words of approval. The Father thus understands this view of his death. No one else at that hour understood either him or the Father. The darkness of the eclipse is coming on.

The Victorious Debate

The rulers felt keenly their disadvantage now before the people. There was the raising of Lazarus, the triumphal entry, the cleansing of the temple, the marvelous teaching. The spell must be broken somehow. He must be exposed and made ridiculous, if nothing more. Tuesday morning, as Jesus walked and taught in the corridors of the temple with admiring crowds of listeners, he suddenly found himself confronted by a company of the rulers who challenged his authority. But all at once they are themselves on the defensive as Jesus by a pertinent question asked their opinion of John's baptism. John had introduced, baptized, and identified Jesus as the Messiah. If John's baptism were of God, that was the answer to their question, for he was the Messiah. But the question of Jesus put them in a hopeless quandary, and they timidly begged to be excused, and so they are laughed at, not Jesus. Christ pressed his advantage by then telling parables which the rulers saw were against them, but which they were helpless to turn. They stepped back, cowed, saddened, but no wiser. The Pharisees and Herodians rallied and came to the rescue by sending some of their brightest students to ask a question about tribute to Caesar. The people, of course, were opposed to the Roman taxes and hated the publicans who collected them. But to oppose the taxes publicly was treason against Caesar. It was with a deal of pious palaver that these youngsters gave him what they thought was a hopeless dilemma. But at the reply of Jesus they looked simple, held their peace, and stepped back wondering greatly at finding one wiser than they were. The Sadducees enjoyed the defeat of the Pharisees and Herodians and tried now their hand with a mock story about the resurrection which the Pharisees had never been able to meet. But Jesus showed by the word of God to Moses that they were in error, not knowing the Scriptures. They, too, were silent, but the Pharisees (scribes) could not keep still. "Master thou hast well said" (Luke 20:39).

At this the Pharisees gathered in a jubilant group and one of the lawyers among them volunteered his services to his embarrassed friends. He tempted Jesus by a question in his own specialty, the law. He could only acquiesce in the reply of Jesus and retire. Our Lord now turned on the assembled Pharisees and asked them a question about the person of the Messiah, the very thing that they had so often asked him. How could he be the Lord of David and the son of David at the same time? The problem really was that of the humanity and the divinity of the Messiah. He had carried the war into Africa and put them all to rout. No one dared ask him another word. "The common people heard him gladly."

They were still cowering before Jesus, and for once he let loose the vials of his wrath upon his relentless foes. He called attention to the high position of these teachers and how they had degraded their office. They hid the truth, they made proselytes worse than they were before, they were mere hair-splitters, they put wrong emphasis on truth, they were ceremonialists without the spirit, they were professional religionists, boasters of heredity, in a word hypocrites, serpents, offspring of vipers, with the judgment of hell upon them. It was terrific; before this hailstorm and lightning his enemies shrunk away and the crowd dispersed. The heart of Jesus bursts out in lament over Jerusalem soon to be desolate, while the disciples gathered in silence apart. Jesus sat down in exhaustion and watched the people cast their gifts into the treasury, especially one poor widow whose piety doubtless cheered him. All was quiet now after the storm. He went out of the temple, his Father's house, for good and all. His enemies were like maddened hornets.

The Prophecy of Doom

As they went out Jesus pointed to the fine temple buildings and prophesied the destruction of them all. It sounded, as it was, like an echo of his recent denunciation of his enemies. The desolation of Jerusalem would be due to their treatment of him. The debate had closed with Christ as complete victor. But Jesus knew that people are seldom convinced against their will by debate. They would answer him in some other way. Behind the death of Christ lies the destruction of Jerusalem. Further in the background still lies the end of the world. As Jesus sat on Olivet and looked down at the city that he had longed to save, all these catastrophes pressed upon him and blended into one common picture. Language after all is pictographical. It is hardly possible to separate all the details of each part of this composite picture of doom. And Jesus expressly disclaimed knowledge of the time of the end of the world, though he expected the destruction of the city to come in that generation, as indeed it did. Eschatology is not a lucid subject at best and on this occasion the double theme makes it extremely difficult for us. But the kingdom of God will be taken from the Jews and given to the Gentiles. The doom of the city will be in one sense a coming of Jesus again in judgment and will symbolize the final coming. The main practical lesson then and now for us is to be ready. The very uncertainty demands diligence, not carelessness. It is easy to say that Jesus was mistaken because he has not yet come, but one who believes in Jesus as Lord will prefer to wait and trust and be ready. They left the summit of Olivet and went down to Bethany that night. What a day it had been! What thoughts were in the hearts of Jesus and the disciples!

CHAPTER SEVEN

The Answer of Jerusalem

Crucify him, crucify him.
LUKE 23:21

But it was not yet to rest that Jesus went to Bethany. His friends there had a social service to render him.

An Appreciative Group in Bethany

They did not meet at the house of Mary and Martha but with Simon, who had been a leper (not Simon the Pharisee), and who wished to show his love and gratitude to Jesus. Christ had told his disciples that after two days he would be crucified, thus for the first time setting a date for the event. Their hearts, at least, would be heavier than usual during the feast. John mentions this feast out of place in connection with his last account of Bethany, but we follow the Synoptic order.

Lazarus was there back from the grave, and Jesus was there soon to die. The occasion thus brought forth mingled emotions.

It was Mary of Bethany, not Mary Magdalene, whose spiritual devotions found fit expression in the ointment with which she anointed his head and his feet. She wiped his feet with her hair. She had caught the truth about his death and thus delicately expressed her love for the master. It would seem that even those who would not thus have shown their feelings toward Christ could at least have been willing for Mary to do so. But everyone of the disciples followed the lead of Judas in his blunt and brutal protest against Mary's wasteful extravagance. She found a champion, however, in Jesus, who understood her motives and approved her deed, interpreting it for the dull disciples. But it was a distinct rebuke to Judas and, as it proved, the last straw that was needed to break the back of his impatience.

The Sanhedrin Receive Unexpected Help

At the very hour of this feast when the rulers had met in Jerusalem to talk over the situation, they were stung beyond endurance by the triumph and defiance of Jesus that morning in the temple, and all the more so that now they felt so helpless. They had before the Passover made public proclamation of their purpose to arrest Jesus, but now they timidly feared his power with the people. It is evident that they must take Jesus by stealth, and after the Passover is over and the crowds have gone. This is the part of the wisdom as all agree. They are still determined to kill him to save the state and themselves. But all at once Judas, one of the twelve disciples, steps into the room. At first, perhaps, the conspirators are stunned and fear some new attack from Christ, but Judas relieves their fears by blurting out: "What are ye willing to give me and I will deliver him unto you?" (Matt. 26:15). What else he said to convince them of his sincerity we do not know.

He may have said that he was tired of the whole business, that there was nothing in it for him, and he would like to see the bubble burst as soon as possible. In his heart he was disappointed that Jesus was going to die and not be the kind of a Messiah that he expected; perhaps envy had arisen toward Peter, John and James. Jesus had proven to be an idle dreamer and had thrown away his opportunity. At the feast, this very night, he had given him a public insult while the money bag was empty. He knew the haunts and habits of Christ at night, his place of prayer, for instance, and so could easily catch him if they would furnish the soldiers. They must not wait till after the Passover feast. It could be done right away. The Sanhedrin were convinced. It seemed providential to these pious murderers, this opportune convert, and one right from the very circle of Jesus' friends. Who could have believed such good fortune possible? They were glad, which was more than they had been for a long time. The price agreed on was the price of a slave, 30 pieces of silver, and perhaps was meant in that sense. It now remained for Judas to fulfill his contract. Whatever the motives that prompted Judas were, clearly he was now wholly in the power of the devil. It is amazing how common turncoats are, men who are easily rebuffed and wish to show their spite. The act of Judas was secret, but it did not escape the knowledge of Christ. Did Judas suspect next day that Jesus knew? The day was spent in rest at Bethany, for it was useless now to go again to Jerusalem to teach anyone. The die had been cast and Jesus would take the consequences.

Jesus' Concern for the Disciples

How will they stand the awful catastrophe before them? Christ will make one more effort to prepare them for his arrest, condemnation, and death. Peter and John are sent to make ready for the Passover, and at the evening hour at the time of the regular Passover meal the disciples assemble in Jerusalem with Jesus in the supper room, perhaps in the house of Mary, the mother of John Mark. The heart of Jesus is stirred with emotion before he suffers (Luke 22:15). Judas had put on a bold front and come in, but besides his presence the contention of the Twelve for the chief place grated on the spirit of Christ (Luke 22:24), and finally led to his rebuking them by an object lesson of humility (John 13:15). It was a poor start for this last Passover to begin in such a fashion.

But this, bad as it was, was a small matter compared with what Christ had to disclose to them. One of them was going to betray him to the Sanhedrin. The thing seemed incredible, but Jesus had said it. With startled faces they looked at each other and then at Jesus, one after the other asking, "Is it I, Lord?" Of course Judas had to ask also. Peter motioned to John to ask Jesus who it was, but the disciples did not seem to understand the sign given by Christ nor to have heard what he said to Judas when he went out. But he was gone and it was night.

Jesus drew closer to the Eleven and his heart went out to them. He urged that they love one another, those who had just contended for the chief places. Satan was after them all, had Judas for good, and was hard after Peter.

But Jesus had prayed especially for Peter so that he would stand the sifting. Peter really thought the anxiety of Christ needless in his case. He had forgotten how he had once played the part of Satan. So all felt, but Peter was vehement in his assertion of readiness to die for Jesus, if necessary. If they only knew! They will need to struggle now and to fight, though not with literal swords as they understood Christ, but Jesus cannot explain further, for they would not understand. Probably the Lord's Supper was instituted by Christ after Judas left, if we follow the order of Mark and Matthew and not Luke. There was a hush in the upper chamber as Jesus talked on of his death, symbolized by this ordinance. He really meant to die. That was perfectly plain. It is John who has preserved for us this unbosoming of the heart of Christ. He told them all that they could bear and more than they then understood about the Father, the Son, the Holy Spirit, and the future of Christianity. But the insistent note in it all was their need of faith in Jesus after his death. They must believe in him as they believed in God, for he was one with the Father whom he had manifested to them in himself. They can pray to him also and he will hear. He will send the Holy Spirit besides to take his place as comforter and guide to truth and life. They must, in a word, abide in him and love one another, for the world will hate and persecute them. But after all it was best for them that he go away, best for their own development, best for the progress of the kingdom of God. The new Teacher will explain Jesus himself to them and then they will know what he is now trying to make clear. Besides, he will come back to them. They will see him in a little while when he returns from the grave. They will have his presence through the Holy Spirit even after his ascension. Moreover, he will at death take each one of them to the Father. He will come again at the end of the world. He himself came from the Father and is going back to the Father.

Thomas, Philip, Judas (not Iscariot), at first asked questions, as he talked, but soon all was silent attention. Now at last they seem to apprehend the meaning of Jesus. They know and believe, they say; if they only did! Christ has said all to them that was worth while. But he could talk to the Father about them. Either while still in the upper room or possibly in the moonlight on the street outside, Jesus stopped and prayed a wonderful prayer about himself, these eleven men and the other disciples through all the ages. As for himself he longed to go back to the Father, to the glory, to the fellowship. As for the eleven apostles, he had great solicitude. He had done his best with them while with them, but now he is to leave them in the world without him. Will they leaven the world or will the world master them? Satan will seek to win them. He prays that the Father will keep them now from the evil one. If only all the disciples in all the ages can keep down bickerings, personal rivalries, jealousies, rancors, divisions on unimportant matters, the world will soon know that Jesus is the Savior of men and the Son of God. It is not organic unity that Christ has in mind. It is something far deeper, unity of Spirit and freedom from strife such as the disciples had shown this very night.

The Struggle of Jesus with Himself

The Master had held up boldly while exhorting and consoling the disciples, but in reality he was in the depths himself. Every true preacher knows what it is to comfort other hearts while his own is breaking. But the reaction had to come after the strain of much emotional talk. There were a few brief hours before the crisis came, and these Jesus would spend in prayer. He had the habit of going to the garden of Gethsemane for prayer at night and this custom Judas knew and took advantage of it. In his greatest agony Jesus naturally sought this spot. Besides many obvious advantages, it was a comfort to him to be in the place where he had often communed with the Father. The very surroundings would help him in his hour of depression which he felt coming on. He never needed the support of prayer so much, not even in the dreadful temptations in the beginning of his ministry.

Christ knew that Judas would come here and so he divided the disciples, leaving eight near the gate and taking Peter, James, and John further in to watch while he prayed. Instantly Jesus "began to be great amazed" (Mark 14:33). He had never felt that way before. He turned to the three and said: "Pray that ye enter not into temptation" (Luke 22:40). The temptation of all temptations was now upon him, to recoil from the cup which he had offered to drink. He did not know it would be so bitter, and he had to take the very dregs of the cup. He was free from sin, and now for sin to smite him was hard. On his face on the ground he prayed, "O My Father," "Abba, Father" in the Aramaic of his childhood. How could he endure to be looked upon as sin? He cried out against the cup, but instantly he acquiesced in the Father's will, "as thou wilt." That was victory, to submit to the Father. An angel from heaven strengthened him, and that was the Father's answer to his prayer. But the agony increased till his sweat became, as it were, great drops of blood (probable next of Luke). But in it all Jesus had won and now was calmer. He turns to the disciples and finds them asleep! They were only a stone's throw away, but they had gone to sleep as the Son of God battled with himself for human redemption. It did seem hard if they could not watch at such a time for one hour. They had no excuse to offer, save weariness, but they slept again through the two succeeding struggles of Christ. How little they understood what it was all about. How little sympathy they gave Jesus in his hour of great need. But Christ had won the last great battle with himself. He could go to Calvary now. He would drink the cup. It matters little now whether they sleep or not.

Jesus Gives Himself Up to His Foes

It should never be overlooked that Christ made a voluntary surrender of himself to his enemies. Vain the Roman soldiers with all their weapons and torches, vain all the treachery of Judas, vain the persistent hatred of the Sanhedrin, if Jesus had not been willing to die. He could call legions of angels to his help. He did indeed smite the soldiers to the earth with a word as he stepped forth to meet them. Jesus rallied them for their timidity in coming there by night instead of arresting him openly in the temple.

But Judas did not lose his nerve. He had taken advantage of his knowledge of the devotional habits of Jesus in order to betray him. His infamy was to sink still lower when he gave the kiss as a sign to the soldiers. Christ was shocked at this depravity. Peter's blood was stirred at the baseness and he wanted to fight. He did indeed try to kill Malchus, a servant of the High Priest, and cut off his right ear as he dodged his head. But Jesus would not allow that much use of the sword for himself. He healed the ear and insisted that the Scriptures be fulfilled. He must drink the cup. It was the hour and the power of darkness (Luke 22:53). Christ's hour and the power of light will come later. The disciples were paralyzed with fear when Jesus refused to use his power to protect himself and forbade their doing anything. The spectacle of Christ in bonds was too much for them. He had always defeated his enemies before but now he would not do anything. It was clearly time for them to take care of themselves. Even Peter fled too, after all his talk of courage. A young man, possibly Mark, came near getting into trouble for following Jesus after the arrest. He had to flee naked. Surely blackness of night had now come. To Judas it was all easier than he had thought.

Jesus Faces His Accusers

Peter and John followed him to the palace of the High Priest. John went on inside, but Peter remained in the outer court. Now Jesus is in the toils of his enemies. At last they have him in their clutches after years of effort. How they chuckled with satisfaction.

They will now show him who understands the law and whose theology is right. They will answer all his arguments by death. The logic of persecution limps badly. The trouble is that the truth cannot be killed though you kill the man who teaches it. The vitality of truth is marvelous. But the persecutor never learns anything and unhesitatingly flings himself against eternal truth and the eternal God. There are two trials, the Jewish and the Roman, though, as a matter of fact, only the Roman was pertinent, for the Sanhedrin had already decided on his death, and did not have the power of death. Still it would look strange for them to demand his death without a trial and so they would go through the form of it. But nearly every form of law and every principle of justice is disregarded to get a conviction.

The Jewish trial has three stages in it, though the appearance before Annas is merely a preliminary examination by the ex-high priest probably, while the Sanhedrin is assembling. He asks Jesus about his disciples and his teaching with a fling at both. Christ with dignity appealed to the publicity and success of his work. His protest led a bystander to strike Jesus, who did not turn the other cheek, but made a calm, yet firm denial of the justice of that blow. Soon the Sanhedrin meets, possibly in the same palace, a full meeting, with the probable exception of Joseph and Nicodemus. Caiaphas presides and acts as chief prosecutor as well. It was illegal to try such a case at night, anyhow. The witnesses were hired and told nothing after all. The farce was at an end when two witnesses brought up what Jesus had said about the destruction of Jerusalem three years before, misconstrued it, and disagreed in the misconstruction. But the high priest had to pretend that something had been made out, and in a great rage demanded that Jesus defend himself. There was nothing to defend himself against, and, if there had been, he did not have to incriminate himself. It was only when the high priest put Christ on oath as to whether he was the Messiah or not that Jesus spoke. This, after all, was what was the matter. To refuse to answer now would have been proper legally, but would have been understood as a denial of his Messiahship. Then Jesus spoke with clearness, "I am." Moreover, the day will come when this Sanhedrin will stand before him who will sit at the right hand of power. This transcendent claim made it easier for them to have a show of right in voting that he was guilty of blasphemy. After dawn a ratification meeting was held, but no ratification can ever make a wrong right.

Somewhere in the midst of the Jewish trial the denials of Jesus by Peter took place. It is a sorrowful story and humiliating in the extreme. Peter had been specially honored and warned by Jesus, and had been loudest in his protestations of fidelity. He sought to hide in the crowd of servants by the fire in the open court, but the fire had light as well as heat. His exposure then led him to go to the door by the street, but even here he was recognized. He did conceal himself for an hour, but finally a kinsman of the high priest's servant, Malchus, whose ear he had cut off, said, "Did not I see thee in the garden with Him?" (John 18:26). That was enough, and Peter lost all control of himself, swore, and cursed like an adept in the business to prove his ignorance of Jesus. He caught the eye of Jesus through the open door, and the look broke his heart. He went out and wept bitterly, and appeared no more until after the resurrection. The Gospels vary in many details, but somehow thus these things seem to have occurred.

Before Pilate the accusers come with quite different charges. They now make political, not religious accusations. The first charge of perverting the nation was mere fiction. The second one of forbidding to give tribute to Caesar was a downright falsehood, the very thing that they had tried to get Jesus to say. The third charge of claiming to be a king was true, but not a king in the sense that Caesar was, as they well knew. In fact the chief complaint the Jews had against Christ's claiming to be the Messiah was just this, that he would not be a temporal king. The triumphal entry gave enough color to the charge for them to use it. When Pilate learns that he is king of truth, he sees that this does not at all infringe on the province of Caesar. He even endeavors to persuade the Jews to be willing for Jesus to be set free, announcing his own decision that he is innocent. Surely this is a strange attitude for a judge to assume. Pilate catches at the mention of Galilee to send him to Herod Antipas, who quickly sends him back. He was nothing but a puzzle to him. He seeks to win favor for Jesus by putting him against Barabbas in the choice of the people as a released prisoner. But the chief priests stir up the people to ask for Barabbas. Pilate tried to make a joke out of the thing and brings out Christ with a crown of thorns on his head. In disgust he surrenders, repeating the innocence of Jesus, not his guilt. In superstitious dread he once more recoils from the deed and the people shout "Caesar" at him. They will tell Caesar that Pilate pardoned a man who claimed to be a rival king. It was their strong appeal, and Pilate withered before it. Vainly did he remind the Jews that they had done it, not he. He could wash his hands, but not his soul. In truth, Sanhedrin, mob, Pilate, Judas, all had their share in the crime of the ages. There was guilt enough for all. The cry of the people to crucify Jesus was a nightmare to Pilate and is a stain upon the Sanhedrin, Sadducees, Pharisees, all, that has never been erased.

Jesus Dies a Shameful Death

It is a dreadful story, a harrowing narrative, the tragedy of the universe. Jesus came to redeem Israel and Israel crucified him. He came to his own, and his own received him not, preferred a highway robber to him, took his blood on their heads with spiteful glee.

Jesus began the journey to the cross, carrying his own cross, but Simon of Cyrene was shortly impressed to carry it after him, probably because of the fatigue of Christ, exhausted by the fearful night. The women of Jerusalem who bewailed his fate little knew what would befall their fair city because of this deed. Jesus reminds them of the fate of the dry tree when once the flames light it up. In a sense Christ took the place literally of Barabbas, who would have been crucified between these two robbers as the ringleader of them. Upon the hill shaped like a skull, overlooking the city, they nailed Jesus to the cross. He would not take the wine mingled with gall or myrrh, which some sympathetic person offered him to relieve his sufferings. He would go into the shadow with unclouded brain. He would taste the whole cup.

The first three hours on the cross, from 9 a.m. to 12 noon, were hours of torture and scorn. But Jesus showed the sublimity of his spirit by praying for forgiveness for his murderers, who did not know in their blind rage what they were doing. He practiced now what he had preached. But while he prayed, the soldiers gambled for his robe at the foot of the cross. Pilate had a spasm of stubbornness after his weak surrender on the main point. He stoutly refused to alter the accusation written on the cross. It was indeed the charge on which Jesus had been sentenced by him, but it stung the Sanhedrin. He would show them that he could not be run over all the time. The heart of Jesus went out to his mother who stood by the cross. The sword had indeed pierced her soul now. The brothers and sisters of Jesus did not believe in him yet and so John, the beloved disciple, is the only one who can console Mary in this unutterable hour. He led her away from the dreadful scene to his home in Jerusalem.

One of the bitterest drops in the cup was the mockery of the crowds as they swept by in lofty scorn. Jesus was now a fallen idol and they gleefully hurled into his teeth his great claims as Savior, Son of God, the Christ, King of Israel, his power to build the temple in three days. Why not step down from the cross that we may see and believe? That will convert us all! So the crowds, the members of the Sanhedrin, who lost control of themselves in their hour of triumph, so the soldiers with loud rudeness, so even the robbers on the cross by his side. Even the robbers looked down on this scapegoat between them, till one of them came to his sense and turned in rebuke to the other. The revulsion was so great in him that he swung over to faith in Jesus. That was trust, indeed, to believe that Jesus had a kingdom in such an hour as this. He trusted that a better day would come for Christ, and Jesus honored his faith then and there, and opened the portals of Paradise. Even on the cross Jesus saved a soul, aye, on the cross he saved all who are saved.

At noon came the black darkness, as if nature could not longer behold the scene. The veil of night is drawn over these three slow hours when silence reigned. The mocking ceased and a strange awe fell upon all. It was not an eclipse of the sun, for it was the time of the full moon. The stillness was at last broken by a cry of desolation from Jesus. He felt that somehow in all the dreariness of these hours the Father had withdrawn his presence. He was made to be sin, who knew no sin, and he was left to feel the sting of death for sin. We may not penetrate the mystery further, but someone has well said that the answer to this cry was John 3:16. It was God's love for the world that had made possible this hour of unutterable gloom. Jesus retained his consciousness of what he was doing. He took a sip of vinegar and cried, "It is finished" (John 19:30). He saw victory where the devil and the Sanhedrin saw only defeat. He died with a cry of resignation on his lips, and gave up his spirit to the Father.

And Jesus was dead. His head was bowed and the light was gone out of his eye. The great artists of all ages have sought to put on canvas this sublime and awful tragedy. The temple had the veil rent from top to bottom by the earthquake which came when Jesus died. The graves of many saints were opened, who themselves came forth after his resurrection, so Matthew records (Matt. 27:53). The Roman centurion in charge of the crucifixion was greatly impressed by the darkness, the earthquake, and the bearing of Jesus. He realized that a dreadful mistake had been made and a God man put to death. The people were smitten with dread and fled to the city. The faithful women stood alone and watched it all.

When the soldiers came to finish the work that the bodies might not remain over the Sabbath, they found Jesus already dead. John had come back to the cross and saw a soldier pierce the side of Jesus when blood and water came out, proving thus two things: one that he was a real man, and no mere phantom because of the blood, the other that he had died rather suddenly because some blood still remained in him, probably from a broken heart, according to the suggestion of Stroud. The blood, so Dr. Stroud argues, would not otherwise be found in the body after death. But John, whatever the explanation, insists that his witness to the fact is true (19:35). The courage of Joseph and Nicodemus at this dark hour is not strange after all, just as timid women will often be bold as lions in a great crisis. They took this stand for Jesus after his star had sunk out of sight. Let it be put to the credit of those two men of high position that, though they waited long, they did take their stand openly for Christ when it cost most to do so, when in fact many of the leading disciples were in hiding. But the women were faithful. They watched the place, the new tomb of Joseph in the garden, where Jesus was laid, watched till the Sabbath drew on (dawned), and then rested with heavy hearts that night. It was a restless Sabbath that the rulers spent, for, though Jesus was dead, he had spoken of rising from the dead. They did not believe any such nonsense themselves, but the case of Lazarus made them uneasy. They feared Jesus, though dead, as Herod Antipas did John the Baptist. They gave it out to Pilate that they were afraid of the disciples of Jesus. At any rate, they had their way and a guard was placed by the sepulchre sealed with the Roman seal. Then the Sanhedrin could go to prayers and thank God that "that deceiver" was out of the way. No more would he violate their rules and teach heresy to the people. No more could he ridicule them to the populace. Rabbinism and sacerdotalism were still triumphant. They had saved the kingdom of God from this upstart! They could stroke themselves with pious satisfaction this Sabbath day. Did he brand them "hypocrites"? He will never do it again, thank heaven. Yet they could still hear those words ring out in the corridors of the temple as the people cheered Jesus. Was he really dead, or was it all a fancy that he was saying those words again? Perhaps their nerves were just a bit overstrained. That was all.

Jesus in the Tomb

The Sabbath seemed an eternity. The excitement had died down. The Sanhedrin were grim masters of the situation. Pilate's flickering conscience worried him at times, and perhaps his wife still had dreams. The Roman soldiers gossiped about the strange prisoner who had been crucified. The people of the city had a new respect for the power of the Sanhedrin who after all had carried out their threat against the Prophet of Nazareth. The Galilean multitudes which had joined so enthusiastically in the triumphal entry accepted the matter philosophically. Many of them said, "I told you so." They always knew that some bad end was in store for this reckless teacher who did not hesitate to oppose the ecclesiastics of Jerusalem. They were the scholars and the custodians of orthodoxy. All that other people had to do was to believe what was doled out to them by the rabbis. Others were sorry and disappointed, but silent. What could they say now?

Jesus was dead. It beat into the soul of Mary, his mother, like the pouring rain. What had the angel Gabriel said? And now this! It was too much for her mother's heart to understand. He was a prophet; he did work miracles; he did claim to be the Messiah, the Son of God. She would believe him against all the world. Besides John the Baptist said that he was the Messiah. Still he is dead. The other women had too much grief of their own to comfort her. And what could they say?

The disciples were scattered like sheep without a shepherd. Judas the traitor had committed suicide. Peter the denier was in tears in secret. John was covering up his own woe in fulfilling Jesus' dying bequest to his mother. The other disciples were not seen after the arrest in the garden. Ah, but they knew what had happened, how they had deserted him in this hour of need. John alone had been perfectly true and brave in it all, John and the women. The hopes of the disciples lay buried in Joseph's tomb. No more petty disputes over the chief places in the Kingdom. To their minds the Kingdom was dead as well as the King. It was all over with Christianity, for the kingdom of the world had triumphed. The hope of the world was buried in that tomb.

The enemies of Jesus have manifestly triumphed. It is Satan's triumph and he knew it. The Sanhedrin had been but tools in his hands, though they piously imagined that they were serving God by what they had done.

There was joy in hell and Jerusalem this Sabbath. Christ had chosen battle rather than compromise and this is Satan's answer. Will Jesus remain in that tomb? Did he remain in that tomb? The light of the world has gone out. Will that Sun of righteousness rise again with healing in his wings? On the answer hinges the future of Christianity and the future of the world. During that Sabbath no one expected it. All had lost hope and forgotten all that Christ had said on the subject. The theology of the disciples went down with a crash before the great fact of his death. That was the outstanding fact that obscured their minds, and that they could not throw off. The funeral knell of the solemn Sabbath hours tolled on the bleeding hearts and hopeless minds of those whom Jesus had chosen for this very day. But they could not raise him from the grave, and to them a dead Christ was a dead Christianity. It is easy for others to offer doctrinaire sympathy in the hour of death as the clods echo our gloom upon the grave. But in this grave lay buried the best flower of the race, the hope of those who had trusted all to him. Put yourself by that tomb and imagine what you could have said. It is vain to recall the promises of a dead Christ.

CHAPTER EIGHT

The Final Triumph of Jesus

The Lord is risen indeed.
LUKE 24:34

It was blackness of despair for the disciples. The night was long and there were no stars. True, Jesus had said that he would rise on the third day, but no one thought of that now but his enemies, nor did they believe it. The cruel, blighting, staggering fact of the death of the Master stared them in the face at every turn. He had indeed raised Lazarus from the dead after being in the tomb for four days, but now the grave held Jesus himself fast. With him they had buried all their hopes. It was not a momentary eclipse of faith that had come upon them, but settled night. It is important to realize to the full this situation so that one can see clearly that any light on the matter had to come from someone else than the disciples themselves. No conspiracy on the part of these dejected disciples to revive Christianity with the announcement that Jesus was alive, though he was not, is conceivable. If Christianity was born again with the belief in the Risen Savior, one must understand how difficult it was for the disciples to come to this belief. If it be said that the women imagined that they had seen angels and Jesus, and so restored the hopes of the disciples, it is to be observed that the disciples did not believe the women. If it be said that the narratives are conflicting, one must remember that this shows independence in the testimony. If one says that this is the after-reflection and theological interpretation of the disciples, one must recall the fact that the narratives tell unhesitatingly their own blunders, shortsightedness, lack of faith, difficulty of belief in the resurrection of Jesus. In simple truth, no theory has yet been advanced that harmonizes with the fact of the revival of a dead Christianity save the fact of the resurrection of Christ. The disciples saw Jesus. To say that they saw his spirit, not his body, does not make it easier of belief. It is a miracle to see a disembodied spirit. Let us linger over the fragmentary narratives of the events of those wonderful forty days. The hopes of the human race center in what took place at this time. Let us observe the steps toward the light.

The Fact of the Empty Tomb

This was the discovery of the women and admitted by all. It is the first cardinal fact in the new situation. The enemies of Christ had overreached themselves in having the Roman seal on the tomb and the Roman guard to watch it. That guard guaranteed that no man could steal the body of Jesus. When the affrighted soldiers fled to the Sanhedrin, not to Pilate, they told the truth. They said that Jesus came out of the tomb. Did the Sanhedrin believe in Jesus? Not much. Christ had said that they would not believe though one rose from the dead. The Sanhedrin had killed Jesus, and now undertook to kill the fact of his resurrection. A fact is the hardest thing in the world to destroy and has perpetual power of rejuvenation. It is far easier to kill a man than a fact. But Jesus did not appear to the Sanhedrin and they ceased to worry, for the soldiers were compelled for their own safety to say what they were told to say. One may remark in passing that, if the soldiers were really asleep, they knew nothing about what had happened. The Sanhedrin took care of them with Pilate. But to return to the women. Late on the Sabbath afternoon the group of faithful women gave themselves the sad privilege of viewing the sepulchre again. For some reason they did not observe the Roman guard, perhaps not going close enough. After sundown they bought spices with which to anoint the body of Jesus, and then rested till morning. With the dawn they started, doubtless, from Bethany, and before they reached the knoll north of Jerusalem, the sun was risen. They had made no plan for rolling away the stone, and all of a sudden they are troubled over that. But, lo, the stone is already rolled away! What could it mean? Had his body been stolen by his enemies? Their ignorance of the guard would make such a suggestion natural to them. They entered timidly the open tomb and beheld two men. At a glance they see that Jesus is not there. This is the first indisputable fact that stands out and confronts us. The empty tomb calls for explanation.

The Story of the Angels

The two men turn out to be two angels and they have an interpretation of the situation. They offer an explanation of the empty tomb. The strength of this evidence is weakened for some minds by the fact that angels are brought into the narratives. But if men can rise from the dead, it may be possible for angels to appear also. Still, it is indirect, for the women have only heard the angels say that Jesus is risen. "Why seek ye the living among the dead? He is not here but is risen" (Luke 24:5). It is the angels who seek to remind the women of the forgotten promise of Jesus that he would rise on the third day. They now begin to understand. Strange they had not thought of it before. The women are charged with a message to the apostles and Peter in particular. Jesus promises to meet them in Galilee as he had said he would before his death (Mark 14:28). The women were naturally agitated. Astonishment, fear, trembling, joy, haste seized them and they ran in silence on their mission. Was it all true? The women at least seem to be convinced that Jesus was alive. But what will the disciples think of it?

John's Intuition

The skeptics of the resurrection of Jesus were his own disciples. The problem of the Risen Christ was how to convince them of this fact. It was impossible to revive faith and hope in them while they looked on Jesus as still dead. The resurrection of Christianity depended on the Risen Christ as a fact and as a force. Mary Magdalen quickly caught the fact that the tomb was empty and hurried on, without seeing the angels, to tell Peter and John. Peter is with John now, no longer alone. Common grief has brought Peter back. They are both greatly distressed over the idea that the body of Jesus has been stolen from the grave, as Mary supposed. They must first see if it be true. John reached the tomb first, both far outrunning Mary, but hesitated about going in after seeing the linen clothes lying to one side. Peter did not hesitate to go in, whereat John did likewise. John noticed that the napkin that had been on his head was not with the linen clothes, "but rolled up in a place by itself" (John 20:7). To this sensitive spiritual temperament here was evidence that Jesus had indeed risen from the grave. It was no grave robbery, no sign of a struggle with the guard or haste in the removal of the clothes, which indeed would probably not have been removed at all in such a case. Jesus himself laid that napkin carefully to one side. "He saw and believed." But Peter was more matter of fact and still doubted. Peter and John had both forgotten the pledge of Jesus that he would rise on the third day, had forgotten indeed the glory of the transfiguration mount. But if he was risen, where was he? No one had seen Jesus. It was still an unsolved mystery. The soldiers alone knew what had taken place and they did not tell the disciples but the Sanhedrin. The mouths of the only eye witnesses to the salient facts were closed. Possibly the Sadducees had not believed what the soldiers had said, but the Pharisees had taken it more seriously. It was a grave situation on the whole. Were they to be baffled after all?

Perhaps, however, he had appeared only as a spirit and had vanished to bother them no more.

Jesus and Mary

After Peter and John had left the empty tomb, Mary arrived, for they had been too swift for her. Another interesting item is the fact that the angels did not appear to Peter and John, but reappeared to Mary. One might argue that this proves that the women started it all out of their excited imaginations, but no one believed the women till their testimony was confirmed. So another solution must be sought, though I have none to offer. Gabriel appeared to Joseph as well as to the mother of Jesus. Mary was standing without, weeping in inconsolable grief. It was bad enough before, but now it is far worse. To have dishonored his body was to go to the last extremity of shame. She stooped and looked into the tomb. The angels are surprised at her grief and she at their joy. She gave the angels the same answer of perplexity concerning what had been done with the body of Jesus, and then turned and saw one whom she took to be the gardener. Here, perhaps, was a ray of light. Possibly he had removed the body of Jesus to another part of the garden. The very soul of Mary went out in her reply when she said: "Sir, if thou hast borne him hence, tell me where thou hast laid him, and I will take him away" (John 20:15). It was a pathetic appeal. The answer was the first word that Jesus is known to have spoken to a human being since his resurrection and it was simply "Mary." But it was the old accent and tone of voice. She had not been thinking it possible that Jesus was alive and did not recognize him. Besides Christ had another appearance to some extent. It was not easy to apprehend him at first, and sometimes he held the disciples back in a sense from knowing him. But now there was no doubt. By the open grave Mary saw Jesus. She could only say, "Rabboni." She ventured to lay her hand tenderly upon him, but he restrained her. He is here at all because he has not yet ascended to the Father.

He is on the way from the grave to glory and stops some days with the disciples. He calls them "My brethren" and identifies himself in sympathy with them in relation to God the Father. He sends a message to them that he is going to ascend to the Father. The other women had a promise from the angels that he would see them in Galilee. Both messages were true and would test them. Mary is all ablaze with the wondrous reality and comes running to the disciples with the tremendous words, "I have seen the Lord" (John 20:18). But no one believed her. If John heard this, he kept quiet. Doubt held the apostles fast. It simply could not be true. It was some new delusion that had seized Mary. Perhaps the demons had her again.

Jesus and the Other Women

He met the women on the way from the tomb with the message of the angels before they had seen the disciples, though Luke 24:9 may indicate that they had delivered the message of the angels. Jesus repeats the message of the angels to them that he would meet them in Galilee. And yet he was soon to see them in Jerusalem. Was it that he was gradually getting them ready for seeing him? Before the great reunion in Galilee they would need much strengthening. His appearances to them in Jerusalem were all in the nature of a surprise. The Synoptics all give the Galilee appointment and some of the Jerusalem appearances on this first day also. No more did the apostles believe the testimony of the group of women. It was to them as idle talk (Luke 24:11).

Unexpected Light on the Problem

They had come into town this first day of the week to see if there were any developments among the disciples on the situation. It was late afternoon and they were plodding their way home with heavy hearts. It was still all dark in Jerusalem. They were talking it all over as they went along. It was a time for reviewing the whole career of Jesus of Nazareth. Each sought to explain the work of this marvelous man and asked the other questions on difficult points. Why was there so much promise if it was all to end thus?

A stranger joined them and listened to their talk. Finally he asked what it was all about. "They stood still, looking sad" (Luke 24:17). Where had he been these days not to have heard of Jesus of Nazareth? Had he lived all alone in Jerusalem? There was but one theme on people's lips in these days and that was Jesus. They briefly recounted the story of the Nazarene, his works, his character, and his end. They added what had been their own hope about him, a hope now buried in the tomb. "We were hoping that it was he that should redeem Israel." The nation's hope had risen fast around him. It did look once as though he were the long looked for Messiah. But now it is all over, for he has been dead three days. It is true that some of the women had a story that the tomb was empty, which turned out to be so, but nobody believed what they said about a vision of angels who alleged that Jesus was alive. When they left town, no one had seen Jesus himself.

The stranger now began to talk. He took up the Old Testament and explained how the career of Jesus, as they had outlined it, tallied with the description of the Messiah in the Scriptures. He even argued that it was necessary for the Messiah to suffer. It was a new and very interesting interpretation to them and they would consider it. It was wonderful, for their hearts burned as he spoke. They had never heard it put that way before. But they are at home and must stop. The stranger hesitated and started to go on. Only upon their urgent invitation did he stop for the evening meal. Across the table they now sat and he took the bread and said grace. It was the old voice and the old charm. They looked at each other and he was gone! It was Jesus, and they had seen him. The women were right after all. Christ had risen from the dead and was alive. They must tell the brethren in Jerusalem and bring joy to their hearts.

A Conference on the Situation

It was in the same upper room where they had assembled on that fateful night when Jesus had foretold all that had come to pass. Probably Simon Peter was the cause of the meeting. The women had brought a special message from the angels for him from the Master. But to crown it all Jesus himself had appeared to Simon Peter. The news created the utmost excitement among the apostles. He was the leader and surely he would not be deceived, even if the women had been. It was a crisis of Christianity, the crisis of all crises. If Jesus was indeed risen from the dead, then all was not lost: in truth, all was won. There would still be a future, a glorious future, for Christianity. It was important that the apostles do not disband. They must meet at once with those disciples that could be reached and confer on the next step. Probably Mary and other women were here also, but Thomas was absent. Possibly in the hurry he could not be found. There would certainly be an interesting time with all these personal witnesses to the fact that Jesus was alive. Perhaps Mary, the other women, Peter, all told how he looked and what he said. What had Jesus said to Peter? It was the first time that Peter had seen the Master since the denials. The rest would eagerly weigh all that was said. Was it valid evidence? Was it conclusive? Could they not be mistaken after all? In the midst of the meeting the two disciples from Emmaus come with their wonderful story. Before they can tell it, they are greeted with the glad announcement: "The Lord is risen indeed, and hath appeared to Simon" (Luke 24:32). This last was the salient point to the disciples. Then the two went on with their remarkable confirmation. It did indeed look as if it were true, wonderful though it was. The doors had been shut for fear of the Jews, for they must take no chances.

As they talked of Jesus, all at once he stood in the midst of them. He had risen from the dead! But were they now convinced? A strange reaction set in, for they were now terrified and supposed that they saw a spirit or ghost, just what some modern critics now allege. This entire appearance as recorded by Luke and John opposes the idea that it was only the spirit of Jesus that was seen by the disciples. He showed them his hands and his side and expressly alleged that he was not mere spirit, but even had "flesh and bones" (Luke 24:39).

This passage adds to the difficulty, one must admit, for flesh and blood will not enter heaven. The resurrection body is a spiritual body. But one must remember that the case of Jesus is entirely exceptional. He spent forty days on earth between the resurrection and the ascension. His body was not as it had been nor as it would be. He could go through closed doors and yet eat broiled fish. We must leave the mystery unsolved, as we have to do with all the deeper mysteries of God and nature. But after all this is no more difficult than the fact of resurrection, and we can see how this transition state could be a mighty help to the faith of the disciples. Their doubt was so great on this occasion that Jesus upbraided their unbelief. As one has quaintly said, they doubted that we may believe. At last our Lord had convinced his own disciples that he was no longer dead, but alive. It is well for us that the proof was conclusive, for the resurrection of Jesus is the foundation of all our hopes and struggles. Christ has convinced them, but this is only the beginning. They have a mission to the world to go and win it. As the Father had sent him, so he now sends them (John 20:21). They are to announce to men the terms of forgiveness. Their task is now to convince others. Can they prove to others that Jesus is alive, that Christianity is alive also and destined to conquer the world? They have at least one qualification: they believe it themselves. They have hope and faith, but they lack experience and power.

The Case of Thomas

They soon meet Thomas, who was absent on the Sunday night when Jesus appeared to the company in the upper room. They try to convince him by saying, "We have seen the Lord" (John 20:25), and fail utterly to move his unbelief. He was still as skeptical as they had been before Peter's experience and before they had seen the prints of the nails in Christ's hands and feet. I will not believe, Thomas bluntly said, till I see what you claim to have seen. After all Thomas was not much more skeptical than the rest had been even after they had Jesus right before their eyes. It is true that he had their testimony added to all the rest. There is an honest doubt which is the foe of all credulity. Christianity is the foe of idle superstition as well as of blatant infidelity. Christianity wishes its adherents to look the facts in the face.

Still the disciples had all carried their doubt too far and were openly rebuked by Jesus for it. Thomas is not a comfort to the man who prides himself on his skepticism. Jesus was good to Thomas. On the next Sunday the disciples meet again in the same upper room where Jesus had appeared to them just a week before. They have not seen him during the week, for Christ does not remain with them bodily now though he is with them in spirit. Will he come tonight? Who can tell? They have not yet gone to Galilee because the time had not arrived for that. They have not wavered in their conviction that Jesus is alive. They have not formulated any plans for the future of Christianity, but are waiting for further developments. The doors are closed again, for the rulers must be kept in ignorance of the present situation. Thomas is there tonight.

Suddenly Jesus stood before them again and speaks to Thomas. He had accepted the challenge of doubt and showed his hands and his side. It was enough and Thomas could only say to him, "My Lord and my God" (John 20:28). If Thomas had doubted longer, his faith now grew faster than that of the rest. He hails Jesus as Lord and God without any reservation. Christ allowed himself to be declared divine, and added that the greatest faith was that which would reach this height without having seen him, the faith of those who "have not seen and yet have believed." The beautitude belongs to all of us who are convinced of the resurrection and deity of Jesus. John adds here, as if closing his Gospel, that this is the reason why he has written, to bring to pass just this state of faith in Jesus as the Messiah, the Son of God. Surely his ambition has been nobly realized even though his Gospel for that very reason has been fiercely assailed through the ages. But, sooth to say, John has given us such a picture of Christ as would make him, if it is not genuine, the greatest creative artist of all the ages, a thing that no one believes.

By the Sea of Galilee

The days went by and the disciples turned to Galilee. The time had not yet come when Jesus would reveal himself to the body of believers (over 500, Paul said) on the appointed mountain in

Galilee. There was nothing to do but to wait in the midst of the scenes of so much of the work of Christ. At every turn along the beloved lake they would be reminded of Jesus. They had left their all and cast their fortunes with the new teacher on these shores. Had it been worth while? What has the future in store for them now? Truly it had been wonderful. Most of them had been fishermen and so one night Peter took the initiative and said that he was going fishing. That was enough to call back the old days. Six of them at once offered to go with him. They fished all night and had fisherman's luck and caught nothing. They were used to that and were pulling for the shore in the early dawn when they saw a figure in the dim light walking on the shore. A voice came to them that was strangely familiar, though the word "children" as applied to them in address was apparently unusual, but John's fine spiritual sense perceived the truth; he said: "It is the Lord" (John 21:7). The impulsiveness of Peter responded to John's insight and he was soon on the shore beside Jesus.

The scene between Jesus and Peter on the shore in the early morning is wonderful indeed. It was after the breakfast of fish and bread that Christ turned to Simon. One other morning he had sat by a fire and this of itself was significant to Simon, but Jesus was pointed enough to bring the whole scene of the denial back to his all too vivid memory. He seized the right moment to probe Simon's heart by three searching questions. It was Simon who had spoken for the disciples at Caesarea Philippi. It was Simon who had said on the night of the betrayal that, though all men forsook Jesus, yet he would be faithful even unto death. Time makes short work of the boaster and now Simon was in poor shape to say a word. Jesus was gentle, but persistent with Peter, challenging his superior love and even his very love itself with the word chosen by Simon. A question came for each denial and each cut to the heart. The result was gratifying indeed and revealed a humility in Simon not manifest before, but which reappears in 1 Peter 5:1–11. He is now converted after the sifting by Satan and the prayers of Jesus for him have availed. Jesus exhorts him to feed the sheep and he will later urge the elders to "tend the flock of God" (1 Peter 5:2). Once Peter had promised

Jesus that he would die a martyr's death, if need be, and then turned and ran in disgrace. But now that he is humble he will have a martyr's death by and by. But Simon is Simon still in his personal characteristics, and his curiosity leads him to ask about John, "And what shall this man do?" (John 21:22). Peter's question bordered upon impertinence and was sharply rebuked by Jesus, though he did not mean that John actually would live till the second coming, a mistake that John takes pains to correct. James and John had once rashly said that they were able to be baptized with Christ's baptism of blood, and James in fact was soon to drink that cup.

On a Mountain in Galilee

The location of this mountain we do not know nor the precise date. Doubtless the bulk of the believers are here assembled. There had been time enough for word to reach them. It was a signal occasion, for here were assembled the people who represented the visible fruitage of the ministry of Jesus, something over 500 disciples. The grain of mustard-seed had begun to grow and would ultimately cover the earth. This Jesus knew. Some few still doubted, having a hard battle, but most had come already to a militant faith in the Risen Redeemer. Jesus met this goodly company as the Leader of a world-conquering host. No statesman ever outlined such a magnificent program as Jesus here laid down, the Christian's Charter for the conquest of the world. No general was ever more certain of victory. The sublime optimism of Christ is transcendent when one recalls that his disciples had no money, no weapons, no influence. They had, however, the supreme message and the presence and power of Christ by the Holy Spirit. It is objected by some critics that the Great Commission is too ecclesiastical to be genuine, but baptism is the only item that is open to such a charge and no detailed directions are here given for the execution of that command. All that we get elsewhere. It is a missionary propaganda that Jesus here lays upon the hearts of the 500 men and women, primarily upon them as members of the kingdom of God, redeemed individuals. The local church is God's appointed means for carrying on the work of the kingdom, but the responsibility rest ultimately on every believer apart from a church's failure, or performance of duty. The disciples are the salt of the earth, the hope of the world, and the future of Christianity rested on their shoulders.

In Jerusalem Again

The apostles now returned to Jerusalem, the scene of their sore discomfiture, yes, but the scene of Christ's triumphant resurrection also. Henceforth Jerusalem, not Galilee, will be the place of their activity. They will seek to win a foothold right in Jerusalem itself, for now they know that God is with them to the end. James, the brother of Jesus, had received a special manifestation and is now a devout believer along with John and the rest. Mary, his mother, has a new song in her heart. She can sing a new *Magnificat*, with a clearer faith. She had indeed seen the salvation of the Lord. Already, then, a nucleus exists in Jerusalem. Lazarus does not appear more in the history, because, perhaps, of the relentless hatred of the rulers toward him for coming out of the tomb.

Jesus meets the disciples again in Jerusalem and takes pains to give them a last lesson in the interpretation of the Old Testament, for he knew the Old Testament. He was, and is, the great interpreter of Scripture for all time. He found himself in the writings of Moses, the prophets, and the Psalms, though he had to open the minds of the disciples before they could see it (Luke 24:45). The open mind is as necessary as the open Scripture and more difficult to get. The closed mind is the chief foe of Scripture truth. Jesus expects us to use our minds in the study of the Bible. Once more Christ urged them on to the conquest of the world. That is the main thing. Missions are the very life of Christianity. They must indeed wait in Jerusalem for power from on high with which to win the world. The spiritual dynamo is absolutely necessary. They will soon receive the Holy Spirit and then they must undertake this world enterprise. They are not, however, to tarry in Jerusalem till all of Jerusalem is won. That is not true yet! They are not indeed ready for this world mission, for they still look for a temporal kingdom (Acts 1:6), an error that the Holy Spirit will remove when he comes. Indeed, the disciples will understand Jesus better after he is gone.

A Last View on Mt. Olivet

Jesus led the disciples out of the Eastern Gate, past Gethsemane with its tragic memories, up the familiar slope towards Bethany, beloved Bethany. The view was sublime in every direction: the Jordan, the Dead Sea, Mt. Nebo, Jerusalem, the Mediterranean. "They were looking up" (Acts 1:9) and Jesus was giving them a parting blessing. A cloud swept by and he was gone. Long after the cloud disappeared the entranced disciples kept gazing into the heaven whither Jesus had gone.

Till He Come

Their upward look was interrupted by the word of the two angels that "this Jesus" will so come back in like manner (Acts 1:11). He had said so himself. They now know that he has risen and believe that he will come back. In a short time they will be under the tutelage of the Holy Spirit and will come to understand the spiritual nature of the kingdom of God. And now they worshipped Jesus (Luke 24:52) with joy and praise. The task of the disciples is to understand, to interpret, and to obey Jesus. The Christian world is still engaged in doing these things. His life and teachings, his death and resurrection, his power over men to uplift and to make God-like, the greatest of all themes, still fill the horizon of the modern world. Science has done wonders, but science is barren beside the life of Jesus. He has stood the searchlight of minute historical investigation. Most of all he endures the test of life. His pitying eye still looks upon us, his powerful hand still reaches out to save. When he came before they crucified him; when he comes again he will be crowned King of Kings and Lord of Lords. Meanwhile let him rule in all our hearts. "Amen: come, Lord Jesus."

PART II
Biblical Theologian

CHAPTER NINE

The Bible as Authority, *The Homiletic Review,* February 1892

There is the keenest interest in the Bible. All the attacks upon it have on the whole sharpened public interest about the Book of books. Every effort to make a new Bible comes to naught. Even Mr. H. G. Wells' elaborate plan for a new Bible for the twentieth century has fallen flat. The Bible holds the field in popular interest as the best seller in all the world with 30 million copies coming from the presses each year. There is, besides, more real study of the Bible in school and church than ever before. The Bible has a firmer grip on the life of man than it had 150 years ago.

It has not always been easy for people to get at the Bible. One of the sharpest indictments that Jesus made of the Pharisees and the scribes was that they put their oral tradition in the place of the Word of God (Mark 7:8, 9, 13). The Talmud recites how the oral law was held to be superior to the written law. There is always this point and this difficulty. Most of us have smoked glasses. We see part of the truth, but it is colored by our glasses.

So when we talk about nature we mean our theories of science, and when we speak of the Bible we mean our theory of the Bible. There is a difference between Christianity and churchianity as there is between the Bible and theology.

But About the Bible Itself . . .

But about the Bible itself men have conflicting theories. Some find in it only a myth and legend of no more ethical and spiritual value than Homer's *Iliad*. Others think of the Bible as dictated by the Holy Spirit in a purely mechanical way without personal differences on the part of the individual writers in knowledge or style.

The Bible is more like a library than a single book with one author. The dates of the various books cover many centuries and the writings fall into two great groups—what is called the Old Testament and what is called the New Testament. The unifying fact and force in both Testaments is God, with His redemptive purpose in it all, as the author of Hebrews shows (Heb. 1:1–4). In the old times God spoke to the fathers in divers portions and divers manners. The record of God's dealings with men of that age appears in the Old Testament. In the new age God spoke to men in His Son. The writer of Hebrews is contributing his share to the interpretation of His Son. The New Testament conception of prophecy is that the Spirit of God moved upon men to speak, "for no prophecy ever came by the will of man; but man spoke from God, being moved by the Holy Spirit" (2 Pet. 1:21). In this sense God is the Author of the message which is thus a revelation of the will of God to men. The Word was spoken by the Lord through the prophet (Matt. 1:22).

The Real Authority . . .

The real authority in a message of this kind is that of God. If one is sure that he has a word from God upon any point, that settles it for him. At least it does for the normal man whose conscience is in good working order. The conscience is influenced by environment and impulse or emotion. The intellect is not an infallible organ of intelligence. It is necessary and should be used by everyone. Nothing is gained by obscurantism in the realm of nature or of grace. Ignorance is not the mother of devotion. We need and desire all the light that can be gotten by discovery in science and in criticism that will help us determine when we are in touch with the will of God in His world as in His Word. But we should note that the mind of man is fallible and not able always to interpret rightly the steps of God in the rocks or the voice of God in His Word or in the conscience. So I must think of the authority of the Bible as being the authority of God if so be it is from God, as I believe. There is no ultimate authority in the spiritual realm outside of God. We hear His voice in the Bible as nowhere else and can never get away from our need of it.

The Truth

Jesus claims to be the truth, marvellous as that statement appears. The Bible centers around the Messiah, the Son of God and the Son of man. The promise that the seed of the woman would bruise the serpent's head is carried on from heart to heart, from book to book, till Jesus of Nazareth comes as the Savior of men. Critics have many and conflicting theories about the books of the Bible, most of which mutually answer each other. Jesus Christ is the central fact of Christianity and of the Bible. I am in the habit of saying that Christianity was just as true before the books of the New Testament were written as afterward. They added nothing to the fundamental facts about Christ. He is Christianity. But the New Testament has preserved for us the first fresh and full apprehension of Christ as the Redeemer.

And Jesus claims complete authority in heaven and on earth and full knowledge of the Father and the power to reveal Him to whom He will (Luke 10:22; Matt. 28:18–20). The New Testament adds nothing to the authority of Christ. The disciples went everywhere proclaiming the wonder of Christ's life and love and message. The New Testament books are records of what Jesus began both to do and to teach as interpreted and proclaimed by men full of the Holy Spirit. The authority carried by the New

Testament is that of Jesus Christ as revealed by the Holy Spirit to men. Men must come to terms with Jesus Christ.

Modern Criticism

Modern criticism has tried to get back of John and Paul and the author of Hebrews and Peter and Jude to Christ. The synoptic Gospels have been pitted against Paul and the Fourth Gospel. And then criticism has sought, as it had the right to do, to find the sources that lay behind the synoptic Gospels. Luke pointedly says that he made use of both oral and written sources (Luke 1:1–4), that he searched and sifted them carefully, and that he used them to present an orderly and accurate narrative of events connected with Jesus Christ. Certainly no one can find fault with the spirit and temper of Luke's introduction. Did he live up to his claim? Some scholars have not been slow to attack Luke as incompetent and a consummate blunderer. But patient research on the part of Sir W. M. Ramsay and others has put to rout most of these criticisms, as I have shown in my *Luke the Historian in the Light of Research*.

It can now be said with confidence that every new discovery in the papyri and the inscriptions has confirmed Luke whenever he stood all alone. That of itself ought to induce patience for the rest. No discovery has shown Luke to be in error. Luke makes no claim to inspiration and he is defended by scholars just as any other historian of the past is treated on the basis of the known facts. But the absence of a claim of inspiration is certainly not a denial of inspiration.

Manifest Progress

There is a manifest progress in the interpretation of Christ by Paul and by other writers of the New Testament books. That is natural and inevitable. Whatever inspiration is, it does not destroy; rather it uses one's mental faculties and powers. I have myself no theory of inspiration as I have none of life, but heartily believe in both as of God. The greatest facts cannot be defined by our little systems. The essential problem about the Bible is not whether this detail of history has been established by research or whether this allusion in popular language to matter in nature is in harmony with modern scientific theory, which is constantly shifting its form of expression. That is quite beside the problem of the Bible. The authority relates to God's revelation of Himself to men and to man's relation to God. That is the scarlet thread that runs through the Book. It is the love of God in search of the soul of man. Prophet after prophet spoke for God with promise and with warning. The people slew all these one after another. But the love of God superabounded. He finally sent His Son as His living Word to men. Men likewise slew the Son, incredible as it seems. But the love of God goes on. The Son rose from the grave and ascended on high, and the Holy Spirit came in power to carry on the work of grace in the hearts of men. This gospel is the power of God unto salvation. It is that power today as in Paul's day. It has the authority of life.

The Full Import of the Bible's Message

It is foolish for men to pick at the Bible with its long record of God's mercy with men because it is not uniform and on a dead level. The prophets themselves did not always clearly perceive the full import of the message which they delivered (1 Pet. 1:10–12). They saw the promises from afar and greeted them in the dim distance (Heb. 11:13). God dealt patiently with a wayward and rebellious people. He gave them light as they were able to bear it and more than they could live up to. In the Old Testament there is a progress in the revelation of God and in the grasp of God's righteousness. Higher ethical standards came as men could follow them.

But Jesus is the way, the truth, and the life. He is the fulness of God in bodily form. Jesus calmly asserted His superiority to the Old Testament. Most assuredly, for that is partial and imperfect prophecy, like a lamp shining in a dark place until the day dawn and the day star arise in men's hearts (2 Pet. 1:19). But the Son of righteousness sets the lamps to one side. The prophets are properly studied in their order and in their place in relation to Jesus Christ.

Scientific Historical Method

The Bible must be studied by the scientific historical method, but also with an enlightened soul in touch with the Spirit of God. It must not be made a catspaw to prove one's individual theological crotchets. But Christ throws light on the Bible backwards and forwards. Jesus opened the Old Testament on the way to Emmaus and he rebuked the two disciples for not understanding the opened Scriptures (Luke 24:25–27). And then later Jesus opened the minds of the disciples that they might understand the Scriptures (Luke 24:45). It is true now as it was then that men cover up the Bible with their theories and their prejudices so that they cannot see it or understand it. The ignorant do it and the learned do it. I sometimes say that one proof of the divine origin of the Bible is that it has stood so much preaching and, I may add, so much criticism. One has sometimes a good deal of sympathy with the old woman who said that she liked commentaries because the Bible threw so much light on them. A man does not understand the Bible simply because he is a scholar. He ought to do it better for that reason, but he can let his own theories befog his eyes so that he cannot see Jesus Christ Himself.

Jesus Found Himself in the Old Testament

Jesus is the goal of the hopes of the race. We need to distinguish between ecclesiasticism and Christianity. Few of the critics of ecclesiasticism venture to criticize Jesus. The rather, they hold him up as the Perfect Man and the aim of all that is highest and best. But these men face a quandary when they hold up the ethical ideal of Jesus as the highest expression of the race and overlook the claims of Jesus about Himself.

We can make a wrong use of the Bible and then complain that it does not stand the test. We can go to it blindly and open at any verse and expect to find as much edification in one verse as in another. That is folly on the face of it. The Bible is a Book of life and not of maxims. Many things are mentioned in the Bible only to be condemned. There are sayings of the devil in the Bible.

One needs to use his sense to interpret properly the Bible. Some men want everything fixed up in pellet form so that they can swallow it without thinking.

The Bible Has Stood the Test of Time

It has been and is the foundation of all that is good in modern civilization. The trouble with the world is not that Christianity has failed or that the Bible is antiquated. The trouble is the world has not given Christianity a real trial. Men push the gospel out of their business and political life and then remark on the failure of the Bible which they do not read. If these people read the Bible and tried to live it, they would love it.

The very men like Huxley and Wells, who scout the Bible as antiquated and a book of fables, tremble for the future of mankind without it or something as good. Mr. Wells has had the audacity to offer to produce something better. It is to be hoped that he will try his hand at it. Men have preached the funeral of the Bible often before, but it goes on and lives on. The reason is that it tells the story of God's love for man. Then we see God reaching out after sinful men who have wandered away from His love. And the way back to God is in Christ. Those who neglect the Bible neglect God.

The Way to the Father

Millions upon millions of men and women today are treading that way to the Father. They have found Christ to be the way to the Father. They have trusted Him as Savior from sin. They find peace in Him. They find the words of Christ food for their souls and Christ Himself the Bread of life.

Many of those who ridicule the Bible do not read it. The proof of the pudding is in the eating. Those who read the Bible daily are those who find it full of the breath of God ("inspired of God"), and useful for teaching, for reproof, for restoration, for discipline in righteousness, that the man of God may be perfect, fully prepared for every good work (2 Tim. 3:17).

Living up to the Bible's Standard

The way to prove the authority of the Bible is to live up to its standard. Christ is the way of life in the Bible. All must be judged in reference to Him. And Jesus keeps before us the goal of perfection which we never quite reach, but which is far beyond that presented by any other teacher of earth. Service is the test of life for us all. We may be able to quote maxims of wisdom and proof texts of orthodoxy and be useless in the midst of sin and of sorrow. The Bible is not a book of magic. It is not an amulet or charm. It points the way to God, the path of righteousness, the cross of Christ, forgiveness of sins, new life in Christ, new help in the new life, help to the end, and love without measure. It is beside the mark when men spend their time in hunting for fly specks and cannot see the cross of Christ, the Lamb of God that takes away the sins of the world. God, sin, and salvation through Christ—these are the burden of the Bible.

The Lamp

The Word of God has been the lamp to the feet of the saints through the ages. It is the same light today. Men live by it and die by it. It is still the Book, as Sir Walter Scott said as he was dying. He asked for the Book. It will never be set aside, for in it we see God in Christ. In it we see our own sinfulness. In it we see the righteousness of God. In it we see the Father's purpose to make His children like Christ in the end. The Bible is the mirror of God's long suffering with sinners. The Bible gives us heart and hope to struggle on to make earth like heaven and to make our hearts and our homes a habitation for Christ. It is spiritual and moral suicide for men to put out the light that has led them thus far through the darkness. Every Scripture is still inspired of God and carries the authority of God for His purpose with men. Dr. R. F. Horton says that Protestants have lost the Bible and so have lost their religion. That is too pessimistic. Some Protestants have lost their Bible and their religion. The great masses of preachers and people are loyal to the Bible and to the Christ of the Bible. It must be admitted that some schools of learning destroy the faith of their students in Christ and the Bible and leave the divinity students without God and without hope in the world, pagans once more. But that thing has happened before. Those who love Christ will not give Him up and His Word will abide with men.

CHAPTER TEN

Preaching and Scholarship, the *Inaugural Address to the Faculty,* The Southern Baptist Theological Seminary, October 3, 1890

The relation that scholarship bears to preaching is, I fear, not always understood. For real attainments in scholarship, so far from being a help to preaching, are sometimes supposed to be a positive hindrance. And if a man happens to like books, it is by some people doubted whether he will ever be a successful preacher, or strongly suspected that he will become a bookworm and lose all sympathy with the people and hence all warmth and power in his preaching. Reading Greek and preaching are often supposed to be uncongenial companions. A presbytery was once examining a young minister for ordination and he was asked what he would do if he did not succeed as a preacher. He at once replied that he would try to get a place as theological professor.

He evidently thought that played-out preachers were good enough to teach others how to preach.

Is Learning Good for a Preacher?

There exists a half-suppressed feeling among many good people that much learning is not good for a preacher. And this feeling is not always suppressed, but finds expression in various insinuations aimed at educated ministers and the schools they attended. Some people, having heard that "a little learning is a dangerous thing," conclude that much learning is much more so. Hence they would limit the "much" to a very small amount, and so do many preachers. A tender fear is entertained that the young minister will become heretical if he knows too much. And so he may, if he studies along heretical lines. But all learning is not sceptical. There is still such a thing as reverent scholarship. Surely infidelity and rationalism have not absorbed all knowledge. You may even hear that a theological seminary is a very nest of heresy, and that, too, where Calvinism of the straitest sort is taught. But such an objection to theological education may arise from ignorance of the real workings of the institution.

It is even sometimes predicted that the preachers will become too learned—too "high larn't"—if they go to school much, a fear, I am persuaded, based on limited acquaintance with theological students. There is small ground of uneasiness here. Your much learning, my brother, has not made you mad, nor anyone else. Such cases do occur where a man becomes top heavy with supposed knowledge, but they are very rare, and it is usually when one is not deep rooted in the faith or is lacking in spiritual power. True knowledge comes so hard that it will serve to keep you humble and all you can digest will not hurt you, provided, of course, that you do not run after knowledge falsely so-called, but seek the real knowledge of God's truth. The schools get overmuch credit. Not every preacher that is spoiled, you may be sure, is spoiled by an excess of learning. Do not believe it. If an education gives a man the swell head, he must have a very soft head. It is amazing how little it takes to turn some people's heads.

Will Theological Education Make a "Dry" Preacher?

You sometimes hear it said that a theological education will make the minister "dry." Perhaps it is thought that much learning will make him dull, if not mad. There are many men who never went to school that can be as dry as the most learned. An education will not make a fountain in a desert, and if it does, it will be an artificial one. It will only run when forced. There is certainly nothing in a theological seminary to stop a fountain, if the professors have any religion. A prominent man once admonished a student who was going to a theological seminary as follows: "Don't lose your juice," he said, "when you go to the seminary." He seemed to think a seminary was a drying machine to fry all the life out of a man and leave him all starch and powder. If by "juice" is meant the unction and fervor of a soul set on fire by the Spirit of God, it is hard to see why biblical study should have such an effect. Why can not the Holy Spirit work through a man that has learning as well as through one that has none? Does God put a premium on ignorance in the ministry? We know that He has no use for the pride of learning, but neither does He care for the arrogance of ignorance. Certainly, ignorance and laziness are no recommendations for a preacher. Does a man gain power by boasting that he has no "book learning"? If the Spirit that stirs the soul be in a man, his preaching will not be dry nor barren of results, even if he has tried to learn books. Perhaps what is meant is that the educated preacher often becomes too abstruse and shoots over the heads of the congregation. He is so far above their level, that it is all Greek to them. Now, no one has a right to use strange tongues in the pulpit. It sometimes happens that highflown language comes from the pulpit, but as often from the uneducated as from the educated preacher. And the best educated ministers with the best taste use the simplest language. But many people hold study and simplicity incompatible. A certain church heard that a theological professor and a D.D. was to supply for them for a while. And they had long faces at such a combination coming to preach for them until they were told that though a professor, he could preach. This shows the existence of the feeling mentioned.

The Stereotyped Preacher?

It is gravely feared by some that young ministers will become stereotyped in style, if they go to a theological school. A cut-and-dried preacher made to order out of a "preacher factory" is abhorred and ought to be. But this is hardly a real objection to scholarly ministers. For if a man has so little force of character as to lose his individuality at school, he would anywhere. If a man lapses into mental desuetude and takes everything at second-hand, the school is not to blame. For theological training will not grind him out sermons according to demand without native wit and hard work. Do not expect any amount of training to take the place of brains, work, and the grace of God. In fact, a glib sermon does little good anyhow. It must take root in the heart and life of the preacher, if it is to reach the hearts of other people. If a numbskull comes to the seminary and goes away a numbskull, do not blame the seminary. For some men are hard to teach. Gideon taught the men of Succoth with thorns and briers; for it was the only kind of instruction that would penetrate their obscure consciences. But thorns and briers cannot make preachers or scholars out of some men. A seminary can only work with the material that the churches send, good, bad and indifferent. I noticed a criticism upon our seminary this fall in one of the denominational papers to the effect that some of its students had a very poor delivery. If a man will pass through the course in elocution here with a very poor delivery, is it not his fault? Elocution cannot make good speakers out of men with no gifts of speech, nor out of those with gifts if they do not apply themselves. Again, it is insisted that to spend two or three years at a seminary is a waste of time. You can do well enough without seminary training, it is urged. Is anything well enough save the best of which you are capable? Some good brethren shook their heads when you started to school, and lamented this waste of time from preaching. A good woman once remonstrated with a young preacher that he could preach well enough without going to the seminary three years. But when he insisted that he must go, she said, "Lor', if you can preach this well now, I just would like to hear you then." She, at any rate, had faith in the power of a seminary course to improve a preacher. Many young men listen to this silly flattery and fail to take a theological course or complete their college work. They even think their friends about half right and that perhaps they are smarter than they at first supposed.

The Amount of Preparation . . .

It all depends on what you want to do. Bottom, in *Midsummer Night's Dream*, said that extempore speaking was nothing but roaring, and hence he could do that to perfection. Now, if you simply want to roar all your life, you can do that without much sense or religion either. It is right for a man to look high and deep into the mission of his life. And the amount of preparation that is necessary for your life work is not to be decided by the urgency of the work alone. For Christ waited until He was thirty years old before He began His mediatorial work. The demand for ministers is always greater than the supply, and always will be, no doubt. The harvest is always great and white for reaping and the laborers few. There is great need for all who will put in the sickle, but greater need than ever for men that are well-equipped and approved of God. No man in these days should cut his preparation shorter than the line of duty indicates.

For the two or three years subtracted from school life may not make up for the loss in power. And power is what is wanted in men today. The apparent loss in time will be more than atoned for by increased momentum and facility for work. The sum of a life work is equal to time plus momentum. It is time and power. I saw this summer in Antwerp women and dogs pulling the carts over the streets. I felt that I had gone back 500 years past the age of steam and electricity. The age compels you to live at high tension. You must learn how to do this with the best results and the least harm to yourselves. If a theological education will increase your power for Christ, is it not your duty to gain that added power? If a high dam will give more power to the mill, then do not begrudge the time that it takes to build it. Never say you are losing time by going to school. You are saving time, buying it up for the future and storing it away. Time used in storing power is not lost. Reverently seek to know, not in conceit, what you can do for God. If you have a high opinion of His service, your own insufficiency will lead you to larger and wiser preparation. So theological education saves time in enabling the pastor to come to his work with improved methods and appliances. A man must work both rapidly and well, if he is to come up to the demands made upon him now. It is a great thing to be able to do well in two hours what used to take you three.

Current Objections to Theological Education

Now, these are some of the current objections to theological education. Many young ministers feel this outside pressure, and consider themselves justified in their inclination to make a dash here and a splash there and go gloriously ahead. They may regret all their lives that they did not stay longer at school. But if it were only some stray brethren here and there that shy at young upstarts from the schools and shake their heads dubiously at some "high larn't" preachers of doubtful behavior, it would not be worth while to waste words about the value of an educated ministry. The matter, however, is of a more serious nature than this. With us in the South, theological education is comparatively new, and has had to remain new to great masses of our people on account of the trying circumstances through which we have passed in the last third of a century. But the denomination is more and more seeing the need of such instruction as is offered here, and there is an increasing desire among our young ministers to avail themselves of the opportunities of the seminary. It is chiefly to accelerate this desire that I now speak. For there are still many that fail to see the importance of theological study. They are not to be blamed too much, for one rarely rises above the standards around him. In such cases, few of one's friends may have gone to the seminary, and those that did may not have been very good specimens of the educated preacher. And these specimens with some arrogance and much palpable ignorance still, in spite of a few months in a seminary, have not helped to remove the prejudice against learning that lingers as an heirloom of other days. And so it has come to pass that young men have often had to go to college and seminary against the prejudice and advice of their best friends. For there has always been opposition to educated ministers, based partly on inherited prejudices and partly on the indiscretions of a few men of bad taste and small learning.

I said that prejudice against theological education was a relic of other days. Do not understand me to say that all the old Baptist preachers in our part of the world were unlettered men, nor that most of them were. At least they did not remain so always. Many of them were college men and earnest advocates of education. And others still that were far from any school, save the "old field school" that ran a few months only, made struggles to obtain a little education that ought to bring the blush of shame to every young man that is too unambitious to go to school or too lazy to work after he goes. There were men like Lewis Lunsford of Virginia, that plowed all day and studied by the light of the pine knot at night, and then would preach on Sunday sermons that you and I can never equal. But it is so easy now to go to school, with our boards to help and our numerous and excellent schools, that we may not all appreciate the value of such opportunities. A man is beneath contempt who trifles with such advantages today. I have no respect for a man who receives more help from an educational board than he actually needs or thinks a seminary should pay him for coming to school. For those who yearn for the chances you have I feel the deepest sympathy. Nothing stirs me more than to see a noble young man striving against great obstacles to obtain an education with which to glorify God and to serve mankind. And so this subject in a measure makes me sad. I think of the thousands of young ministers scattered over the South and West trying to fit themselves to preach the gospel. And many of them get no guidance from pastor or friends. They never go to school, but do the best they can. God bless them and help them. Much of the work of our denomination has been done by men like them. They deserve high praise for what they have acheived. They would go to school if someone showed sufficient interest in them to suggest how they might get an education. The yearning faces of these struggling men make a strong appeal to all friends of Christian education. I remember the life and death of James P. Boyce, how he toiled and died that these very men might have a place to find theological instruction. What is the matter? One thing is, they need their attention called to the subject, for they do not comprehend what such training will do for them. And then they are very poor and need wise financial help. Some are flattered into going to work at once because of their remarkable power. Others still get married and cannot come. One young minister went to college one year and tried to marry a widow's daughter. Failing in this ambition, he married the widow herself and quit school. When our young preachers really want theological training and the churches are willing for them to get it, our seminary will have 500 students.

Antipathy Between Scholarship and Preaching

Some of the popular objections against theological education have been alluded to in order to show that it was not a mere man of straw that I was fighting. And since so many complaints of like nature are made, it is not simply commonplace to insist that there is no real antipathy between scholarship and preaching. It is entirely possible for a man to be a respectable scholar and still be able to preach. When scholarship is spoken of, a critical scholar is not meant, but simply that degree of learning that comes as the result of a college and seminary course with diligent study afterwards. The question is simply this: Is the average man with these qualifications, other things being equal, better prepared to preach than without them? In other words, does the college and seminary training tend to make better preachers? If not, it is a failure. The German idea is to make scholars first and preachers incidentally. But ours is to make preachers, and scholars only as a means to that end. We have small need in the pulpit for men that can talk learnedly and obscurely about the tendencies of thought and the trend of philosophy, but do not know how to preach Christ and Him crucified. The most essential thing today is not to know what German scholars think of the Bible, but to be able to tell men what the Bible says about themselves. And if our system of theological training fails to make preachers, it falls short of the object for which it was established. But if it does meet the object of its creation, it calls for hearty sympathy and support.

Now, all scholars cannot preach. No such claim is made. Not every man with a taste for books has the popular gifts necessary to make him a public speaker. Certainly, there is ample room for American Christian scholars that cannot preach. They are not slaves of the past as is Rome, nor despisers of the past as is Germany; but with due reverence for the past and yet with sufficient independence for accurate work, American scholars occupy a unique position for the best and soundest results. And we need such men to preserve the equilibrium of scholarship. For all scholars are not Christian, but godless men invade the domain of Christian doctrine and presume to pass judgment on the oracles of God.

But my plea is for a scholarship that helps men to preach. For after all, the great need of the world is the preaching of the gospel, not saying off a sermon, but preaching that stirs sinful hearts to repentance and godliness. Our complex civilization has made more difficult and more necessary the task of the preacher. For a highly-refined culture that breeds itching ears has turned many away from the old message to tickle those diseased ears with softer sounds. They worship the golden calf as Jehovah, and proclaim a feast unto the Lord. Give us men in the pulpit today above all things that fear God and think the gospel good enough for anybody and make no apology for preaching it. The preacher must be bold, but not with a zeal above knowledge. In a time of countless heresies that have sprung from distortions of the Bible, there is need of keen intellects and honest hearts rightly to divide the word of truth. It takes a sharp blade to cut asunder God's work with no injury to either part.

Learning Will Not Make a Preacher

But while there is great need of the best and soundest scholarship irrespective of preaching, it is certainly true that learning will not make a preacher. It is equally true that knowledge does not necessarily prevent one from being a good minister of Jesus Christ, but helps him to preach. In *The Mill on the Floss* the rector had been preaching historical and argumentative sermons of an abstruse nature, and the Independent minister political sermons, and neither had any power to "shake the souls of men" at St. Oggs. Nothing save the gospel of Christ can do that, and this they were not preaching. For it is not superfluity of learning, but lack of religion that leads men into such ways as these. They did not preach Christ, but shook in the faces of the people the skeleton of a defunct theology, or held up for their worship a new Christ of the kingdom of the world and men knew Him not, for He had not the marks nor the power of the old Christ. It was scholasticism on the one hand, and politics on the other, neither of which will ever regenerate the world. Do not take up the dry bones of scholasticism and shake them in the faces of the friends of theological education today. If the Spirit does not breathe upon the bones they are dead and will rattle in the pulpit where the power of the living Christ should be. And no amount of learning will make a preacher unless he is filled with an unction from on high. He may quote poetry and Latin and cite authorities by the score, but his preaching will never result in the conversion of a soul.

Moreover, all preachers cannot become scholars. Some men who can preach grandly and powerfully have no great gifts with books. They cannot become learned, yet they have so learned Christ and have such deep spiritual knowledge that they can preach gloriously. God is not bound by ironclad rules in using men. He is not dependent on the exigencies of human attainments for the proclamation of His Word, although he freely uses all such acquirements for the promotion of his glory. He does not put men into a mill and turn them all out with the same brand. Ministers are not all cut according to the same pattern.

And the glory of the Baptist ministry is its diversity and versatility. Composed of all classes of men with varied talents and accomplishments, it can easily become all things to all men. But our educational system has no such formal tendency as is sometimes supposed. For it takes men just as it finds them, with little or much preparation for theological instruction, and seeks to make the most out of each one. His own individuality is intensified and he should become a man of personal force. As there is diversity of gifts, there should be diversity in preparation. No one has a right to say that you must go to school so many years before you will be allowed to preach the gospel. You cannot conceive of the apostle Paul's saying that a man must go to Jerusalem to school before he could become a preacher or missionary. Such a principle is not Baptistic, not Apostolic. Let there be liberty, and let duty and not compulsion regulate the amount of preparation for the ministry in each case. It is not a question of short cut or long cut by the wholesale. Each man must make it a personal matter and settle it in the light of his duty to God and men. And if every man takes what he is or can be prepared for, he will not go far wrong.

The Clergyman of Older Times

The clergyman used to have almost a monopoly of learning in the old times when he was the clerk or school teacher of the nobility. But nobles and peasants are able to write their own names now. And the clergyman is no longer the embodiment of the knowledge of the day. In truth, he has a hard time to keep up with much of the new learning. Shall the seminary fall behind or keep to the front in intellectual force and attainments? If you are to have any power as a minister, people must have confidence in your character. And your acquirements must comport with your professions. You cannot hookwink people by gyrations and beatings of the air. If you say nothing all the time, they will know it and will let you know it. An editor, complimenting the preacher, said, "Your sermon did not seem long, for after you had spoken an hour it didn't seem that you had said anything." The only way to avoid saying nothing is to draw deep from the fountain of spiritual knowledge. And people do not want a simpleton to preach to them. You must have common sense whether you ever heard of a college or not. And some preachers that never saw a seminary have more sense than you or I can ever have. They were born with one talent, but they used that, instead of wrapping it up in a napkin. If you are too dainty to touch sinners with your delicate fingers, you had better quit preaching.

A Busy Pastor

Now, a busy pastor cannot become a specialist. He has to leave that for other men, if he is to prosecute the work laid upon him. He can do scholarly work on his sermon, but cannot branch off much. For he is a man of affairs and must know the hearts of men. And few have the time and fewer still the taste for minute scholarship. This is not contended for. Let a man acquire scholarly methods and apply them to his work. And that work will be less slipshod in style and more effective in results.

So all preachers cannot be scholars. But do not be afraid that you will learn too much. For your seminary course will not make you a scholar. You will be a long way still from any such goal. There will seem to be more for you to learn when you leave than when you came. You will know less about Cain's wife than you do now. But you will have more rapid and effective methods of sermonizing, clearer ideas of biblical study, and juster conceptions of Scriptural exegesis and doctrine and the relation of Christianity to the history and wants of men. And these are the main things that you need to get from a theological education.

A True Education Is Never Finished

But woe unto you, if you are so wild as to think that these results will come ready-made and drop at your touch. There is a long road of toil and sweat if you wish to accomplish much. A true education is never finished, and a finished education is of little use. John Richard Green said, "I die learning." For an education is more the ability to grapple with the present than mere knowledge of the past. The dry preachers are those that learned it all long ago and have relied on that little ever since. There is plenty of fresh truth in the Bible to water your soul, if you will find it. And the oldest will be the freshest, if you get below the surface of superficial meaning that your ears may have become used to. For there will be life and power in the words then. Gladstone says, "I have been a learner all my life, and am a learner still." Whether you keep up your Greek and Hebrew or not, as you ought if possible, you must be continually extending your sphere of knowledge in one or more directions, and so gaining new power. He alone has fresh power who does fresh work. A man can have a scholarly method of work and not be scholastic. What is wanted is the mill to grind the corn, whether it be by steam or water or hand. The corn must be ground. God's truth must be kneaded well in the mind and heart of the preacher, if it is to be adapted to the wants of his audience. He must not make the truth bleed by rough handling, and so destroy the right proportion that one truth sustains to another. This is the function of scholarship in preaching. It is mechanical, perhaps, and yet in this age of mechanism we see the importance of having the right kind of machinery. But there is no virtue in a dead machine. It needs the fire to give motion and power. The wire is of no service, save when charged with electricity. It is the electricity that is wanted. Away with a scholarship in the preacher that refused to be the vehicle for the Spirit and Word of God, but is laden rather with the crotchets of men. This is over education, or too much of the wrong sort. A few men go to school too long. You can rub all the edge off of some blades, but they are thin blades. If you are a thin blade, do not whet all your edge away.

For the Glory of God

This then is true: not all scholars can preach, and not all preachers can become scholars. There are varying degrees of both, but the best preachers have generally been men of the best training in the schools. This is all that can be said and it is enough. For each man wants to do the most that is in him for the glory of God. The leading examples of preaching will confirm this statement. Paul was an educated man, and so was John Chrysostom, the

Golden Mouthed preacher of later days. Luther was a theological professor. Calvin preached every day for a long time while professor of theology at Geneva. John Knox learned Greek and Hebrew between the ages of 40 and 50. Whitefield and Wesley, the great popular preachers, were Oxford men. The famous French preachers, Bossuet, Bourdaloue, and Massillon, were likewise scholarly men. And the exceptions usually prove the rule, for even Spurgeon has made a respectable scholar of himself in spite of the lack of early training. Incidental cases here and there do not alter the general fact that the best and foremost preachers of Christendom have been not simply men of the largest gifts of mind and heart, but likewise of the most thorough training their times could give for their work. Given the grace of God in a man's heart and natural parts, and he will be a better preacher if he pursues the study of God's Word with a sound and reverent scholarship. And so the whole question of theological education amounts to this: is a man better fitted to preach, other things being equal, with a working amount of scholarship or without it? For it is not such an education as is necessary for a professor that the preacher needs, but such as can be brought to bear upon the exposition of Scripture. This is the question that every young minister has to face. It is not whether you can preach well enough now to satisfy Deacon Jones or Sister Brown, but whether your usefulness for life would be enhanced by a college and seminary course. If this be true, it becomes a matter of duty, and a conscientious man will be slow to cut short his usefulness by a short cut or any other contrivance that will give him the shadow instead of the substance of an education. But each man will seek to adjust his preparation to his capabilities and circumstances. With the question thus stated, one needs to be slow in refusing to get hold of this apparatus for Biblical study that comes from a course of theological training.

The Preparation and Delivery of a Sermon

But some people have queer notions about preaching. They seem to think that the operation of natural laws does not apply to the preparation and delivery of a sermon. It is as if a prophectic inspiration swept down upon the preacher and suspended the working of his faculties. Now, the minister should seek and expect divine help both in the preparation and delivery of a sermon; but it is not reverence to look for the divine blessing upon wild impromptu ravings more than upon the sober reflections of a thoughtful mind drawn from the Word of God and the promptings of a heart full of the deepest Christian experience. And if such people half believe the preacher inspired in the manner of his message, they certainly do not act as if they believed the inspiration binding on their lives. But the highest excellence is where reverent learning is united with great pulpit ability and deep piety. For full preparation is apt to make a man careful about fanciful interpretations of Scripture. He will not so readily make a hop, skip, and jump to remarkable conclusions. And real knowledge should keep the preacher from the pride of unconsecrated scholarship and the presumption of ignorance. The true minister of the Word will seek not to dazzle, but to enlighten. And the Bible will become clearer to him by deep study and earnest seeking of the Holy Spirit. His learning will result in not mere poring over books all the time to get ideas. He will get them there but also from the men he meets and everything he sees. The world will be an open book to him.

But simple going to school will not make a man of you. Hanging around a college or seminary few or many years will not make you a scholar nor a preacher. And the inertia of ignorance that clings to you there will cling to you still. I make no apology for such greenhorns as imagine that mere attendance on a theological seminary will give them a patent right to success by some sudden process that involves little effort on their part. What prestige without power you might acquire will melt away so rapidly in the heat of earnest work that you will wonder where your little learning has gone to—you will be left so far behind in real work in the cause of Christ. Such men are not spoiled by an education. They did not get enough to leave a trace. They spoiled before they got any. You will never become a preacher worth listening to without travail of soul. There has to be some severe thinking and suffering before you will command the ears and hearts of men. Mere dabbling in books will not make you a deeper man. But if you get a studious habit upon you, it will help you to go to the bottom of things.

No, do not hinder any honest preacher from becoming a scholarly man, if he can. It will not hurt him, but will help him if he is a man. And if he is not a man, it will not make much difference whether he knows much or little. For if he will be puffed up because he has the good fortune to go to school, perhaps he would be made vain by looking in the glass, and with as little ground for it, or have his head turned by the prattle of flatterers. If a preacher has religion, learning ought not to and will not chill his ardor, when tempered by the grace of God. Unspiritual scholars can never become preachers. God deliver us from a set of schoolmen who simply squabble over how many angels can stand on the point of a needle, and neglect the weightier matters of the gospel. May the chilling pall of godless learning never fall upon our schools! God forbid that our American schools should ever become places where pupil and teacher merely rummage among the cobwebs of the past just to find the spiders.

The educated preacher needs to be a man. You cannot put clothes on a dead man and breathe life into him by education. It is necessary to have a live man to start with, a man with grit and purpose. Tom Tulliver's idea of a man was to be able to play at heads and tails as much as he wished. Some men never get over this childish foible, and play at heads and tails all their lives. Life is a chance and not a purpose with them. A dillydallying man has no business in the ministry. He would better play mumblepeg. Polish must not come at the expense of power. And why should it? The shining blade can be very sharp and strong. Let a man retain his manhood and vitality along with his scholarship. For pale-faced jaded scholars stand a poor show beside vigorous manly men with plenty of religion but less learning. Christian education should not emasculate the ministry, but develop a sturdier type of man with a larger and firmer mental grasp. The phrase, "gentleman of the cloth," is not a good expression. It is always repulsive to my conception of a minister of Jesus Christ. A preacher is not a gentleman of cloth and ease, but a man of work and sturdy manliness and rugged virtue, anything but smooth and sleek. He should be more like John the Baptist with his raiment of camel's hair and his homely message of repentance than like the Pharisee with his soft raiment and softer speeches for the people. If a man is not willing to work he has small business preaching the gospel, whether he ever goes to school or not. Most people believe that it is a good thing to get a little education, a first dash to get a start in life. But to make an honest effort to know things is not so popular. It is for this that a plea is made, that our young ministers may become strong in character and attainments. And this is not simply a matter of natural talent, but largely of slow and labored toil. It takes patience to get an education and to make a preacher.

Fresh Preaching

The churches clamor for fresh preaching and often will not let the preachers stay at school long enough to learn how to study and to think—two very important items in the preparation of a sermon. What can a preacher do, if he has not learned how to think? When his stock of ideas is exhausted, he will have to seek pastures new; for the churches are unreasonably intolerant as to the repetition of old ideas. You might get someone else to do your thinking for you, but that is a rather humiliating business, unless it be your wife. Some people pay for their thinking as they do for their clothes, only not so much, for it takes less to do them. But the unhappy preacher must work his brain or change his pastorate. Yet you will not let him get his thinking machinery into good working order. Young preachers' brains are in no better condition than other people's and need a deal of rubbing to get them into good trim. Ask these theological teachers of many years' experience. They could tell you volumes that they have or have not found within young preachers' heads.

Hence a minister, if he is to last, must be fertile in resources. A few sermons at first will represent the top soil. The deep subsoil of his nature must be stirred, if his mind is to be fruitful. Greek and Hebrew roots may be tough and may jar a little in the breaking. But break them. It will pay. You will get deeper down when they are cleared out of the way, and the harvest will be larger and richer. A man should never be satisfied to give the sum of his thoughts that float on the surface. Stir up the depths. Let God's truth sink and settle in the depths of your soul. Dislike to theological study is often the expression of laziness. The plea that is made for scholarship among ministers is for men of sturdy mentality, trained to think, whose minds shall drink at the fountains of knowledge. And the Bible is the best fountain.

Go to school, if you can and as long as you ought. If you cannot go a long time, go a short time. It is better to preach with one year at school than with none. And it is better, a thousand times better, to preach with no education at all than that the glorious gospel of Christ should not be given to the world. If our colleges and seminaries so make a hedge around the ministry that the gospel cannot be given to the perishing thousands, they will have lost their mission among men. Let the gospel be preached though seminaries fall. Let men be fitted to preach in the way best suited to the times and in accordance with the spirit of Christianity. This way seems to lie in the existing institutions of the denomination. In these institutions is supplied ample training for our ministers if they will avail themselves of all that is within their power.

And the best training is furnished for the existing ministry, because there is allowed the largest liberty, regulated by counsel when needed, so as to meet the wants of all. If you cannot take the best, take the best you can. For thus the demands of Christian work among us as a denomination will be best met. Let each one do his duty in this matter in the fear of God. I am persuaded that a larger number than ever before are seeing the importance of the widest preparation for the great and exalted work of the gospel ministry. This hope will meet fulfilment in the freest discussion of this great subject. For the proper education of the rising ministry is a matter that lies close to the hearts of our wisest men, and is worthy of the most serious consideration. Let all that is said and done for the solution of the grave problems that affect theological education be with a breadth of mind and earnestness of purpose commensurate with the dignity of the subject. Let us all seek to gain just views as to the training of the men who are to be the preachers of the future. And let us all sustain all wise plans for the promotion of Biblical knowledge among the men who are to interpret the Scriptures to the churches, and pray that they may do it with the demonstration and power of the Spirit. But let the gospel be preached, whatever we do or think; else the very stones will cry out and give glory to God, if we refuse to give Him praise for His wonderful redemption.

In the course of time prejudice against ministers that have had scholastic advantages will die away. It lies largely with those that share such advantages as to how soon this will be the case. If you conduct yourself discreetly and preach with greater power, men will bless God for such an institution that sent you forth. You may have heard the story of John Kerr, a wonderful preacher of a generation ago. When he came from school he was put up to preach. An old farmer at the outskirts of the congregation, with deep-rooted prejudice against "high larn't" preachers, said, "That school boy can't preach." He pulled his hat over his eyes and determined not to listen. But by and by he got a little interested and looked up. He soon leaned forward. After a while he stood up. At last he took off his hat and shouted, "Bless God, he can preach." The educated preacher had overcome the prejudice of the farmer by doing the one thing, which is the end of all theological education. He could preach. And his preaching was all the clearer and more convincing because of the training he had gotten in the schools. But whether such prejudice ever wholly dies away or not, it becomes the duty of every young minister to prove himself superior to it, and to lay hold of every opportunity the college and seminary afford to increase his power and efficiency as a minister of Jesus Christ.

CHAPTER ELEVEN

The Inerrancy of the Scriptures, *Western Recorder,* June 30, 1892

It would be very difficult to find a loophole in the attitude of the Scriptural writers toward one another and themselves for the original errancy of their writings. They certainly seem to think that they speak by the authority of God, and that what they say is true and to be received as true.

There is a vast difference between the authority of a revelation originally inerrant on everything on which it speaks, but which has suffered a little from the ravages of time, and one which originally contained various errors scattered through it, but which was in the main correct.

In the first case, the divine authority remains intact and affects the whole of the revelation. In the second case, the divine authority only affects the part that is true, with the added uncertainty running through it all. If the Bible was originally truth mixed up with error, all the talk about the "essence" of Christianity being preserved in it will not avail with the average man.

Who can ever tell what came from God and what did not? Scholarship can be relied on to give us the correct text out of the critical apparatus in its hands. If some difficulties still remain, and always remain, no scientific biblical student is impatient by this for such a condition of affairs exists in every branch of knowledge. He who can explain everything cannot really explain anything. But no scholarship can be relied on to go through an inaccurate Bible filled with error and root out the divine for us. No sort of higher criticism has any such second sight or divine instinct as this. It is presumption to assume it, and no amount of Pentateuchal analysis which rests chiefly on the individual whim of the analyst will appeal to the sober thought of the world.

It is no new thing for discrepancies to be pointed out in the Scriptures. Nothing new has been brought forward. It would have been a miracle if slips in transcription and mistakes in translation had not occurred through all the thousands of years that various portions of the Bible have been in existence. But when one considers the length of time it has existed, and the many hands through which it has passed, the preservation of the Bible has been wonderful. As compared with other ancient books, its text is in a far better condition. And what slips have crept in are chiefly patent ones that give no trouble. And, no doubt, the others would disappear if we had greater facilities for their correction.

The only new thing about this subject is to hear the original errancy of the Scriptures insisted on by evangelical Christians. Not that there have not been in various ages such men, who were ready to admit this in a few unimportant cases which did not affect the integrity of the Scriptures, as they claimed. But outside of Germany, until our generation, the Christian world has hardly witnessed such a crusade against the original accuracy of the Scriptures as is now going on. It may be worth while to say several things in this connection.

1. *The argument about the original Scriptures* is obliged to be largely a presumptive one, since we have not and never can have, the original manuscripts. But it is not to be laughed out of court for this reason. It is asserted that it is useless to talk about the

original manuscripts, since God has not thought it worth while to preserve them. Is this a fair argument? Did God make man originally sinless or sinful? If He made him sinless, he has not remained so. Did God make the first horse perfect or imperfect? It is not a question as to whether there are any diseased horses since. When creation had the first stamp of God's hand, He said that it was good. The analogy of nature is on the side of the original inerrancy of the Scriptures. Revelation is progressive, slowly unfolding God's will, but this is far from saying that God revealed what was erroneous. It is like God to make His revelation correct, however slow it may be in coming.

2. *But the argument is not all presumptive.* It would be granted at once that the writers mean to be accurate. They certainly mean to tell the truth. And some of them claim to be accurate. Luke 1:3 claims to narrate "accurately" all things, and John 21:24 says his witness is true, and in his first Epistle (1:3) speaks as an eye witness. The prophets and apostles in numerous places claim to have the Spirit of God and to speak with the authority of God.

3. *It might naturally occur to one as a strange thing* that Christian scholars should make such a stir about the original inerrancy of the Scriptures if it can never be settled by the original manuscripts anyhow. If they can never be found, why insist so strongly that they contained errors? To claim that it is more scholarly to admit this, settles nothing, because real scholarship takes into account all the evidence, which is by no means all in favor of such a verdict. Much is said about one's retaining his "mental integrity" by admitting it. Now, if a man is honestly convinced that there were errors in the original Scriptures, of course it would violate his mental integrity to deny it. But suppose he is convinced the other way, where is any sacrifice of mental integrity? Or suppose he is undecided about it and thinks the whole thing is beyond our power to settle, does he sacrifice his mental integrity in refusing to say that there were errors in the original Scriptures?

No, there is more behind it all than this. These reasons are not sufficient to cause the clamor about this subject by some scholars of our time. The real object behind it all is to get the point granted once for all that the original Scriptures contained errors, in order to claim the right to reshape the Old Testament history according to the anti-supernatural notions of Kuenen and Wellhausen. If you once grant that the original Scriptures contained many errors, as Dr. Briggs and others claim, how are you going to deny the possibility of the Mosaic account of the creation, the patriarchs and wilderness journey being full of errors? What is now done with many apologies will then be done fearlessly. It is the purpose of the type of Higher Criticism called Destructive, following Kuenen and Wellhausen, to reset the entire history of Israel according to an evolutionary hypothesis that only explains a few of the facts and contradicts the others as well as the testimony of Jesus Himself. This is the real reason why such a furor is made about the errancy of the Scriptures. In Germany, Rationalism has so long held sway that no man has to apologize for any theory he advances, however anti-supernatural. But you cannot transplant those naturalistic tendencies to English and American soil without provoking a conflict. And the conflict has come. The strange thing about it all is that here it is men considered evangelical who accept the results of anti-supernatural scholarship. It is certainly a grave question how long one can reconcile such results with his reverence for the Bible as God's only revelation of grace to men. It is befitting to American Christianity to be slow before it accepts these radical notions, even if they come from the lips of revered teachers. It is befitting Baptists to be slower than anybody else, and until better evidence is adduced than has been or is likely to come, to be too slow to give up the old faith at all. The fate that met the theories of Bauer as to the New Testament is almost certain to overtake the notions of Kuenen and Wellhausen as to the Old Testament. Let us wait and see it.

CHAPTER TWELVE

Is the Virgin Birth Credible? *The Watchman-Examiner,* November 18, 1920

Can a modern man accept the story of the birth of Jesus? Each age is sure of itself and credulous of others. Our own is characterized by a species of cocksureness in its own wisdom that has no foundation in matter of fact. This question of the virgin birth of Jesus, attested by both Matthew and Luke in two independent narratives, has been attacked from every standpoint.

On scientific grounds it is argued that it is impossible. At least that argument was once made. Modern science is familiar with *partheno-genesis*, or "virgin birth," in the lower forms of life. Hence science cannot set aside the virgin birth of Jesus. However, Luke does not present the birth of Jesus as in accord with nature. He distinctly asserts that it was due to the overshadowing of Mary by the Holy Ghost, like the Shekinah or presence of God. It is miracle that we have, not nature; but miracle cannot be ruled out unless it is ruled out everywhere. To do that rules out God and leaves us with materialism, the biggest miracle of all. Besides, men of science today do believe in the virgin birth of Jesus just as Luke did before them. And he was also a man of science.

It is objected that Luke has simply followed blindly the heathen myths which tell of gods becoming men. Some have found analogues in Babylonian mythology, some in Greek mythology, some in Jewish theology. But none of them gives us a real virgin birth. They each contradict the other. No real connection with Christianity is shown. "The Jewish theories confute the Gentile; the Gentile the Jewish; the new Babylonian theory destroys both and itself perishes with them."[1] Harnack,[2] who counts the story legend, yet knocks the "myth" theories in the head: "Nothing that is mythological in the sense of Greek or oriental myth is to be found in these accounts; all here is in the spirit of the Old Testament, and most of it reads like a passage from the historical books of that ancient volume."

It is objected that the very beauty and charm of Luke's narrative proves that it is all a legend. "That, as an a *priori* statement, I deny. Luke may be artistic, but so is God."[3] The point is that the persons and the poems in Luke 1 and 2 suit the actual events even better than they suit Luke's story. The steps of God have a rhythm that puts to shame our noblest measures. If God is at work in the birth of Jesus, everything else is simple enough. The supreme art of Luke lies in telling the story as it was. Ramsay[4] has biting sarcasm for critics that cannot be satisfied: "Luke has already been proved in the process of discovery to be correct in almost every detail of his statement" (in Luke 2:1–3). "The story is now established, and the plea now is that Luke's story is a legend because it is true to facts." We do not have to say that Luke had the same concepts that Mary had at each point. "That there was a more anthropomorphic picture of the messenger in Luke's mind than there was in Mary's I feel no doubt. Yet I believe that Luke was translating as exactly as he could into Greek that which he heard. He expresses and thinks as a Greek that which was thought and expressed by a Hebrew."[5] I heartily agree with Carpenter[6] when he says of these events: "I believe that they were beyond the power of either Luke or Mary to invent, though their meaning was not beyond the power of Mary to apprehend. That experience, described so briefly, so simply, so plainly, yet without a single word that could offend the most delicate purity, I take to be the conception of the Holy Child."

It is even objected that the silence of Jesus concerning his divine birth discredits the narratives in Matthew and Luke. That is an utterly absurd demand. From the nature of the case Jesus could not say anything on that subject. But when only twelve years old he does reveal a consciousness that God is his Father in a peculiar sense (Luke 2:49). He often insisted on this point (John 5:18; 8:19; 10:25) in a way to enrage his enemies, who finally accused him of blasphemy for this very thing (Matt. 26:63f).

It is not claimed that all the difficulty concerning the virgin birth of Jesus has been removed. We live in a world that has recovered the sense of wonder. The greatness of God overshadows all. The discovery of radium has made men of science humble. Astronomy has enlarged our ideas of God. Einstein has modified Galileo and Newton. Scientists gaze into the heavens with fresh awe. If light is subject to the law of gravitation, spirit and matter are not far apart. And even men today can fly in the air. Loeb claims that by artificial stimulus he has made fertile infertile eggs of some forms of sea-life (the sea-urchin). If Loeb can do this, cannot God? "God laid his hand on the deepest spring of man's being when his Son came to us 'conceived by the Holy Ghost, born of the virgin Mary.'"[7] All things considered, it seems to me that the virgin birth of Jesus is overwhelmingly attested. We have seen the strength of the witness of Luke and the independent testimony of Matthew. John's Gospel really supports them. There is nothing contrary to this view in the New Testament save the erroneous reading of the Sinaitic Syriac for Matthew 1:16, which is itself contradicted by its own text for Matthew 1:18–20.

But the question goes deeper than the witness of documents or the interpretation of Luke. Carpenter[8] puts it fairly: "Matters of this sort, involving belief or disbelief in the doctrine of the virgin birth, are not determined, and cannot be determined, by sheer literary and historical criticism."

We are confronted by the fact of Christ, the most tremendous fact in human history. All efforts to prove that Jesus never lived, but is a myth, have failed signally. All efforts to separate "Jesus" and "Christ" have likewise failed, from the days of Cerinthus and his "Aeon Christ" coming upon "Jesus" at his baptism to the recent "Jesus or Christ" controversy.[9] The historic Jesus and the Christ of faith confront us in Mark and in the *Logia* of Jesus, our earliest known documents concerning Jesus. Besides, Christianity is the vital force for human uplift in the world. Christ today is the hope of the race.

Thinking men have to account for the fact and the force of Christ. We have the view of Luke. It does account for the phenomenon of Jesus. If we reject it, we must have an alternative view. Carpenter[10] has no doubt that the "incarnation principle" is more clearly exhibited in the doctrine of the virgin birth than in any other." For myself I cannot conceive of a real incarnation of God in any other way. Some men think that they can conceive of an incarnation of God in Jesus even if Joseph was His actual father. They are certainly honest in their view, but it does not satisfy one. It greatly increases the difficulties for me. Sir W. F. Barrett[11] quotes F. C. S. Schiller as saying:

"A mind unwilling to believe or even undesirous to believe, our weightiest evidence must ever fail to impress. It will insist on taking the evidence in bits and rejecting item by item. The man who announces his intention of waiting until a single bit of absolutely conclusive evidence turns up, is really a man *not* open to conviction, and if he be a logician, he *knows* it."

The testimony of Luke concerning the virgin birth of Jesus is part of the larger problem of Jesus as the Son of God in human flesh. That question raises the greatest of all issues, the fact and the nature of God, of man, of sin, of redemption, of law, of miracles, of life, of matter, of spirit. The angel Gabriel said to Mary: "Wherefore also that which is to be born shall be called holy" (Luke 1:35). Peter says that "he did no sin" (1 Peter 2:22). John asserts that "in him was no sin" (1 John 3:5). Paul declares that "he knew no sin (2 Cor. 5:21). The author of Hebrews (4:15) says that Jesus was "without sin." Jesus himself claimed sinlessness (John 8:46). "This problem of an absolutely Holy One in our sinful humanity: How did it come about? Can nature explain it?"[12] Bruce[13] has the answer: "A sinless man is as much a miracle in the moral world as a virgin birth is a miracle in the physical world." It remains true that the only adequate explanation of the whole truth about Jesus lies in the interpretation given by Luke in the opening chapters of his Gospel. This view of Luke the physician holds the field today in the full glare of modern science and historical research.

PART III
Lexical Scholar

CHAPTER THIRTEEN

The Greek Article and the Deity of Christ, in *The Minister and His Greek New Testament*

The objections to the real Deity of Jesus Christ have taken various forms (philosophical, historical, theological, exegetical, grammatical). There are those who will not take Jesus as Lord of life and death because they cannot comprehend the mystery of the Incarnation and who refuse to admit the possibility of the union of God with man in the person of Jesus Christ. There are those who reject the historical evidence for the existence of Jesus and seek to explain the record of His life and death as myth and legend. There are those who say that Jesus lived and was the noblest of men and was deified by Paul and John (or whoever wrote the Fourth Gospel) after the fashion of the Roman emperors. There are those who accept the New Testament writings as adequate interpretations of Christ and Christianity, but who say that Trinitarianism is a misinterpretation of the New Testament. Jesus was, indeed, the Son of God, but only in the sense that all believers are, greater in degree, to be sure, but not in kind.

And then the grammarians have had their say, pro and con, on this great subject. As early as 1798 Granville Sharp wrote a monograph on the subject entitled, "Remarks on the Uses of the Definitive Article in the Greek Text of the New Testament, containing many New Proofs of the Divinity of Christ, from passages which are wrongly translated in the Common English Version." He laid down a "rule" (p. 3) which has become famous and the occasion of sharp contention, but which is still a sound and scientific principle: "When the copulative καί connects two nouns of the same case [viz., nouns (either substantive or adjective, or participle) of personal description respecting office, dignity, affinity, or connection, and attributes, properties, or qualities, good or ill], if the article ὁ, or any of its cases precedes the first of the said nouns or participles and is not repeated before the second noun or participle, the latter always relates to the same person that is expressed or described by the first noun or participle: i.e., it denotes a farther description of the first named person."

Now it is not easy to lay down a universal principle of syntax, particularly in a language so rich and varied in significance as is the Greek. But, though Sharp's principle was attacked, he held to it and affirms (p. 115) that though he had examined several thousand examples of the type, "the apostle and high priest of our confession Jesus" (Heb. 3:1), he had never found an exception. He does not, however, claim (p. 6) that the principle applies to proper names or to the plural number. Proper names are definite without the article. Ellicott (*Aids to Faith*, p. 462) says: "The rule is sound in principle, but in the case of proper names or quasi-proper names, cannot be safely pressed." But Sharp did not apply it to proper names. Middleton followed Sharp in an able discussion, "The Doctrine of the Greek Article applied to the criticism and illustration of the N.T." (1808). A few examples may suffice to show how the principle works. Take the common idiom, "the God and Father" (Rom. 15:6; 1 Cor. 15:24; 2 Cor. 1:3; 11:31;

Gal. 1:4; Eph. 5:20; Phil. 4:20, 1 Thess. 1:3; 3:11, 13), all in Paul's Epistles, and add Rev. 1:6 and "the Lord and Father" (James 1:27; 3:9).

All this is plain sailing. Now take the precisely parallel idiom, "the Lord and Savior Jesus Christ" in 2 Peter (2:20; 3:2). There is no dispute here that the author describes one and the same person by the two epithets with the one article. In 2 Pet. 1:11 and 3:18 the pronoun "our" comes after "Lord," but that makes no difference in the idiom. It is "our Lord and Savior," and it is so translated in the English versions. But we have precisely the same idiom in 2 Pet. 1:1, "our God and Savior Jesus Christ" as the Canterbury Revision rightly has it and so Moffatt translates it. But the King James Version renders it "God and our Savior Jesus Christ," while the American Standard Version reads, "our God and the Savior Jesus Christ" (note the insertion of "the" not in the Greek text) after the marginal rendering of the Canterbury Revision. Now why this confusion where the syntax is so simple? A strange timidity seized some of the translators in the Jerusalem Chamber that is reproduced by the American Committee. There is no hesitation in translating John 1:1 as the text has it. Why boggle over 2 Pet. 1:1?

The Explanation

The explanation is to be found in Winer's *Grammar* (Thayer's edition, p. 130; W. F. Moulton's, p. 162), where the author seeks by indirection to break the force of Granville Sharp's rule by saying that in 2 Pet. 1:1, "there is not even a pronoun with σωτῆρος." That is true, but it is quite beside the point. There is no pronoun with σωτῆρος in 2 Pet. 1:11, precisely the same idiom, where no one doubts the identity of "Lord and Savior." Why refuse to apply the same rule to 2 Pet. 1:1 that all admit, Winer included, to be true of 2 Pet. 1:11? There is no escape from the logic of the Greek article in 2 Pet. 1:1. The idiom compels the translation, "our God and Savior Jesus Christ." One may agree or not with the author, but that is what he said and what he meant to say. The simple truth is that Winer's anti-Trinitarian prejudice overruled his grammatical rectitude in his remark about 2 Pet. 1:1. The name of Winer was supreme in New Testament grammar for three generations and his lapse from the plain path on this point is responsible for the confusion of the scholars in the English versions on 2 Pet. 1:1. But Schmiedel in his revision of Winer (p. 158) frankly admitted Winer's error as to 2 Pet. 1:1: "Grammar demands that one person is meant." Winer really gives the matter away in his comment on Titus 2:13, where the Canterbury Version again has it right: "Our great God and Savior Jesus Christ." Here the King James Version and the American Standard Version have it: "The great God and our Savior Jesus Christ." The American committee here again are responsible for standing by the King James Version in the margin of the Canterbury Revision. Moffatt follows the King James Version, but adds "of" before "Savior." Winer (Winer-Moulton, p. 162) attacks the Sharp rule in Titus 2:13 by arguing that "the article is omitted before σωτῆρος, because this word is defined by the genitive ἡμῶν, and because the appositive precedes the proper name." But the appositive "precedes the proper" name in 2 Pet. 1:1, 11; 2:20; 3:18, and in the same passages, except 2:20, we have also ἡμῶν. The grammatical criterion is plain, and Winer knew it, for in a footnote he adds: "In the above remarks it was not my intention to deny that, in point of grammar, σωτῆρος may be regarded as a second predicate, jointly depending on the article του; but the dogmatic conviction derived from Paul's writings that this apostle cannot have called Christ the great God, induced me to show that there is no grammatical obstacle to our taking the clause καὶ σωτῆρος . . . χριστοῦ by itself, as referring to a second subject." In the text above the footnote Winer had said: "Considerations derived from Paul's system of doctrine lead me to believe that σωτῆρος is not a second predicate, coordinate with θεοῦ, Christ being first called μέγας θεός, and then σωτήρ." Here, then, Winer gives the whole case away both about Titus 2:13 and 2 Pet. 1:1. The grammarian has nothing to do per se with the theology of the New Testament as I have insisted in my grammar (*Grammar of the Greek New Testament in the Light of Historical Research*, p. 786). Wendland challenged Winer on Titus 2:13, and considers it "an exegetical mistake" to find two persons in Paul's sentence. Moulton (*Prolegomena*, p. 84) cites papyri illustrations from the seventh century A.D., which "attest the translation, 'our great God and Savior' as current among Greek-speaking Christians." Moulton adds this pointed conclusion: "Familiarity with the everlasting apotheosis that flaunts itself in the papyri and inscriptions of Ptolemaic and Imperial times, lends strong support to Wendland's contention that Christians, from the latter part of 1 A.D. onward, deliberately annexed for their Divine Master the phraseology that was impiously arrogated to themselves by some of the worst of men."

A Pernicious Influence

It is plain, therefore, that Winer has exerted a pernicious influence, from the grammatical standpoint, on the interpretation of 2 Pet. 1:1 and Titus 2:13. Scholars who believed in the Deity of Christ have not wished to claim too much and to fly in the face of Winer, the great grammarian, for three generations. But Winer did not make out a sound case against Sharp's principle as applied to 2 Pet. 1:1 and Titus 2:13. Sharp stands vindicated after all the dust has settled. We must let these passages mean what they want to mean regardless of our theories about the theology of the writers.

There is no solid grammatical reason for one to hesitate to translate 2 Pet. 1:1, "our God and Savior Jesus Christ," and Titus 2:13, "our great God and Savior Christ Jesus." It is true that thus we have two passages added to the side of the Trinitarian argument to make up for the loss of 1 Tim. 3:16 and 1 John 5:7–8. Scholarship, real scholarship, seeks to find the truth. That is its reward. The Christian scholar finds the same joy in truth and he is not uneasy that the foundations will be destroyed. It is interesting to note also that in Acts 20:28 both the King James Version and the Canterbury Revision have "the church of God, which He purchased with His own 'blood,'" whereas the American Standard Version has "the church of the Lord." Here the difference is a matter of text, not of the article. But the two oldest and best manuscripts (the Vatican and the Sinaitic) read "God," which is almost certainly right. There is a good deal more that can be said concerning the Greek article and the Deity of Christ, but enough has been said concerning the crucial passages to show the part that the article plays in the argument.

John 1:1

A word should be said concerning the use and non-use of the article in John 1:1, where a narrow path is safely followed by the author. "The Word was God." If both God and Word were articular, they would be coextensive and equally distributed and so interchangeable. But the separate personality of the Logos is affirmed by the construction used and Sabellianism is denied. If God were articular and Logos non-articular, the affirmation would be that God was Logos, but not that the Logos was God. As it is, John asserts that in the Pre-incarnate state the Logos was God, though the Father was greater than the Son (John 14:28). The Logos became flesh (1:14), and not the Father. But the Incarnate Logos was really "God only Begotten in the bosom of the Father."

In Rom. 9:5 the punctuation is in dispute and the article plays no decisive part in the meaning. Westcott and Hort punctuate the sentence so as to make God in apposition with Christ, as do the English Versions. This punctuation makes Paul apply the word God to Christ as we find it in John 1:1 and 2 Pet. 1:1 and Titus 2:13. In Col. 1:16–17 Paul treats Christ as Creator and Upholder of the Universe.

CHAPTER FOURTEEN

Grammar and Preaching, in *The Minister and His Greek New Testament*

Paul vs. Peter and John

It may provoke a smile on many a preacher's face when there is suggested any connection between grammar and preaching. Moody broke grammar and broke hearts, we are reminded. That is true, but he did not break hearts because he broke grammar. Plenty of preachers have broken grammar who have never broken hearts. Power in the preacher rests at bottom on the Master, the message, and the man. The power of Christ is mediated through the Holy Spirit and is at the service of all men. The message of the gospel is open to all who can apprehend it. We gain fresh glimpses of the Word of life, but in essence it remains the same. The one variable quantity in preaching is the man's personality. This is itself complex and includes what we call genius and magnetism for lack of more precise terms, for there is a subtle power in a real man that cannot be defined. God uses men of differing gifts. "Now there are diversities of gifts, but the same Spirit" (1 Cor. 12:4). But we must not confuse cause and effect. The Spirit of God blesses the work of different men, not because they are ignorant of Greek or English, but although they are ignorant. We can thank God for this fact.

Knowledge Power/Ignorance Weakness

Knowledge ought to be power and ignorance is weakness. Knowledge may minister to pride and so become an element of weakness (1 Cor. 8:1). God has always been able to take the weak things of the world and confound the strong (1 Cor. 1:7). But we must not forget that Paul himself was a man of the schools with the best technical training of his day at Tarsus and Jerusalem. The chosen vessel of Christ for the conquest of the Roman Empire was the ablest mind of the age with Hebrew, Greek, and Roman culture, and not the fishermen of Galilee, who had courage, but lacked the special scholastic equipment (Acts 4:13) that Paul possessed. Paul was a linguist, at home in Aramaic (Hebrew), in Greek, and probably in Latin, and did not need an interpreter like Mark for Peter. Even his oratorical impetuosity and intensity of feeling in Second Corinthians did not betray him into the grammatical crudities seen in the Apocalypse. Paul wrote and spoke the vernacular Koine, but as an educated man in touch with the intellectual life of his time. I am not pleading that Paul was a professional stylist, as Blass has done. I do not believe that Paul consciously imitated the rhetoricians of Rhodes or the grammarians of Alexandria. He was not artificial, but real, in his learning. However, Paul knew the power in a word and in a phrase and was able to write 1 Cor. 13, the noblest prose poem on love in all literature. Man of genius that he was, he was also a man of the schools, as Peter and John were not. He became the great preacher, missionary, theologian of the ages. Linguistic learning is not all that the preacher requires, but the supreme preacher like Paul does need it. Instance Alexander Maclaren as a modern example of the scholarly preacher.

Not Pleading a Lost Cause

There is no denying that the drift today in educational circles is heavily against the study of the classics. This undoubted fact by no means proves that the modern minister acts wisely when he ignores or neglects the Greek New Testament. There are fashions and fads in education as in other things. It remains to be seen whether the new utilitarian education will equal in value the old cultural standards and ideals. There may be as much mental drill and gymnastics in the study of scientific details and sociological theories as in the study of the language and of the literature of the ancients. The modern topics demand a place, but the old term "humanities" for the classics is not without significance. They have had a refining and a humanizing influence beyond a doubt. In Dean West's volume, *The Value of the Classics*, the most striking argument is that made by business men, captains of industry, who plead for the retention of Latin and Greek in the college curriculum on the ground that classical students make better leaders in business life than those without the humanities. And ex-President Woodrow Wilson is quoted in a recent magazine as saying that, if he had his college course to go over, he would give more attention to the study of Greek. In his case he was not thinking of Greek as a pastime, as when Gladstone would write Greek hymns to relieve the tedium of dull speeches in the House of Commons, but rather as a means of sharpening his intellect for problems of statecraft. The best outcome of educational discipline is not the storing of facts, useful as that may be, but the training of one's powers for instant service on demand. For this result the study of the Greek language claims preeminence. It is true that in the United States the high schools now seldom offer Greek. Here in Louisville my own son could not study Greek at the Male High School because it was not offered, though he did take it up at college. Even Oxford University, with the approval of Professor Gilbert Murray, has at last dropped compulsory Greek. One can now, alas, secure his B.A. in some colleges without either Greek or Latin. But if the study of the dead languages become itself dead in our colleges, the problem is still not settled for the minister of the gospel.

The Minister a Specialist

The physician has to study chemistry and physiology. Other men may or may not. The lawyer has to study his Blackstone. The preacher has to know his Bible or the people suffer the consequences of his ignorance, as in the case of the physician or the lawyer. The extreme in each instance is the quack who plays on the ignorance and prejudice of the public. It is true that the minister can learn a deal about his Bible from the English versions, many of which are most excellent. There is no excuse for anyone to be ignorant of his English Bible, which has laid the foundation of our modern civilization. But the preacher lays claim to a superior knowledge of the New Testament. He undertakes to expound the message of the gospel to people who have access to the English translations, and many of these are his equal in general culture and mental ability. If he is to maintain the interest of such hearers, he must give them what they do not easily get by their own reading. It is not too much to say that, however loyal laymen are to the pulpit, they yet consider it a piece of presumption for the preacher to take up the time of the audience with ill-digested thoughts. The beaten oil is none too good for any audience. Now the preacher can never get away from the fact that the New Testament was written in the Greek language of the first century A.D. The only way for him to become an expert in this literature of which he is an exponent by profession is to know it in the original. The difficulty of the problem is not to be considered. One will not tolerate such an excuse in a lawyer or in a physician. The only alternative is to take what other scholars say without the power of forming an individual judgment. Some lawyers and physicians have to do this, but they are not the men that one wishes in a crisis. The preacher lets himself off too easily and asserts that he is too busy about other things to do the main thing, to learn his message and to tell it. Fairbairn says: "No man can be a theologian who is not a philogian. He who is no grammarian is no divine." Melanchthon held that grammar was the true theology, and Mathias Pasor argued that grammar was the key to all the sciences. Carlyle, when asked what he thought about the neglect of Hebrew and Greek by ministers, blurted out: "What! Your priests not know their sacred books!"

The Shop and the Sermon

One is familiar with the retort that the preacher must not be a doctor dry-as-dust. It is assumed that technicalities sap the life out of one's spirit. The famous German professor who lamented on his death-bed that he had not devoted his whole time to the dative case is flaunted before one's eyes. So the preacher proudly reminds us of the "Grammarian's Funeral," and scouts "Hoti's business" and all the other dead stuff while he preaches live sermons to moving audiences. "Grammar to the wolves," he cries. No gradgrind business for him! He will be a preacher and not a scholar. He will leave scholarship to the men who cannot preach. Such a preacher seems to rejoice in the fact that he does not look into his Greek grammar, lexicon, or Testament, and not often into his commentary.

It is not argued that the preacher should bring the dust and debris of the shop into the pulpit, only that the workman shall have a workshop. There is music in the ring of the hammer on the anvil when the sparks fly under the blows. Certainly the iron has to be struck while it is hot. No parade or display of learning is called for. Results and not processes suit the pulpit. The non-theological audience can usually tell when the sermon is the result of real work. The glow is still in the product. There are men who study grammar and never learn how to read a language, men who cannot see the woods for the trees, who see in language only skeletons and paradigms, who find no life in words, who use language to conceal thought, who have only the lumber of learning. These men create the impression that scholarship is dry. Ignorance is the driest thing on earth. One does not become juicy by becoming ignorant. That is a matter of temperament. The mind that is awake and alert leaps with joy with every scholarly discovery that throws light on the thought of a passage.

The Preacher a Linguist

He is so by profession and he is debarred from unconcern about grammar. He is a student of language in the nature of the case. Just as the lawyer must know how to interpret phrases to make a will effective and to keep one from losing money, so the preacher must be able to expound the will of God to men that they may not lose their souls. The preacher only reveals his incompetence when he disclaims being a student of language. He uses the English language and he must be understood in that tongue. Often he is not understood because he preaches in the language of the books while the audience thinks in the language of the street. The homely language of Spurgeon went home to men's business and bosoms. Spurgeon was deficient in his college training, but he made himself at home in Greek and Hebrew that he might speak with first-hand knowledge. Language is man's greatest discovery, or invention—or whatever it may be called. Nothing else save the gospel of Christ has played so great a role in human history as the use of language. It is folly for the preacher to affect a superiority to linguistic knowledge. There is no other key to literature save the knowledge of letters. Grammar is simply the history of human speech. It is the record of human thinking. The first thing to do with any passage in a book is to read it, to construe it. This has to be done by the elements of speech. One picks up a certain amount of English without much technical study. He hears English of a certain type spoken and he learns to speak that dialect. But he has to learn his dialect whether he gets it out of books or by hearing of the ear. The very preacher who glories in his own eloquence condemns his lack of interest in the Greek New Testament. He is a linguist by profession.

Exactness in Exegesis

It is pitiful to think how the Bible has been abused by men who did not know how to interpret it. Many a heresy has come from a misinterpretation of Scripture. The worst heresy is a half truth. The literalist carries it to one extreme and the speculative theorist to the other. The only cure for wrong criticism is right criticism. The people find themselves at the mercy of every new "ism" because they are themselves so poorly instructed in the Bible. Sometimes the preacher does not know how to expose the subtle error before it is too late. There is in some quarters a prejudice against all scholarship because of the vagaries of some men who have not been able to be loyal to Christ and open to new learning. To a little man a little learning is a dangerous thing, Broadus used to say. Obscurantism is no answer to radicalism. The man who loves the light is not afraid of the light. No amount of toil is too great for the lover of the truth of God. The true preacher wishes to plant his feet on the solid rock of real learning. Grammatical exegesis precedes the historical and the spiritual. A preacher with college and seminary training can hardly keep his self-respect if he does not have upon his study table a Greek Testament, a Greek lexicon, a Greek grammar, and several modern commentaries on the book that he is studying. He will have many other books, of course, but these are prime necessities if he plans to do serious work upon a page in the New Testament before he preaches upon it. Only thus can he be sure of his ground. Only thus can he be relatively as original as he ought to be. The contact of his mind with the Greek Testament is a fresh experience of first importance. The mind of the Spirit literally opens to his mind in a new and wonderful fashion.

The Preacher a Psychologist

The psychology of preaching is attracting fresh attention these days. Language itself has its psychological side. Grammar cannot be fully understood until one considers language as the expression of the thought in the mind. The thought shapes the mold into which it is cast. The very inflections and cases have a meaning. The Greek prepositions are instinct with life. There are pictures in Greek prepositions and sermons in Greek roots that leap out at one. The preacher has to know the mood of the audience as well as the mind of the Spirit. He mediates the written word by the living word to the hearer. He must know his own heart and keep it ready for this spiritual transmutation. If a man is a wizard in words, he will win hearts to attention and to service. Those men spoke like Jesus in depth of thought, simplicity, charm, and power of expression. Men, even rough soldiers, hung on His words, listening. His enemies gathered round Him to seize Him, but their hands were palsied as they listened to His speech. The gift to pick the right word and drive it like a nail in a sure place is what makes a speaker effective. Hence the exact and prolonged study of language is of inestimable value for the preacher. Instead of scorning grammar he should devour it with avidity.

A Closed Greek Testament

Imagine yourself with a Greek Testament, priceless treasure of the ages, and yet with no lexicon and no grammar and no teacher. Imagine yourself without even a copy of the Greek Testament of your own, and yet with a deathless passion to read for yourself this Book that is the greatest not only in the Greek language but in all the world! Imagine yourself too poor to buy a copy of the Greek Testament and unable to go to school because you had to make your living as a shepherd boy on the hills of Scotland. Surely one would be excused for not learning to read the Greek Testament in such a case. One day in 1738 a youth of 16, John Brown, walked 24 miles to St. Andrews, and in his rough homespun clothes startled the shopman by asking him if he had a Greek Testament for sale. He took it eagerly and read a passage in the Gospel of John, and proudly walked back to his sheep with the most precious book in all the world in his hand. This lad had borrowed a Greek Testament from a minister and at odd hours had made a grammar for himself slowly, like a new Rosetta Stone, in order that he might unlock this treasure for himself. One of the dearest treasures at St. Andrews today is John Brown's Greek Testament. Grammar, self-made grammar, unlocked the closed Greek Testament for him and opened the door to the treasure of the ages. Today thousands of ministers who have had Greek courses in college and seminary and who have Greek grammars and lexicons on their desks lack the energy to hold themselves to a steady course of daily reading in the Greek Testament till it becomes one of the delights of life. One could wish that the picture of John Brown, the shepherd lad, making his own grammar, might rise to put us all to shame and send us back to grammar and lexicon and Testament. For in the Greek Testament Jesus speaks to us with almost more of reality, Erasmus says, than if He stood by our side and we heard His audible voice. He spoke both in Greek and in Aramaic. Certainly we have some of His "ipsissima verba" and His very words are life.

PART IV

Denominational Statesman

CHAPTER FIFTEEN

Baptism, *Baptist Argus* (Louisville, Kentucky), 1900

In the modern world there are three attitudes assumed towards immersion in the Scriptures. One is that immersion alone is meant by the word "baptize." The second is that the word means either immersion, pouring, or sprinkling. The third denies that immersion is Scriptural. It is not often that genuine scholars now go to the extreme of saying that immersion is not baptism. Dr. Shedd, in his *Commentary on Romans*, endeavors to show that Paul, in Romans 6:4, did not connect baptism and burial. But this species of exegetical gymnastics is so rare as not to be taken seriously by the student of Scripture. There is a much larger number of writers who freely admit that immersion is the proper meaning of baptize, but who insist that another meaning is permissible also in special cases. Hence, it is argued, one cannot properly insist on immersion alone as baptism. Something else will do as well, or almost as well. Dr. A. Plummer is a fine example of this type of scholars who wish to find some Scriptural justification for modern practices in Christian worship. Writing in the new *Hasting's Dictionary of the Bible*, he says:

> The mode of using it was commonly immersion. The symbolism of the ordinance required this. It was an act of purification; and hence the need of water. A death to sin was expressed by a plunge beneath the water, and a rising again to a life of righteousness by the return of light and air; and hence the appropriateness of immersion.

That would seem conclusive, if he had not added: "But immersion was a desirable symbol, rather than an essential," mentioning the stock objections about household baptism. The Baptists are by no means alone in claiming that nothing but immersion is taught in the Scriptures. In fact, the overwhelming bulk of modern scholarship is with the Baptist contention on this point. The trouble is not so much here, as in the conclusion from this fact. The Romanist will say: "Yes, but the church had the right to change the mode of the ordinance." He falls behind the doctrine of an infallible church. The appeal to Scripture does not reach him. The Lutherans, and many other Paedobaptists, admit it freely, but affirm that the form is a matter of indifference, and claim that pouring and sprinkling are more convenient, and more suitable to model conditions and customs. It is denied by them that the form is essential to obedience to this command. This is the position of the majority of Paedobaptists. The wise line of argument with those who hold this view is to show that the form is essential to the symbol, that the very idea of baptism is destroyed when the form is broken, that an ordinance is meant in the nature of the case to be unchangeable; in accord to make it clear, that one who loves the Bible must follow the Bible teaching. It is just at this point that most of the irritation arises in the discussion of its subject. In our view we assume that no one is baptized at all who is not immersed on a profession of faith. This is considered arrogance by many who differ from us, and it is frequently said that we make immersion essential to salvation. If we expect to reach those who disagree with us, we must take pains to be understood, and to make it clear that our stress on immersion is not because we consider it essential to salvation, but essential to the ordinance. Baptism is not essential to salvation, but we insist that, when one is baptized, he should be really baptized. Baptists also feel very strongly the beauty of the symbolism of baptism as a death and resurrection. We are unwilling to see the pictured truth of the ordinance destroyed by the substitution of some other act. Besides, we contend that the command of Jesus cannot be obeyed unless the thing commanded by Him is done.

The Substitution of Sprinkling for Immersion

It is a commonplace among scholars that the counsel of Ravenna in 1311 was the first council to put sprinkling on a par with immersion. This permission to use sprinkling, says the *Schaff-Herzog Cyclopedia of Religious Knowledge*, "was favored by the growing rarity of adult baptism." Up to this time, sprinkling was only allowed in case of the sick, and gradually for infants. It was the doctrine of baptismal regeneration that led both to infant baptism and sprinkling. The belief that only the baptized were saved caused something to be done that would answer for baptism to insure salvation. Luther took the side of immersion and tried to stem the tide towards sprinkling, but he failed. Calvin considered it a matter of indifference. Roman Catholics stand by the council of Ravenna. The Continental Anabaptists were divided as to immersion. Modern advocates of sprinkling stand for a rite that gained its triumph at the close of the Middle Ages.

The Greek Church

The Greek Christians did not accept the decision of Ravenna, and did not cease the practice of immersion. This is a very striking testimony to the meaning of *baptize*, since the Greeks are credited with knowing the meaning of words in their own lanugage. It is true, they practice trine immersion, but this fact has no bearing on the question of immersion or sprinkling.

The Early Fathers

There is such a wealth of testimony here that one hesitates what to use. I have before me, as I write, the *Greek Lexicon of the Roman and Byzantine Period* from 140 B.C. to A.D. 1100, by

Prof. E. A. Sophocles, himself a native Greek. This book is the standard authority for this period of the Greek language, and is invaluable in the study of ecclesiastical terms. He, in accordance with all Greek lexicons, gives "dip, immerse, plunge" as the meaning of the word. He refers to Barnabas, Ignatius, Justin Martyr, Ireneus, Origen, Cyril, Gregory, Epiphanius, etc., to prove the mode. Moreover, Barnabas and the Shepherd of Hermas both speak of "going down into the water" and "coming up out of the water." Tertullian uses the Latin word "mergito," "to plunge."

When the teaching of the Twelve came to light, there was much ado made because this document of the second century permitted pouring when immersion could not be done. This is true. Already the doctrine of baptismal regeneration had arisen, and so much stress was laid upon baptism that when there was not enough water for immersion, pouring was allowed. But this is not the Scripture teaching. No such emphasis is laid upon baptism by the New Testament. Moreover, in the Teaching of the Twelve, when pouring is allowed a different word is used from "baptizo." The word used for pour is "ekcheo," a word never used in the New Testament in connection with baptism. Now the fact that "ekcheo" is here used for pouring, as distinguished from "baptizo," proves that "baptizo" does not mean pour.

Ancient Greek

"Baptizo" is not used as often as "bapto," from which it is derived. But each means to dip, to plunge. Both words are used in figurative expressions also, as all words are. One can be plunged in grief, immersed in cares, etc. *Liddell and Scott's Standard Greek Lexicon* (seventh edition) gives not a single example that permits pouring or sprinkling. What the precise difference is between "bapto" and "baptizo" has not been determined. In practical usage no real distinction can be observed, save "baptizo" is more common in later Greek; "bapto" in the earlier idiom. We have the same situation concerning "raino" and "rantizo," to sprinkle. The ancient Greek uses "raino," the later

Greek uses its derivative, "rantizo," but with no real difference in sense.

Contemporary Greek

The Biblical Greek is based on the Universal Dialect, which was occasioned by the spread of the Macedonized Attic by the conquests of Alexander the Great. Plutarch, Dio Cassius, Lucian, Philo, Josephus, Polybius, Diodorus, Strabo, all use "baptizo," and all use it in the sense of dip. These writers wrote in the language which lay immediately behind Biblical Greek, and were in a sense contemporaries of Biblical Greek. Plutarch speaks of one dipping ("baptizo") himself into the lake. Josephus (*Antiquities* XV., 3, 3) tells of young Aristobulus, brother of Mariamne, who went swimming with some of Herod's servants. At the proper time, in the dark of the evening, they "dipped him as he was swimming," and so he was drowned. The word "baptizo" is here used for "dipped."

The Septuagint

Both "bapto" and "baptizo" are used in the Septuagint translation in literal and figurative senses, but always with the sense of dip. In 2 Kings 5:14, we read of Naaman: "Then went he down, and dipped himself seven times in Jordan." There the Septuagint uses "baptizo" for "dipped."

The New Testament

The New Testament is based immediately upon the Dialect. Prof. Sophocles (*Lexicon for Roman and Byzantine Periods*) says of "baptizo": "There is no evidence that Luke and Paul and the other writers of the New Testament put upon this verb meanings not recognized by the Greeks." The word assumes a technical application to a special ordinance in the New Testament, but the act used as an ordinance is the original and persistent meaning of the word. The Jews had ablutions before John the Baptist introduced the ordinance of baptism. Some of those ablutions were immersions, but there is no evidence that the Jewish Proselyte baptism of later times (which was also immersion) existed before the time of Christ. In Luke 11:38 we are told that the Pharisee marveled at Jesus because "He had not first washed before dinner." The word for wash is "baptizo," and refers to the Pharisaic scrupulosity about ceremonial defilements. To make sure of ceremonial purity, a whole bath was felt to be necessary. In Mark 7:4 we read that when they come "from market, except they wash, they eat not." There again "baptizo" is used for wash. Some ancient documents here read "rantizo," sprinkle, showing clearly that "baptizo" and "rantizo" mean different things. The reading "rantizo" doubtless arose from the difficulty felt by those not Jews in thinking that everybody would go to the trouble of taking a bath after coming from the market before meals. In Luke 16:24 "bapto" is translated dip, "that he may dip the tip of his finger in water." "Baptizo" is used in figurative senses in the New Testament, but always in harmony with the original and literal meaning of the word.

The baptism of death, of fire, of the cloud, of the Holy Spirit, all preserve the same imagery of the literal usage. The way to learn the real meaning of a word is not from the metaphor, but from the literal sense. We have seen from the use of the word "baptizo" in Greek writers of all ages, from the time of Homer till Modern Greek, that "bapto" and "baptizo" mean to dip. So then, the presumption is all in favor of this idea in the Bible, unless the connection makes it impossible, and renders a peculiar sense proper which does not elsewhere exist. We have seen that in the Septuagint translation of the Old Testament "bapto" and "baptizo" mean to dip. We have seen also that in the New Testament, when the ordinance is not spoken of, both "bapto" and "baptizo" mean to dip or immerse in a literal or figurative sense. What, then, is the sense when "baptizo" is used for the ordinance of baptism? We observe at once that "rantizo," to sprinkle, and "eccheo," to pour, are both used in the New Testament, but never in connection with the ordinance of baptism. The word "baptizo" is consistently used throughout. We should expect "baptizo" to have one meaning, since we have observed this to be true of it elsewhere. This one meaning should run through all the figurative uses of the word also. We suggest that one use successively pour, sprinkle, immerse in every instance in the New Testament where the word baptize, or baptism, occurs. The result will completely remove pour and sprinkle from serious consideration. Dip or immerse will suit every time. The circumstances surrounding the ordinance of baptism naturally suggest immersion. Jesus went down into the water, and came up out of the water (Mark 1:10).

The baptism took place while down in the water. If the word "baptizo" elsewhere always means immerse, certainly there is nothing here to make it otherwise. The New Testament descriptions of various baptisms suggest an immersion. Moreover, Paul has drawn a picture of what baptism is like. In Romans 6:4 he tells us that baptism is like death, burial, and resurrection. (See also Col. 2:12.) The very symbolism of baptism demands going down into and rising from the water. It is impossible to picture burial and resurrection by pouring or sprinkling. Immersion does do it, and nothing else does. The argument is complete, as complete as it is possible to make any argument. No real objections can be found in the Scriptures. The number baptized at Pentecost does not show immersion to be impossible. Baptist missionaries among the Telugus have duplicated that experience several times. The water was at hand also, for Jerusalem was well-supplied with large pools, and always had plenty of water. The baptism of the jailer at Philippi is entirely possible. It is not stated when the baptism took place. Baptism by immersion is common in jails now. Water can be found in plenty when it is wanted. But, one may say, suppose water could not be found, then what? Do nothing. Baptism is not essential to salvation. A man in a desert can wait till he gets out of the desert, if he ever does. If we do not know that Jesus was immersed in the Jordan, we do not know anything in the Bible.

What Will You Do?

If Jesus was immersed, you wish to be immersed also. You ought not to be willing to do something else. If He went all the way from Nazareth to the Jordan to be immersed by John, we ought not to say anything about convenience now. It is not a question of what we would rather do. Jesus was immersed. Will you be content with doing something else for your own convenience, and offer that to Him for obedience? It is not a question of salvation, for we are not saved by baptism. But why do anything if you are not willing to do what Jesus did, and what He commands? He has commanded us to be immersed. He has nowhere commanded pouring or sprinkling.

CHAPTER SIXTEEN

The Spiritual Interpretation of the Ordinances, *Baptist World Alliance Proceedings,* June 20, 1911

This is one thing that Baptists stand for against the great mass of modern Christians. The Greek Church, the Roman Catholic Church, the Lutheran Church, the High Church Episcopalians, and the Sacramental wing of the Disciples attach a redemptive value to one or both of the ordinances. It is just here that the term "Evangelical Christianity" comes in to emphasize the spiritual side of religion independent of rite and ceremony. It is a curious turn in history that the one body of Christians that holds a thoroughly consistent attitude on the subject of regeneration before baptism should be so often charged with holding that baptism is essential to salvation. As a matter of fact, Baptists lay less emphasis on the necessity of baptism than any other denomination except the Quakers who go to the extreme of rejecting it entirely. The Quakers are right in stressing the fact that one's spiritual fellowship with God is independent of rites, but they impoverish the message of the gospel in refusing to use these ordinances which are charged with rich truth, just because so many misuse them. Those evangelical Christians who practice infant baptism lay more stress upon baptism than the Baptists do, since they will not wait till the child is converted. They practice infant baptism in hope that the child will be converted. This puts the cart before the horse and empties the ordinance of its real significance. One cannot but feel that infant baptism among the evangelical denominations is a relic of the fears that infants would perish unless they were baptized, the origin of the practice, in truth. Then they are wholly inconsistent, though preaching salvation by grace, praise God.

How Baptists Stand Out

Now, Baptists stand out against the indifference of the Quakers, the heresy of the Sacramentalists, the nervous over-emphasis of the Paedobaptists and contend for the spiritual apprehension of the ordinances. Our position is a difficult one because men are prone to drift into reliance upon rites for salvation. It is the lazy man's religion. It is the way of the literalist. The very use of rites tends, unless resisted, to harden into formalism and sacramentalism, unless one continually strives to see the significance of the symbol. The Pharisees made an ordinance out of washing the hands before meals. The Pharisee who invited Jesus to dine marvelled that Jesus did not take a bath before the meal. Unless you take a bath before meals, you are unclean and cannot be saved. The Judaizers carried this sacramental notion into Christianity. They held that a Gentile could not be saved without circumcision. He had to become a Jew. The blood of Christ was not enough. The Holy Spirit could not give one a new heart without the help of this ancient Jewish rite. So the Pharisaic party in the church at Jerusalem had Peter up before the church for fellowship with the house of Cornelius in Caesarea. They reluctantly submitted after his story and held their peace for a while. When Paul and Barnabas returned from the first great missionary campaign, the Judaizers promptly turned up at Antioch with the ultimatum: "Except ye be circumcised after the custom of Moses, ye cannot be saved." Paul accepted the challenge without a moment's hesitation. He took the matter to Jerusalem to show that the apostles and the mother church did not endorse the radical doctrine of the Judaizers. He would not for the sake of peace agree for Titus, a Greek, to be circumcised. He did not yield for one hour to the demands of the false brethren, that the truth of the gospel might abide. The battle of Paul's life was just this. He preserved spiritual Christianity against the demands of the ceremonialists. He met terrific opposition as did Jesus, as did Stephen, and for the same reason. The intolerance of those who mistake the symbol for the reality is always bitter.

Paul's Fight

Paul won his fight with the help of other apostles, and Judaizers were driven back before the onward march of apostolic Christianity. But the same narrow spirit reappeared in the second century. It dropped circumcision and seized on baptism as the "sine qua non" of salvation. This teaching was in reality Pharisaism "redevivus." It was also in harmony with much pagan theology. It was easy to understand and it swept the field in the course of time. Out of the heresy of baptismal regeneration or remission has sprung a brood of errors that have turned the course of Christian history away from its primitive purity. If baptism was regarded as essential to salvation, then the sick and dying should be baptized before it was too late. Clinic baptism thus arose. But the sick could not always be immersed; hence sprinkling or pouring could be done in extreme cases. Water for immersion was not always ready to hand, and, since death might come, the ordinance had to be changed to sprinkling or pouring. This situation appears as early as the middle of the second century in the *Teaching of the Twelve Apostles*. The supposed necessity of baptism is the explanation of the gradual use of sprinkling and pouring alongside of, and finally instead of, immersion. Thus also is explained the origin of infant baptism. If baptism is essential to salvation, then infants must be baptized. At first, and for long, infants were immersed, but gradually sprinkling and pouring drove out immersion.

The Modern Baptist

The modern Baptist voice cried in the wilderness in the seventeenth century in England, only the multitudes did not flock to the wilderness to hear and heed. To the many, after the long centuries of perversion of the ordinances, we seem interlopers and disturbers of the settled order of things. But the Baptist voice has been heard in the world of scholarship. The lexicons, the Bible dictionaries, the critical commentaries with monotonous unanimity now take for granted as a matter of course that baptism in the New Testament is immersion and immersion alone. To the unlearned, Baptists still have to prove this fact so patent to scholars.

The Restoration of the Ordinance of Baptism

And yet we do not carry all modern evangelical Christians with us in the restoration of the ordinance of baptism. We have won our contention, but we do not carry those who are convinced to the point of action. The tables are turned upon us in this wise. They say that we are sticklers for a mere form. What is the use? Grant all that we claim, and what difference does it make? So it comes about in modern life we are put again on the defensive and pushed over to the edge near the side of the ceremonialists, we who are the champions "par excellence" of spiritual Christianity, of a regenerated church-membership. We must expound our message yet again. We do not insist on baptism as a condition or a means of salvation. We deny both positions very strenuously. We say "no conversion, no baptism." First the new life in Christ, then the baptism as the picture and pledge of that life. We contend that the form is important just because the ordinance is only a symbol. The point in a symbol lies in the form. It is true of a picture. One wants the picture of his own wife, not just the picture of a bird, a man, or that of another woman. Baptism is a preacher. It cannot preach its full message unless the real act is performed. John the Baptist used baptism as the pledge of a new life worthy of the repentance which the people professed. He used it also to manifest the Messiah. Jesus spoke of it as a symbol of His death, the baptism which He was to be baptized with. Peter likened it to the flood in Noah's time. But it is Paul who has given the classic interpretation of the significance of baptism. He has brought out the rich message in his "mold of doctrine" as no one else has. It is a burial and a resurrection, submergence and emergence, buried with Christ and raised with Christ. It is a preacher of Christ's own death and resurrection, of the sinner's death to sin and resurrection to a new life, of the Christian's own death and resurrection in the end. The very heart of the gospel message is thus enshrined in this wonderful ordinance. Leaving to one side the question of the duty of obedience to the example and command of Christ and the practice of the apostolic Christians, matters of no small moment, we press our plea on the ground of the great loss sustained by the perversion of the ordinance. Its beauty is gone. Its message is lost. It cannot tell the story that was put into it. It becomes a mere rite that may have a meaning to those who perform it, but certainly not that with which it was charged. No stretch of imagination can make sprinkling or pouring proclaim death and resurrection.

A Beautiful Ordinance

Since it is an ordinance to which Jesus submitted and which He enjoined, since it is so beautiful in itself and so rich in high teaching, we claim that modern Christians should not let mere custom or convenience, prejudice or inertia rob them of the joy of obedience to Christ and fellowship with Him in His death and resurrection through this mystic symbol. Thus all can proclaim the heart of the message of Christ's death. We should not rob Christianity of its full rights in this matter. Let baptism preach. Our contention thus finds its full justification. We do not call men non-Christians who fail to see this great truth. We joyfully greet all true believers in Christ of whatever name and are glad to march with them in the great army of the Lord Jesus. But we cannot approve the substitution of a device of man for the sacred ordinance of John and of Jesus and of Paul. Once it is clear that immersion alone is baptism, then we should not hesitate to take the next step, to be baptized.

The Lord's Supper

The second ordinance preaches much the same message as that of the first, the death of Christ. It does not, indeed, speak about burial and resurrection. It is only of death that it has a message. But, if the Lord's Supper does not hold so full a message, the celebration is repeated frequently while baptism comes only once. The bread and the cup symbolize the sacrificial body and blood of Christ. The atonement is thus preached. The blood of Christ was shed for the remission of sins. This ordinance reminds us of the blood covenant of grace. We were bought with the blood of Christ. We must never forget that. We keep this ordinance in remembrance of Christ. We proclaim His death till He comes. The ordinance, like baptism, points forward as well as backward, the one to the Second Coming, the other to the Resurrection. It is a symbol also of the high fellowship which the saints will have with Jesus in the Father's kingdom on high. It is an ordinance rich with spiritual teaching. We do not admit the doctrine of transubstantiation nor that of consubstantiation, but we do see in the Lord's Supper much significance. Thus we symbolize our participation (communion) in the body and blood of Christ. Like baptism, the communion is a preacher. It proclaims the death of Jesus for sin, His second coming, and our participation in the blessing of His death. But there is one thing more. "We, who are many, are one head, one body for we all partake of one bread." In a mystic sense we are one loaf in Christ. This ordinance accents our fellowship with Christ and with one another.

Paul uses baptism as a powerful plea against sin. "We who died to sin, how shall we any longer live therein? Or are ye ignorant that all we who were baptized into Christ, were baptized into His death?" Rev. F. B. Meyer has made a most effective use of Paul's argument in a diagram in which a grave is placed beneath the cross. Our old man was crucified with Christ on the cross. The burial with Christ under the cross advertises our death to sin. We come out on the other side of the cross and His grave to a new life in Christ. Paul uses the Lord's Supper in a similar plea for consecration. "Ye cannot drink the cup of the Lord and the cup of demons." "Ye cannot partake of the table of the Lord and of the table of demons." He alludes to the feast in the idol temples, but the principle is general. How can the man who partakes of the cup of the Lord resort to the saloon, the gambling den? How can he align himself with the evil forces of this world? Baptism is a true "sacramentum," the Christian soldier's oath of fealty to Christ in his conflict with the hosts of Satan. The Lord's Supper is the mystic fellowship of the saints with Christ and with each other in Christ.

Overemphasis and Indifference

The ordinances speak loudly against the misuse into which they have fallen. Between over-emphasis and indifference there is the golden mean of truth. The Baptist voice has always spoken in clear tones for the free intercourse of the soul with God. The ordinances preach the same glorious doctrine of soul liberty. They testify to the fact that the soul is in communion with God through Christ: It is a supreme travesty to make these ordinances stand between the soul and Christ as hindrances, not as helps, to the spiritual life. Through centuries of misunderstanding we have come thus far. Three hundred years ago the English Anabaptists, then in exile in Holland, made a confession of faith in which they protested against infant baptism as the Dutch and German Anabaptists had done a century before. It was not till 1640–41 that the English Anabaptists clearly grasped the Scriptural requirement of immersion alone as the true baptism. The Baptists have not cried in vain during these centuries for a return to apostolic purity in the matter of the ordinances, for the immersion of believers only. In simple truth many men of culture in other denominations wish that they instead of the Baptists had the powerful message which Baptists offer to the world. It is a message of reality and is in harmony with the modern spirit. The life is more than meant, more than ceremony. There is no reason in any ceremony that does not express a glorious reality. If we have died to sin and are living in Christ, then baptism and the Lord's Supper have a blessed significance; else they become a mockery and a misnomer. Never in all the history of the world was the Baptist message on the ordinances more needed than it is today. Never did it have so good a chance to win a hearing.

CHAPTER SEVENTEEN

Denominational Loyalty, from *The Christian Index*, September 15, 1921

We have passed through some years of more or less bitter feeling on the subject of organic union of the various denominations in Christendom. Most of the agitation was due to a few well-meaning men who felt called to regulate the affairs of the kingdom of God. Some of it was the natural expression of a growing sentiment all over the world that Christians should show a solid front to the world as far as possible. Part of this sentiment is proper and good and part of it is mere hazy emotionalism. Part of it is real confusion of thought that misinterprets Christ's plea for unity to be a prayer for organic union, a very different thing. Each denomination today has organic union within itself and is in dire need of spiritual unity, the thing for which Christ prayed. Indeed, there are few local churches that do not exhibit signs of a lack of unity and harmony at times. Some are in a chronic state of faction that borders on schism. That spirit is evil and is condemned repeatedly in Paul's Epistles and throughout the New Testament. This spirit of strife has its root in selfishness and the desire to have one's own way at any cost.

In the abstract it would be best if all Christians belonged to one organization provided that organization best interpreted the mind of Christ and represented His will concerning the kingdom of God. But that is a very liberal proviso and, human nature being what it is, exceedingly difficult of execution. Uniformity in Christian faith and practice has been maintained at the point of the sword at different times at great cost of blood and progress. The massacre of St. Bartholomew's Eve is only one of many efforts to compel conformity in Christian creed and conduct. To this day in England to be a non-conformist is to befall a certain amount of scorn. But it is not true that organic union is a good in itself. It may be a veritable curse in the name of Christ.

What Organic Union Means

It is hard to believe in the sheer sincerity of some who talk so much about Christian union, though it seems uncharitable to say such a thing. At bottom one finds that the demand for organic union for the peace and progress of the forces of Christianity means the surrender of cherished convictions. The church of England made overtures through some of its leaders to the Pope of Rome for the reunion of Christendom, to be met with the flat refusal to consider any compromise, but only unconditional surrender to the church of Rome. But that blunt rebuff from Rome did not present the church of England and American Episcopal Bishops from sending forth the Laibeth proposals for reunion on the basis of the historic episcopate. The very humor of the situation might have forestalled such a document. More than one denomination has been started for the purpose of uniting all other denominations by aggressively absorbing them. Several efforts at organic union have met with mishaps as when the Cumberland Presbyterians split in the effort to unite with the Presbyterians. The Congregationalists, Methodists, and Presbyterians of Canada seem about to unite and that experiment will be watched with great interest everywhere.

The Baptists present a problem of a special kind to all plans for artificial union. For one thing, Baptists have no uniform and binding creed apart from the New Testament and their historic practices. Baptists cannot coerce each other. Their only resource is the open forum of debate with the open Bible before them and the appeal to an enlightened conscience. A certain amount of description can be exercised in the individual church and in the cooperation of churches in the same district association. Beyond that oral suasion is the only weapon that will carry Baptists. Baptists are jealous of this loyalty to the New Testament ideals and methods and are open to any appeal for union that is grounded on the simple teaching of the New Testament. But they cannot be whipped into line by any decree of council or ukase of pope or bishop or threat of civil, social, or ecclesiatical ostracism.

The Baptist conscience has been likened to a backbone. The Baptists of Britain are not numerous, but in several crises, as High Price Hughes, the famous Methodist preacher, said, the Baptist conscience has proved the salvation of British life. The tenacity of the Baptist conscience does not depend upon the support of all Baptists. To see the great issues at stake may even arouse the Baptist masses to greater zeal and loyalty.

Modern Christianity Functions Through Such Loyalty

When all is said and done, modern Christianity functions through denominational loyalty. Many essayists and novelists have repeatedly proclaimed the death of the denominational spirit because of its sectarian narrowness and bigotry and various other ugly things. But somehow the funeral of denominational life does not exactly come off. The various denominations have their ups and downs like all other enterprises, but on the whole keep up a steady progress in numbers and in service. The only way to change denominational loyalty in any given case is to convince the individual that he is wrong on fundamental points.

It is a free country and every man has the privilege of such a propaganda if he so desires. The result of his effort may be a firm reply or even an angry retort, or it may lead to fresh study on the part of the victim of the propaganda. The final outcome may be a more intelligent grasp of the hope to which he clings. It may conceivably lead to a change of conviction or even to the loss of all faith.

But it is certain that we need a more intelligent denominational loyalty than ever before. The very activity of certain diligent propagandists like the "Russellites," "Christian Scientists," and others like them, calls for fresh endeavor on our part to safeguard our own children against the zeal that is without knowledge. We cannot meet error by ignorance or mere denunciation. Freedom may itself be a peril unless it is buttressed by intelligence. The youth of the whole country is in sad need of Bible knowledge, but Baptists cannot afford to wait for a national solution of this peril. Judgment must begin at the house of God. If we lose our young people, we can only blame our own negligence. We have our Baptist homes, our Sunday schools, our churches, our preachers, our B.Y.P.U., our newspapers, our tracts, our books, our Conventions, our boards, our secretaries, our colleges, our seminaries.

There Must Be Intelligent and Trained Loyalty

It is not enough to retain or even increase denominational pride and loyalty. Certainly Baptists have a very great deal to quicken enthusiasm and to stir their ardor. We are the heirs of a great past and face a tremendous opportunity and responsibility. The time calls for intelligent and trained loyalty. The whole world seems ripe for the proclamation of Baptist principles that have survived through fire and flood till now they are about to become the common property of mankind. Religious liberty stands at the door of all men, a Baptist contribution to the race. It is a time when many voices challenge Baptists to their best endeavors as individuals and as a mighty body of believers who hold truth that the world needs and must have if it is to come to the New Testament ideals and standards.

There was never a day when it meant so much to be a Baptist as now, so much privilege and power for service.

But the new day emphasizes the need for the full recognition of the rights of others. The truth must be spoken, but in love and in courtesy. Certainly no Baptist feels like apologizing for being loyal to his own convictions. He does not ask any one else to do that. We must all learn the lesson of give and take with hearty good will. Baptists were never more conscious of a real mission for Christ than now. They claim no monopoly on truth or conscience. Each of us must work with the light that he has, scatter all the light that he can get, and welcome all real light from whatever source. Nothing good is gained by loosening of the bonds of denominational allegiance and loyalty. We can all work best in the harness to which we are accustomed and can do our bit and our best to push on the kingdom of our Lord and of His Christ.

The Bible Begets Baptists

It is a waste of time for men to try to change the grooves of history. Christianity is suited to all ages, races, and lands. Men see with the eyes that they have. It is a remarkable thing that, wherever the Bible has been put into the vernacular of any people, views more or less like our Baptist interpretation of Christianity have sprung up. The Bible begets Baptists if it is allowed free course. That is, it makes Baptists out of those who respond to the Baptist view of liberty and of loyalty. We have our place in the sun. Let us prove worthy of it.

CHAPTER EIGHTEEN

"Our Baptist Democracy—How It Works," from *Church Administration,* December 1930

The word *democracy* is Greek and means the rule of the people. A pure democracy can only succeed in a small group as in the case of Athens; and even there, where every citizen had an equal right to speak and vote on every question before the assembly, it finally failed. The populace easily fell victim to demagogues who misled the masses by specious arguments that appealed to passion and prejudice. Successful demagogues became tyrants. Popular favor was whimsical. The hero of today may be ostracised tomorrow, as with Themistocles. The only chance for success in a pure democracy lies in the education of the masses so that the demagogue will have a more difficult task. Athens was the most gifted and the best trained group of the ancient world, and yet it fell before its own demagogues, like Alcibiades, and before the jealousy of rival states like Sparta.

A Practical Democracy

A Baptist church is a practical democracy, not a pure democracy. The existence of pastors and deacons imposes limitations of leadership and service. This limitation is carried still further by various committees and other organizations for special classes (the Sunday school, the children, the young people, the women, the men). In a formal church meeting each member has an equal right for expression of opinion and vote, but responsibility for leadership has already been distributed in the various subdivisions if they function properly. But in every church meeting the problem of majority rule comes up. The theory in a democracy is that the majority rules. It works except when a minority refuses to abide by the decision of the majority. Probably more trouble comes to a Baptist church at this point than at any other. A stubborn minority can create a schism on almost any point whether important or unimportant. Many a church has split on a very minor issue, and bitter personalities follow with a new church organization. No Baptist church can succeed without wise leadership and wise following. Decisions should be reached after full, frank, and fair disucssion in the open. The obvious thing for the minority to do is to acquiesce in the decisions unless it is a matter of principle and real importance. Before a minority decides to cause a schism, the whole problem should be carefully reconsidered from every angle of duty and loyalty. A church boss can ruin the life of any church. Precisely the same thing can be done by the chronic objector who must have his way about every detail. A Baptist church is a practical democracy, not a pure democracy. Jefferson and Madison in Virginia patterned our republic on the model of Virginia Baptist churches.

A Further and Delicate Step

The problem of cooperation between local churches is a further step and a delicate one in such democratic bodies. Paul confronted precisely this issue in his missionary campaigns. The church at Corinth from which he and Barnabas set out approved the work, but gave no financial support towards it. It was not till the second campaign after the church in Philippi was established that Paul began to get help in money, first from Philippi and then from Thessalonica and Berea. But the church in Corinth, instead of contributing to Paul's work, criticized him sharply for his way of doing it, just as the missionary interest of some people is expended in criticizing boards, secretaries, and conventions. Paul in this third mission tour raised a collection for the poor saints in Jerusalem from the churches in Asia, Galatia, Macedonia, and Achaia. Though the apostle to the Gentiles, he gave no order to the churches on the subject. He made visits, sent agents, wrote letters, but left the actual response to the churches themselves as a voluntary offering, though laid by in store and regularly planned for. This effort of Paul was the first cooperation on a large scale among the early churches. Only those churches actually cooperated that were willing to do it. The rest held aloof, and some of them severely condemned Paul for what he was doing.

The Baptist Cooperation Program

The Baptist cooperation program has gotten no further than this voluntary principle. Baptist churches group themselves into district associations, state conventions, and the Southern Baptist Convention for certain purposes. In order to do this with any degree of success at all there must be messengers or delegates who meet together for consultation and agreement. Naturally leaders develop in these gatherings who are charged with certain definite duties to carry out the wishes of the body gathered together. We call these committees, boards, secretaries. These are in no sense endowed with authority to give orders to the churches behind them. They do have the responsibility of leading the denominational forces to which they appeal for help and cooperation. But a Baptist church is a sensitive body and will take orders from no man, not even from the pastor. But there is a wise way for these responsible leaders to make appeals that will win a response.

Today, as always, open discussion is the privilege of every member of a Baptist church concerning any item in the denominational program. But every one who starts a public discussion that will hinder the onward work of the denomination has a responsibility on himself. He should consider whether the information derived cannot best be obtained by private inquiry, and whether the point involved is one of mere detail or of principle.

Unless there is proof to the contrary, it should be assumed that the regularly appointed leaders are acting with intelligence and sincerity and are free from merely personal motives. No leader has ever had more bad motives attributed to him than has the apostle Paul, as we see in 2 Corinthians 10 to 13. It is a serious thing to make damaging accusations against denominational leaders and to foment discontent and to encourage refusal to cooperate in the cause of Christ as set out in the denominational program. There is so much inertia to overcome with the stinginess of many that it is not hard to gather anywhere a lot of people who will oppose aggressive work that calls for money.

On the other hand, denominational leaders should be very careful to walk circumspectly themselves and to "do all things honorable in the sight of God and man" as Paul claimed for himself. There are always some, like the Judaizers with Paul, who desire an occasion, who are looking for specks and faults, who make mountains out of mole-hills. As with Paul, so with us today, the work of Christ will win the help of those who are willing to lend a hand, and of no others.

CHAPTER NINETEEN

Baptist Colleges Are Essential, April 26, 1923

Recently a wealthy and prominent Baptist layman referred to the Baptist college as a hopeless and needless institution. He argued that it was impossible for the denominational school to compete with the state school with its vast income and prestige. He held that it was best to submit to the inevitable and to fall in with the regime of state education. He was absolutely convinced by his own logic, so much so that, though the richest man in his city, he had steadfastly refused to contribute to the flourishing Baptist college of his own state located right near him. I listened to his arguments and then asked him one question. I knew that he was a staunch and loyal Baptist and proud of his denomination. So I asked him if he knew where Baptists got their denominational leaders (ministers, laymen, women), whether from the

Baptist colleges, or from the state colleges. He at once replied that they came almost entirely from the Baptist colleges. I then asked him if he thought that Baptists could succeed today without an educated leadership, and he promptly answered that they could not. I do not know what will result from that conversation, but I think it is worth telling because other Baptists have fallen into a like dilemma concerning the denominational college when they have faced the tremendous expense involved in competing with the state colleges.

When the matter is thought through, it becomes plain that the question at bottom is one of denomination efficiency. The state schools produce almost a negligible number of denominational leaders, nearly all of whom come from the denominational colleges. Without properly trained leadership no denomination can make headway today. It is immaterial what the cost to the denomination may be. It must have its denominational school or go out of business as a serious factor in modern life. This is not the whole case for the denominational college, of course, but it is the heart of it. The acceptance of this position carries with it the great responsibility that those who send their children to the denominational college shall not be penalized for their loyalty by seeing their children receive an inferior grade of culture. Nothing but the best can meet the demands for Baptist culture in the South today. This program is a very expensive one, but there is no dodging it if our people mean to go on over the top for Christ. I have recently come in contact with one of our Southern Baptist colleges.

The vigorous and growing institution is located at Pineville, Louisiana, just across the Red River from Alexandria. It has an ideal situation on a hill among the pines on a great highway where the finest residence around Alexandria are now built. President C. Cottingham has succeed in erecting one of the finest college buildings for offices, classrooms, and auditorium in all the South. It is part of a larger plan that will be finished as the funds are secured. I fairly revelled in the beauty of this building and rejoiced in the prosperity attending the administration of President Cottingham. He has able co-workers, and it was particularly pleasing to see again my old student, Professor J. E. Brakefield, who has the Bible chair in Louisiana College. Some four hundred students crowd the buildings here. The situation is ripe for more buildings and for a large endowment. North Louisiana has become rich from oil and one wishes that this oil could turn into the oil of grace and fill the coffers of Louisiana College to the full. But the progress is already great, and greater things are in store for this young and live institution. It is absolutely the key to Baptist growth in Louisiana as genuinely so as the Baptist Bible Institute holds the key to Baptist prestige in New Orleans.

CHAPTER TWENTY

Baptist Interest in Education, *The Christian Index,* April 10, 1930

There are still people who refer to the "ignorant Baptists" as if that was the characteristic of our denomination. It is true that many Baptists are illiterate, but they are not illiterate because they are Baptists. The chief reason is that Baptist pioneer preachers went after the people remote from the town and city life and won them to Christ. Once, when a cultured woman of another denomination referred to the large number of illiterate Baptists in conversation with Dr. John A. Broadus, he quietly replied that it was true, but added that there were more educated Baptists than all the members of her denomination put together and then we have the illiterate Baptists besides. These uneducated Baptists are a great undeveloped source of power and they are already furnishing pupils for the schools who are becoming leaders in the churches.

Prejudiced Pioneer Preachers?

But in fairness it must be admitted that some of the pioneer preachers were prejudiced against an educated ministry and even boasted of their own ignorance as a mark of divine favor. One can find the facts on this subject in Sprague's *Annals of American Baptist Ministers*. Shubal Stearns was one of the ablest of them who did a wonderful work in the Carolinas and Georgia. The hardshell element in the denomination, which is still stronger according to the reports of gifts to missions than we like to admit, has always opposed education for the ministry. An ignorant ministry can only serve an ignorant constitutency. The gradual growth of popular education has narrowed the spheres of influence of the untrained preachers. But this historic fact has furnished some basis for the phrase "ignorant Baptist." It never was true of our people as a whole, but it is still true enough to hamper all the cooperative work of the denomination. The majority of Southern Baptists do not read a denominational journal of any kind and do not contribute to the cooperative work in missions and education. The chief problem with us is how to enlist, enlighten, and win the unenlisted masses without offending and repelling these good brethren and sisters whose environment has been unsympathetic with the organized work. It is a difficult task. One can find traces of the struggle that the Southern Baptist Theological Seminary has had with the antagonism against theological education in my *Life and Letters of John A. Broadus*. Boyce and Broadus had to face a long and bitter struggle with the remains of the old prejudice.

The various Baptist colleges in the southern states sprang up from the desire to have a trained ministry in order to unite the denomination in the cooperative missions program of Luther Rice in his effort to win support for Adoniram Judson in Burma. American Baptists have not properly appreciated the work of Luther Rice. One of the new dormitories at the Southern Baptist Theological Seminary is named in his honor. But he saw clearly that Southern Baptists among whom he labored chiefly must have educated preachers if they were to be won to cooperation in mission work. The effort to educate the preacher inevitably led to the education of the layman. The boys and girls must also be educated along with the young preacher. Hence our Baptist colleges soon became no longer schools for preachers, but for all. So they have remained with the development of special colleges for the girls and the rise of theological seminaries for the ministers.

The growth of Baptist colleges has gone on along with the increase in missionary interest as Luther Rice foresaw, but not without struggle and difficulty. The colleges and seminaries have furnished an increasing number of young men and young women who are eager to become missionaries to the foreign field. There are probably more than a hundred today who are unable to go, though ready and eager, because the contributions from the churches will not justify sending them. In the enthusiasm of the Seventy-five Million Campaign some were sent who have had to be recalled for lack of support. It is apparently true that education among Baptists has grown more rapidly than interest in missions. It would seem that there has been a lack of mission information somewhere or somehow. The churches will never be genuinely enlisted in mission endeavor until they are properly informed concerning mission work. As I see it, there is far more need of mission information such as *The Home and Foreign Field* furnishes than there is call for discussion of plans and methods. It is true that some who used to give more are now giving less, but the cure for this is more and fuller information. The mission problem is at bottom an education problem of a special sort. The Woman's Missionary Union now gives as much for missions as the rest of the Southern Baptist convention because the women have study courses on various mission fields and take the time and the trouble to learn the facts about missions needs.

The "Enlightened Poor"

There are, of course, thousands of Southern Baptists who believe in education and who would give something to the school but for their deep poverty. These enlightened poor send their boys and girls to school, though denied that privilege and blessing themselves. They are heroes and heroines in our Baptist life. They give the best that they have, their children, and many of them are now leaders in the work of Christ all over the world. Let no one sneer at these fathers and mothers as "ignorant Baptists." They may be illiterate, but their faces are towards the rising sun and they are doing their bit for the ongoing of the kingdom of Christ. They are enlightened and enlisted already.

There is a shadow on our Baptist schools in the form of huge debts. Each state is struggling with it. Progress is hindered by debt. Competition with state schools and heavily endowed private schools is keen. Thousands of Baptist boys and girls go to these schools because of free tuition or because of financial aid bestowed. If Baptist schools could get all these pupils, their income would be greatly increased and great improvements could be made in the curriculum and in the equipment for the comfort of students. It is a vicious circle. Many pupils and parents are unwilling to put up with the limitation inevitable in some of our Baptist schools. Wealthy Baptists do not give the endowment essential for the needed improvements. The call upon Baptists of wealth in the South is a real one today to equip Baptist schools so that they can meet all modern demands for college training. This is the way to show Baptist interest in education. Remove the debits from the colleges.

CHAPTER TWENTY-ONE

Southern Baptists Looking Forward, *The Watchman-Examiner,* September 14, 1933

Debts among Southern Baptists preceded the debacle of 1929 when the financial collapse came on the whole country and the whole world. Many of our churches in the boom times had piled up heavy debts and expensive building plants. Under the influence of the Seventy-five Million Campaign the mission boards (state and southwide) were caught with enormous obligations and no funds to meet them. The schools were likewise overloaded with debt, nearly all of them, the University of Richmond being a notable exception, thanks to the skill of President F. W. Boatwright. But the attendance at the schools has kept up remarkably well, and the work of the boards has been richly blessed with conversions. Our Baptist people are looking with hope to the future and mean to pay their debts.

The Hundred Thousand Club

One evidence of this purpose is the plan adopted by the Southern Baptist Convention at Washington, under the leadership of Dr. Frank Tripp, of St. Joseph, Missouri, to pay off in six years the $6 million debt on the southwide boards and schools. The idea is for 100,000 Baptists to pledge themselves to give a dollar a month for six years over and above what they now give, and this extra money to be applied specifically to these debts. The plan is practicable and ought to succeed. It has not met with universal approval. Some of the best men among us fear that it will simply take away funds from the state work for the southwide work. Several of the state boards do not approve it or condemn it, but leave it to its own fate. This aloofness is a pity, but in spite of it there is abundant ground to hope for the success of the movement. It is the only plan proposed with any show of success. The debts will never be paid save by those who are willing to do this task above and beyond the regular routine. How the debts came to be made and who is responsible are questions now of comparative indifference. They must and will be paid. There is hope for complete success of the Hundred Thousand Club. Surely there are 100,000 Baptists among our 4 million members who will rally to the help of the Lord.

Better Prices and More Money

The farmer is getting more money for his cotton and corn, his wheat and cattle than a year ago. The drouth has been severe in some sections, and much cotton has been plowed under in accord with the government's plan. But prices are better, and more money is in circulation. Our people are lining up with great unanimity behind the N.R.A., with hope in the outcome, without clearly understanding the value of the plan. They are willing to do their part in the effort for national recovery. There is a mood of helpful patriotism abroad that augurs well for the future. It is pretty generally hoped, however, that President Roosevelt will not be called upon to exercise all the vast powers placed in his hands by Congress.

The Alcohol Hysteria

The south, as shown by the results in Alabama, Arkansas, and Tennessee, has fallen a victim to the propaganda against prohibition, carried on systematically by the daily press, the movies, the radio, the politicians, the beer barons of former days who have defied the law along with the bootleggers. The underworld has had the help of unlimited money from the lovers of liquor. In all probability the other southern states soon to vote (Florida, Kentucky, Louisiana, North Carolina, Texas, Virginia) will follow suit under the lead of the president, with the party whip cracked vigorously by the postmaster general. It is a sorrowful outlook for the country. Recently a leading brewer urged the beer people to create a taste for beer among the college students who had lost it under prohibition (less than one per cent now drinking it, so he said). All sorts of slanders have been believed, and the work of a hundred years will be undone. But the fight against liquor will go on in the South. We must save our boys and girls from the demon of rum in spite of the politicians. They are worth more than revenue.

The Revival Spirit

Dr. L. G. Broughton laments in *The Western Recorder* that our leaders have largely lost interest in mass revivals. That may be true in several cases, but numerous revivals are reported all over the country. Dr. B. V. Ferguson, of Fort Smith, Arkansas, reports large revivals there and at Little Rock, led by Rev. M. F. Ham. Great revivals continue to be held by Drs. L. G. Broughton, J. W. Ham, J. B. Leavell, J. C. Massee, and many others. People are converted when the gospel is preached. Baptists led all denominations in 1932 in the number of conversions. Members of our seminary faculty (Drs. Adams, Carver, Davis, Dobbins, Powell, Sampey, Tribble, Weatherspoon, Yates) have recently held successful revivals. One of the seminary students has just reported to me more than 100 conversions in his meetings this summer. The gospel is still the power of God unto salvation to everyone who believes. This is supremely true in the South.

CHAPTER TWENTY-TWO

The Preacher and Politics, *The Christian Index,* July 26, 1928

The present political campaign has raised this question in a rather acute form. In the abstract and in general it is not hard to agree that the preacher should eschew politics, especially in the pulpit. The preacher aims to present the gospel so as to win men of all political parties to the service of Christ. We have the example of Jesus to help us, for He did not join in the political turmoil in Palestine and recognized the Roman rule.

But the problem is not always so simple as that. The kingdom of Christ is not of this world, but it is in this world and has the right to make its power effective for God and man. Baptists are mainly responsible for the first amendment to the Constitution which guarantees religious liberty to all and preserves the separation of church and state. But Baptists maintain their rights as individual citizens and so do preachers.

Patriotism or Partisanship?

It is always difficult to distinguish between patriotism and partisanship. The real duty of a true citizen is to put country above party. That is not easy to do when party lines are sharply drawn with a long history behind and with a fixed environment and with complicated issues in the election. It is more difficult for the professional politician than for the ordinary citizen, for the politician thinks of his future. It ought not to be hard for the people to break away from the party traces and to vote according to their consciences, especially when the Australian ballot is used. The southern preacher today is face to face with the issue of loyalty to his conviction concerning prohibition and adherence to the party of his fathers.

The Eighteenth Amendment

It ought to be remembered that it cost a deal of struggle to get the Eighteenth Amendment into the Constitution. It came as the result of the moral and religious conviction of the Christian forces in the country sustained by the business men who wanted sober employees. It was a struggle of country life against city life and the country ideal of morality and sobriety won. Now that ideal is boldly challenged by a man who represents the city and foreign and sporting elements of the country who are clamoring for liquor again.

At the Baltimore Democratic Convention William Jennings Bryan defied Tammany Hall and that act of his nominated Woodrow Wilson. Today Tammany Hall has taken charge of the National Democratic party and the whisky forces are in charge of the campaign.

What is the Southern Baptist preacher to do when the Democratic candidate for president announces his intention to use all his influence to get the Volstead Law modified? The chairman of the campaign committee is a member of the association against prohibition. The least that the preacher can do is to vote according to his conscience. That every citizen should do everywhere.

The crack of the party whip ought not to be powerful enough to silence a man's conscience.

Past Liquor Forces

We all know what the liquor forces have done in the past. They have violated every law ever made. Now they are defying the moral and religious forces of the country and openly propose to nullify the law and legalize again the sale of liquor. If the church members of the south vote in November as they voted when the southern states went dry, every state in the south would vote against the champion of liquor.

The sanctity of the American home, church, school, and civilization is at stake. The moral issue is the main one in this campaign. President E. Y. Mullins, of the Southern Baptist Theological Seminary, has raised a cry of warning that has gone all over the country. It is not contended that every preacher should do as Dr. Mullins has done and urge people to vote for Hoover in order to defeat Smith who has Tammanyized the National Democracy. That is what I purpose to do. Like Luther at the Diet at Worms, I can do no other. But I am insisting that Al Smith's nomination with his Tammany wet record and purpose releases me from bondage to the party led by him.

The preacher who wishes to exercise his privilege of public denunciation of public officials for immoral conduct and law violation has John the Baptist on his side. He openly denounced the Tetrarch Herod Antipas and his wife Herodias for their infamous marriage. It is true that he was cast into prison for his courage and finally was put to death as a result of the rage of Herodias. But it is better to have a head like that of John the Baptist and lose it for the sake of righteousness than not to have such a head and keep it.

Many a preacher will be consulted by a puzzled church member to know what to do. It will be difficult for him to avoid a definite answer. The wet newspapers are already sneering at the Anti-Saloon League, the preachers, and the church members for trying to prevent the restoration of legalized liquor. Christians are citizens. They have put prohibition into the Constitution.

Are they willing for it to be set at naught by the lawless elements of the country? John the Baptist was like Elijah, Isaiah, Jeremiah, and Habakkuk of old. Chicago is at the mercy of the lawless elements as is New York and Philadelphia. Is it too much to say that in every large city the underworld will rally to the battle for Al Smith? Which has the strongest grip on our church members, party or country? The moral and religious problem has been forced upon Christians. Can the preacher hide his head in the sand and be run over?

CHAPTER TWENTY-THREE

On Choosing a Pastor

The efficiency of a church hinges primarily on the pastor. Like priest, like people. There are exceptions, where a poor preacher and pastor is not able to hold back for long a live church. In that case, the church usually sloughs off such a man and starts over again. But even so, scars are left that only time will heal, even if the church is not actually split wide open. Effective church administration heads up in the pastor. He can hold the church back. He can lead them astray. He can bring confusion and defeat.

Hence it is a matter of grave importance when there comes a vacancy in the pastorate. The church is thrown back upon its own responsibility. It is always interesting to note the picture of a church's attractions drawn by the pulpit committee when writing to a prospective pastor. A wide door is opened to the shepherd who can come in and gather together all the scattered sheep that wandered astray from the former shepherd. The weaknesses of the church and the difficulties of the situation he must learn for himself.

Various Ways of Making Mistakes

There are various ways of making mistakes at the very start in calling a pastor. Plenty of names will be presented to the committee, sometimes by the preachers themselves who are candidates for the vacant pastorate. One way of hurting the church is to have several men preach before a call is recommended. It is a poor preacher who cannot please somebody. When the vote is taken, each preacher will receive some votes. I recently heard of a church that refused to reach a decision till all the candidates had been heard. Dr. William E. Hatcher used to call that method "trotting them down the pike." The whole business of preaching a sample sermon is questionable. Sometimes the very best preachers feel embarrassed and are unable to do their best at such a time. Other preachers have one specially good sermon, and if called on that sermon can never come up to it again, so that disappointment comes very soon. It is usually a blunder to have a minister come and preach until the pulpit committee has decided to recommend him to the church for a call, or until the call has already been made. Then he can come and look over the church and the field at the same time that they look him over. One or two of the committee ought to go and hear the preacher in his own church before he is recommended. It is money well spent.

Right to Investigation

Every preacher makes his own record. The church is entitled to make enquiries where he has labored. No preacher has a right to object to investigation by the committee of his actual work. There may be a misfit because of peculiar circumstances for which the preacher is not responsible. Almost every preacher can get a call to some church after his school life is over. Every teacher and fellow-pastor are glad to help a pulpit committee make a wise selection. But as a rule a pastor progresses by the successful work that he actually does. If a man is a church wrecker, he will find it hard to get a fresh start.

Paul felt the importance of securing elders for the mission churches which he established. When he returned from the first great tour, he and Barnabas appointed elders in every church (Acts 14:23). Paul knew that the churches could not carry on well without elders or bishops. So he helped them select men for leadership. Few things concerned him more in his later ministry than securing pastors for the churches. He gathered young preachers around himself and trained them for the churches. Baptists do not have bishops or overlords to select pastors for their churches, nor an outstanding apostle like Paul to train them. The problem is thrown back upon each church primarily. The larger church usually robs another large church of a pastor who has already made good, so that no risk will be run. Sometimes this plan succeeds, sometimes it does not. It by no means follows that a pastor who succeeds nobly in one field will do equally well in the next. Pulpit committees should be constantly on the lookout for young men who are doing well and bring them to larger fields. But they should not close the door to the older preacher who has grown ripe and rich in the service of Christ. If a man is not to be considered before he is 35 nor after he is 50, he has only 15 years for effective work. Surely that is too narrow a range. There is no reason in the world why a pastor who is 60 should not be in his prime. At 70 he should be mellower and wiser than ever. Alexander MacLaren at 80 held audiences in the hollow of his hand, because he was growing all the time.

Promises of Cooperation

There is one other word for pulpit committees. It is that they should show the same zeal in living up to promises of cooperation that they exhibited in making them before the new pastor accepted the call. If that were done, there would be fewer changes in the pastorate, and the church and pastor would grow together into the full stature of manhood in Christ Jesus.

It is certain that people often expect too much of the new pastor. He is a novelty, and his voice and manner have a certain charm. The new broom sweeps clean, until gradually the members begin to take him for granted, and to begin to leave it all for him to do as they had done with previous pastors. The new pastor is often chosen for his points of difference from the old one. Soon he is expected to have the virtues of the old as well as his own. Such members look on the pastor as the one "hired" by the church to do all the work. Some are even willing to pay liberally for his services provided they do not have to listen to his sermons. They will even excuse him from pastoral visiting as a sort of bother and possible interference with personal habits.

A Man for All the People

The modern preacher has to be a marvellously-gifted man if he fulfils all the demands of the various classes in our churches. There are the rich and cultivated who have heard famous preachers in their travels. He has to interest the ignorant and uneducated who require simple language and real thought. There are the young who have problems and perplexities and occasional frivolity, and yet who long for real spiritual help. The aged come with hunger for consolation and hope. The sick and the sorrowing look up for light and leading. The little children are shy and yet eager for notice and guidance.

Criticizing the pastor is the favorite occupation of some members who really have a disloyal attitude, and finally break the new pastor's heart as they did the old one's. The pastor himself may be a bit stiff and offish, and excuse himself from hand-to-hand contact with the people. Surely one has to be called of God if he is to be patient with the demands of the modern church.

CHAPTER TWENTY-FOUR

The Church and Community, *Church Administration,* March 1930

There is a regular campaign on today to squeeze out the small country and village church. It is now done openly in the interest of organic church union and professedly in the interest of the kingdom of God to cut down expenses and to remove an eyesore where there are so many weak churches in sparsely settled communities. Much of the discussion has the flavor of the market, the barter and sale, of supply and demand, with very little emphasis on duty and conviction and service. I shall not undertake to say that, wherever there are a few scattered Baptists, there a Baptist church should be organized. That is largely a local and a personal problem that cannot be settled by doctrinaire discussion at a distance. This is to be said, that Baptists have more at stake in the matter than many other denominations, for our people stand by conviction apart from all the Paedobaptist denominations which sprinkle infants, whatever other differences they may have. With real Baptists there can be no compromise on the subject of the immersion of believers only, and because of the new birth, not in order to obtain remission of sins. The New Testament is so plain here that a Baptist has to stifle his clear convictions to go into a church that denies them. Some Baptists do, and claim to be Baptists still, awfully still, I should say. Those who frown down on Baptists, though small in number who start a new church, should remember this fact.

The "Community Church"

The so-called community church has a fine-sounding name, but it is usually a very uncomfortable place for Baptists with real convictions and intelligence. My own observation is not extensive, but I seriously doubt if such a community church without a Baptist church ministers as effectively to the whole community as two churches would (a Baptist and a Paedobaptist). Organic union with Baptists is nothing like so important as loyalty and obedience to Christ. The prayer of Jesus in John 17 was a petition for unity of spirit, not for organic union. The disciples had organic union, but they lacked unity of spirit. Besides, whatever may be true of other denominations, there is no higher Baptist body that can tell local Baptists when and where they may organize a church. It may be tried, but it will inevitably fail. The Baptist church is a pure democracy and practices cooperation with other Baptist bodies, but takes orders from none save the Lord Jesus Himself.

The Multiplicity of Local Churches

There are undoubted tendencies today against the multiplicity of local churches. Good roads and the automobile make it wise for some small Baptist churches to combine with other Baptist churches. The removal of people from the country to the city works in the same direction. But the establishment of factories with mill villages calls for other churches, mill churches, where none existed before. But the agitation for the community church comes at bottom out of an atmosphere where the state church existed. In England today the church means the Church of England, the Established Church, while the Dissenters or Nonconformists (Baptists, Congregationalists, Methodists, Presbyterians) have "chapels," which are simply tolerated by "the Church" with varying degrees of complacency or impatience. The state church atmosphere conceives that the church is the community. The community is the church. One of the jokes about this is that in England nearly all the criminals are in the Church of England, for all men are born into that church. Now in the abstract it may be ideal for one church to have a monopoly of the religious life of the community. Certainly the Roman Catholics would say so, and they regard Protestants today as an impertinence and wholly evil. And yet one has only to recall the present resentment in Mexico against the tyranny of the Roman Catholic Church to be reminded of the evils of monopoly, even in ecclesiastical matters; one may say especially in ecclesiastical matters. Who will say that France has not paid dearly for the massacre of St. Bartholomew's Eve? The French Republic a few years ago in self-defense had to separate the church of Rome from the state. With all the evils of intense rivalry between churches one must not overlook the tyranny of monopoly.

Each Community an Entity in Itself

A better way can be found. Each community is an entity in itself and is entitled to work out its own destiny with the help of its various affiliations. Each local church is in the community where it is located. Hence it is of the community and partakes of the characteristics and life of that community. That is inevitable and is not to be deplored within the limits of essential truth and conviction. There is this much of truth in the phrase, the "indigenous church" or "indigenous Christianity." The gospel does not spring out of local environment, but the method of spreading it does depend partly on local conditions.

The Most Important Fact

But more important is the fact that the church is for the community, and this in the highest sense. A church that does not feel charged with the mission and message of Christ to men will do little in any community, and may as well die. Such a church can never conceive of itself as a mere social club, for dinners, for dances, for athletics. And yet the local church does touch the whole life of the community. Young people should find themselves at home in it. Courting parlors are actually arranged in some city churches. Surely marriage and the courting that leads to it are not to be considered outside of the activities of a church that ministers to the life of the community. Not every church can afford a gymnasium, but every church should have a good library to help the reading of the young. Some churches are using the moving picture, and even the radio, for week night services of special kinds. The place of the pastor in the life of the community is still second to that of no one. He is no longer the only educated man in the community. Many in the church will surpass him in knowledge of various things. But he is still the only leader who gathers up in himself the whole life of the people. It is a great opportunity for service and nowhere more than in a country or village church. He can touch the life of the home, the school, the farm, the store, the state, the world. May God make each pastor the leader and the hero of his community life.

CHAPTER TWENTY-FIVE

Denominational Effectiveness, *Western Recorder* January 19, 1893

Have we a mission as a denomination? We most assuredly think so, and God's marvellous blessings upon the labors of our people would seem to indicate such a mission. Baptists have had a peculiar history, checkered by persecution and prosperity. Out of the strange and inspiring past we have come to a time of great opportunity. The great numbers that belong to the Southern Baptist Convention form a mighty host, if only they can be marshalled against the hosts of Satan. Dwelling upon the possibilities for usefulness of our Southern Baptists, at various times, I have been stirred to put forth the following ideas, as being conducive, even necessary, to denominational effectiveness:

1. *Firm adherence to well-defined principles.*

We must have something to stand for, know what it is, and stand for it. If we have nothing to stand for, that marks us off from the great body of Christian believers, we are guilty of dissension in creating a schism. If we do not know what we do stand for, we are poor Baptists indeed, and if we know, but do not hold fast, we are worse still. It used to be worthwhile for Baptists to maintain the necessity of a regenerated church membership, and so of believers' baptism, of supreme loyalty to the Bible as God's infallible rule of faith and practice, and of the right of religious liberty. Are these things of less interest or value today than of old? The battle used to be for religious liberty. The fathers died for that, and won it. The idea of a regenerated church membership has gotten into the Baptist blood. Loyalty to the Bible has always marked our people in the past. It is here that the battle is raging now. Either the Bible is God's Word and infallible as originally given, or it is not. It is not sometimes infallible and sometimes not. If God gave it, He gave it right, however we may have abused it since.

If we waver in our fundamental principles, the enthusiasm and power that come from deep convictions, will depart from our ranks. We believe we are right. Let us stand.

2. *Concentrated and united effort all along the lines.*

We may be orthodox and dead. If so, nothing will be done. Inactivity will never increase the power of godliness or spread the Gospel over the world. We must hear the trumpet call that sounded more than a hundred years ago when Carey caught its note. It comes all the way from a mountain in Galilee, and it says, "go." We may be orthodox and contentious, and thus spend what force we have in settling private scores or gaining personal points of advantage. There is some satisfaction in this, but it is a selfish satisfaction. It is better for us not to have our way, if Christ's cause can be advanced. The printer once, in printing the minutes of a Kentucky association, called it "The Association of United Baptists." How often is that true! We sometimes hang apart instead of hanging together. And yet we are all freemen in Christ Jesus—as free as the air. Everyone has a right to his idea as to the best way of doing things. No pope or bishop can crack a whip over us. We are parts of no machine. Rather, the churches are the machine, and we run ourselves. We all have a right to be independent and stand off like chestnut burrs, but we may not be doing the best thing for the cause of Jesus.

There are two extremes, one is to have all machinery and no individuality, as some religious organizations do, the other is to have no organization and all individualism, as it is possible for us to do. If we are to do a great work as a great people, we must work together with one another and with God.

If we put into operation denominational organs and institutions, these should perform their work with consecration and ability and should receive warm and hearty support. But it is only the "esprit de corps" that can be stirred. Nobody has a right to say to Baptists about such matters "you must."

3. *Loyalty to Jesus and love for Him as the supreme inspiration in every Baptist heart.*

It is the love that Jesus has for us that must be the mainspring behind every man's life, if he is to rise to his duty as a Christian. If we were all thus held down from all that is merely selfish or personal and held up to a high and exalted sense of responsibility and duty, would not added power be given to such a host as rally around Jesus' standard in the Southern Baptist Convention?

Questions for Group Discussion and Personal Reflection

Chapter One

1. Describe what the author writes about the "messianic consciousness of Jesus."
2. What is "the problem of Jesus"? Why is "no merely natural explanation of Jesus possible"?
3. What is our first glimpse of Jesus in the Scriptures? At this time, is Jesus aware of his messiahship?
4. Was Jesus "born of a virgin?" Explain why this is true.
5. Describe the baptism of Jesus and his call into the wilderness. What happened in the wilderness? What was the moral issue in the wilderness temptation?
6. How does John present Jesus?
7. What terms did Jesus use to describe himself and why?

Chapter Two

1. What was the first appeal of Jesus? How did Jesus make connection with the work of John the Baptist? What prophecies did John fulfill?

2. Who were the first disciples? Describe their calling.
3. Why would Peter one day be called the "rock"?
4. What was Jesus' first miracle and why was it significant?
5. What problems did Jesus have with the Jerusalem authorities and why?
6. Describe Jesus' interview with a "Jewish scholar." Who was the "scholar" and what did Jesus say to him?
7. What experience did Jesus have with the Samaritan woman? Why was his approaching her so unusual?
8. Describe Jesus' call to Nazareth. Why did Jesus want to visit Nazareth?
9. What happened in Nazareth and where did Jesus go from there?
10. What happened when Jesus visited Galilee?
11. Who were the "publicans and sinners"?

Chapter Three

1. What was the "conflict over the Sabbath"?
2. Describe the "battle renewed in Galilee."
3. What was the Sabbath controversy?
4. Why did Jesus choose the disciples he chose? Did he "make a mistake"?
5. What does Dr. Robertson write about the "sermon on the mount"?
6. What was the "warning against worldliness"?
7. Why did John the Baptist despair? How did Jesus answer him?

Chapter Four

1. Describe Jesus' second tour of Galilee. What happened?
2. How does Jesus repel the attacks of his enemies?
3. What was Jesus' "new style of teaching" and why did he adopt it?
4. What is a parable? Why is it effective in communicating?
5. Describe Jesus in "heathen territory."

6. What happened during Jesus' last visit to Nazareth?
7. What happened during Jesus' third tour of Galilee?
8. Why did the Jerusalem Pharisees hate Jesus?

Chapter Five

1. Why did Jesus need to train his disciples? How did he do it?
2. Describe the trip to Phoenicia.
3. Why was Jesus relunctant to heal the daughter of the Syrophoenician woman? What was her answer to him? What happened to her daughter?
4. Describe what happened in Decapolis.
5. Read Matthew 16:16 and ponder.
6. Why did Jesus rebuke Peter and refer to him as "Satan"?
7. Why did Jesus go up into the mountain one night to pray? Whom did he take with him? What happened?
8. What did Jesus teach about his coming death? Did his disciples understand the meaning of his words to them?
9. Why did rivalry break out among the twelve?

Chapter Six

1. Read Luke 13:34 and contemplate its meaning.
2. Who were the "Jerusalem conspirators"? Who were the Sanhedrin?
3. What was the significance of Jesus' words in John 8:12?
4. Describe the healing of the blind man and what happened.
5. Was Jesus eager to meet his fate? (Read Luke 12:49.)
6. What happened when Jesus visited Perea?
7. Why did the Pharisees seek to catch Jesus on the question of divorce?
8. Why did Jesus tell the parable of the "Pounds"?

Chapter Seven

1. Why did Jesus love Bethany?
2. Describe the betrayal of Judas. What was significant about the amount of silver paid to Judas?

3. Why was Jesus concerned for his disciples? Why did Jesus especially pray for Peter?
4. Describe Jesus' struggle in prayer.
5. What happened when Jesus faced his accusers? Describe the events of his "trial."
6. Describe Jesus' shameful death. What happened between nine and noon? What happened when he died? How did the people react to his death?

Chapter Eight

1. What did the disciples do during the three days Jesus lay in the tomb?
2. What does the author say about "the fact of the empty tomb"?
3. Tell the story of the angels.
4. What happened at the tomb between Jesus and Mary?
5. Describe Jesus' appearances after his resurrection.
6. Why did Thomas find Jesus' resurrection so difficult to believe?
7. What happened after the resurrection by the Sea of Galilee?
8. Read Acts 1:11 and discuss.

Chapter Nine

1. What does the author mean by this statement: "There is a difference between Christianity and churchianity as there is between the Bible and theology."
2. How did people in Dr. Robertson's time regard the Bible?
3. Why is the Bible more like a "library than a single book"?
4. What is the "unifying fact and force in both Testaments"?
5. Fill in the blanks: "________ _________ is the central fact of Christianity and of the Bible."
6. What is "the scarlet thread that runs through the Book"?

Chapter Ten

1. Explain what is meant by this statement: "And if a man happens to like books, it is by some people doubted whether he

will ever be a successful preacher, or strongly suspected that he will become a bookworm and lose all sympathy with the people and hence all warmth and power in his preaching." Do you agree or disagree? Why?

2. What does the author say are "current objections to theological education"?
3. What is the "antipathy against scholarship and preaching" as stated by the author?
4. Why can't "a busy pastor become a specialist"?
5. What are the "main things" one should get from a theological education?
6. Contemplate the following statement: "You will never become a preacher worth listening to without travail of soul. There has to be some severe thinking and suffering before you will command the ears and hearts of men."

Chapter Eleven

1. What does the following statement mean? "There is a vast difference between the authority of a revelation originally inerrant on everything on which it speaks, but which has suffered a little from the ravages of time, and one which originally contained various errors scattered through it, but which was in the main correct."
2. During 1892, what was happening concerning the Scriptures, about which the author writes?
3. Discuss the three points Dr. Robertson makes in his statement.
4. What is meant by "mental integrity"?

Chapter Twelve

1. Why does the author ask this question: "Can a modern man accept the story of the birth of Jesus?" What is the controversy surrounding the virgin birth?
2. How do the Matthew and Luke narratives of Jesus' birth agree? How do they disagree?
3. Why does "science" argue the virgin birth to be "impossible"?
4. What is the "Babylonian theory" and what does it teach?

5. Do you believe that "we live in a world that has recovered the sense of wonder"? Explain.
6. After reading this chapter, answer in your own words the question: "Is the virgin birth credible?" Explain.

Chapter Thirteen

1. What "various forms" have the "objections to the real Deity of Jesus Christ" taken? Examine each.
2. Discuss the following statement: "There are those who will not take Jesus as Lord of life and death because they cannot comprehend the mystery of the Incarnation and who refuse to admit the possibility of the union of God with man in the person of Jesus Christ."
3. Who was Granville Sharp? What were his works?
4. Ponder: "The simple truth is that Winer's anti-Trinitarian prejudice overruled his grammatical rectitude in his remark about 2 Pet. 1:1."
5. Would you agree with the following statement? "Scholarship, real scholarship, seeks to find the truth. That is its reward. The Christian scholar finds the same joy in truth and he is not uneasy that the foundations will be destroyed"? Why or why not?
6. What does Dr. Robertson write about John 1:1?

Chapter Fourteen

1. What three things produce "power in the preacher"?
2. What is the "variable quantity in preaching"?
3. Describe Paul's education. How did his education differ from Peter's or John's?
4. Why is it important to teach classical languages in the schools, according to Dr. Robertson?
5. Ponder the following: "The physician has to study chemistry and physiology. Other men may or may not. The lawyer has to study his Blackstone. The preacher has to know his Bible or the people suffer the consequences of his ignorance, as in the case of the physician or the lawyer." Do you agree? Why or why not?

6. Why is it important for a preacher to be able to read New Testament Greek?
7. Discuss the "preacher as a psychologist"?

Chapter Fifteen

1. What are the "three attitudes assumed towards immersion in the Scriptures"?
2. Read Romans 6:4 and discuss.
3. Is "immersion essential to salvation"? Why or why not?
4. Complete the sentence: "Baptists also feel very strongly the beauty of the symbolism of baptism as a ______ and ____________.
5. What is the meaning of each of the following words: "baptizo," "ekcheo," "bapto," "raino," and "rantizo"?
6. Why do the "circumstances surrounding the ordinance of baptism naturally suggest immersion"?

Chapter Sixteen

1. Explain the term "Evangelical Christianity."
2. What do Quakers believe about baptism?
3. Why do evangelical Christians often practice infant baptism, according to the author?
4. How do Baptists stand out "against the indifference of the Quakers, the heresy of the Sacramentalists, and the nervous over-emphasis of the Paedobaptists"?
5. What is "the lazy man's religion" and why?
6. What was the "battle of Paul's life"?
7. What is "clinic baptism" and how did it originate?
8. Why is baptism a "preacher"?

Chapter Seventeen

1. Why did Dr. Robertson write this particular article? What is its purpose?
2. Discuss the following: "Each denomination today has organic union within itself and is in dire need of spiritual unity, the thing for which Christ prayed. Indeed, there are

few local churches that do not exhibit signs of a lack of unity and harmony at times. Some are in a chronic state of faction that borders on schism."

3. Describe the "massacre of St. Bartholomew's Eve."
4. What does "organic union" mean?
5. Explain why the "Baptist conscience has been likened to a backbone"?
6. Why does "modern Christianity function through denominational loyalty"? Is it still true today?
7. Why must there be "intelligent and trained loyalty"?

Chapter Eighteen

1. What does the word "democracy" mean?
2. What is a "pure democracy"?
3. What is a "practical democracy"?
4. How should decisions be made in the Baptist church?

Chapter Nineteen

1. Why is the denominational school so important, so essential, to the life of Baptists?
2. Are denominational schools still as important to Baptist life as they were in 1930, when this article was written?

Chapter Twenty

1. "There are still people who refer to the 'ignorant Baptists' as if that was the characteristic of our denomination," writes Dr. Robertson. Is this still true today?
2. What does the author describe as the reason for "illiterate Baptists"?
3. Ponder: "But in fairness it must be admitted that some of the pioneer preachers were prejudiced against an educated ministry and even boasted of their own ignorance as a mark of divine favor."
4. Who was Luther Rice and what did he accomplish?

Chapter Twenty-One

1. What happened to Southern Baptists in 1929?

2. What was the purpose of the Hundred Thousand Club? How was it supposed to work?
3. Describe the "fight against liquor" that was raging in the South in 1933 when this article was published.
4. Ponder the following: "Dr. L. G. Broughton laments in *The Western Recorder* that our leaders have largely lost interest in mass revivals. That may be true in several cases, but numerous revivals are reported all over the country."
5. Who were some of the revival leaders at that time? Where were revivals occurring most often?

Chapter Twenty-Two

1. Discuss the following: "Baptists are mainly responsible for the first amendment to the Constitution which guarantees religious liberty to all and preserves the separation of church and state." What was happening regarding the Volstead Law in 1928, at the time of this writing?
2. What does Dr. Robertson urge preachers and Christian citizens to do?
3. How and why did the Eighteenth Amendment come about?
4. What did President E. Y. Mullins of Southern Baptist Theological Seminary tell preachers to do? Why?

Chapter Twenty-Three

1. What does the "efficiency of a church" primarily hinge upon and why?
2. The author writes: "There are various ways of making mistakes at the very start in calling a pastor." What are some of these?
3. What does the expression "trotting them down the pike" mean?
4. What practical advice does the author give for selecting or calling a pastor?
5. How did the apostle Paul conduct the choosing of elders, pastors, and other church leaders?
6. What does the author mean by "promises of cooperation"? What would happen in the church if this could always be done?

7. Why is the role of pastor so difficult? To whom must he minister and how?

Chapter Twenty-Four

1. What is the "regular campaign on today to squeeze out the small country and village church" that the author writes about?
2. What is Dr. Robertson's opinion about the small church?
3. According to the author, what is the "so-called community church"? Why is the community church "uncomfortable" for Baptists?
4. Discuss: "The prayer of Jesus in John 17 was a petition for unity of spirit, not for organic union." Do you agree? Why or why not?
5. What is Dr. Robertson's "better way"?

Chapter Twenty-Five

1. How would you answer Dr. Robertson's introduction question? "Have we a mission as a denomination?"
2. What does the author say about "firm adherence to well-defined principles"? about "concentrated and united effort all along the lines"? about "loyalty to Jesus and love for Him as the supreme inspiration in every Baptist heart"?

Notes

Introduction

1. In fact it was Robertson's expanded translation of the New Testament. See Everett Gill, *A. T. Robertson: A Biography* (New York: Macmillan, 1943).

2. Frank H. Leavell, "Archibald Thomas Robertson: An Interview for Students," *The Baptist Student* 10 (May, 1932): 3.

3. Gill, *A. T. Robertson*, 28.

4. Ibid., 42.

5. Ibid., 57. In Robertson's journal he noted that one advantage of seminary life in Louisville was the added opportunity to hear great preachers and lecturers who would come to the city. In addition to Moody, he particularly mentioned: Sam Jones, Henry Ward Beecher, Edward Judson, Joseph Cook, Will Carleton, Justin McCarthy, P. S. Henson, George W. Lorimer, Phillips Brooks, Joseph Parker, Arthur O'Conner, Sir Thomas Grattan Esmond, DeWitt Talmage, Francis Murphy, J. William Jones, and James G. Blaine.

6. Gill, *A. T. Robertson*, 65.

7. Ibid., 67.

8. Ibid.

9. Ibid., 198.

10. A. T. Robertson, *Life and Letters of John A. Broadus* (Philadelphia: American Baptist Publication Society, 1901), x.

11. Edgar McKnight, "A Baptist Scholar," Founder's Day Address, The Southern Baptist Theological Seminary, February 4, 1986, p. 6.

12. William A. Mueller, *A History of the Southern Baptist Theological Seminary,* 1859–1959 (Nashville: Broadman, 1959), 124.

13. See the Southern Seminary faculty's letter to their fellow Southern Baptists in Mueller, *A History*, 162–64.

14. Ibid., 164.

15. McKnight, "A Baptist Scholar," 3.

16. Gill, *A. T. Robertson*, 184.

17. Mueller, *A History*, 206.

18. A. T. Robertson, "Is the Virgin Birth Credible Today?" *The Watchman-Examiner*, 18 November 1920, 1168.

19. Gill, *A. T. Robertson*, 239.

20. I wish to express appreciation to Greg Thornbury and Mark Railey for their help with this project. It is a genuine privilege to have worked with Dr. Herschel H. Hobbs on this project, which was one of the last works from his prolific pen.

Chapter Sixteen

1. Orr, "The Virgin Birth of Jesus" (p. 181).
2. "The Date of the Acts and the Synoptic Gospels" (p. 156).
3. Carpenter, "Christianity According to S. Luke" (p. 166).
4. "Bearing of Recent Discovery" (p. 226).
5. Ramsay, "Luke the Physician" (p. 13, cf. p. 255).
6. Op. Cit. (p. 168).
7. Father Paul Bull, "God and Our Soldiers" (p. 244).
8. Christianity According to S. Luke" (p. 158).
9. Cf. Hibbert Journal Supplement for 1909.
10. Op. Cit. (p. 159).
11. Preface to "On the Threshold of the Unseen."
12. Orr, "The Virgin Birth of Christ" (p. 191).
13. Apologetics (p. 410).

Index

E

F

G

H

I

J